The Politics
of
Children's Survival

The Politics
of
Children's Survival

GEORGE KENT

PRAEGER

New York
Westport, Connecticut
London

Copyright Acknowledgments

The author gratefully acknowledges permission to reprint from the following:

Kent, George. "Nutrition Education as an Instrument of Empowerment," reprinted with permission, *Journal of Nutrition Education*, 20, no. 4 (July/August 1988), copyright © Society for Nutrition Education.

Kent, George. *War and Children's Survival*. University of Hawaii Institute for Peace, 1990.

Kent, George. "Who Would Not Save Their Own Children? The Impact of Powerlessness on Child Survival," *Development Forum*, 16, no. 6 (November/December 1988).

Kent, George. "Security and Hunger," *WHY: Challenging Hunger and Poverty*, no. 1 (Spring 1989 CIP).

Library of Congress Cataloging-in-Publication Data

Kent, George, 1939–
    The politics of children's survival / George Kent.
      p.   cm.
    Includes bibliographical references (p.   )
    Includes index.
    ISBN 0-275-93723-2 (alk. paper)
    1. Children—Mortality.   I. Title.
HB 1323.C5K46   1991
304.6'4'083—dc20   90-7578

British Library Cataloguing in Publication Data is available.

Copyright © 1991 by George Kent

Library of Congress Catalog Card Number: 90–7578
ISBN: 0-275-93723-2

First published in 1991

Praeger Publishers, One Madison Avenue, New York, NY 10010
An imprint of Greenwood Publishing Group, Inc.

Printed in the United States of America

The paper used in this book complies with the Permanent Paper Standard issued by the National Information Standards Organization (Z39.48-1984).

10 9 8 7 6 5 4 3 2 1

CONTENTS

TABLES AND FIGURES

TABLES

FIGURES

PREFACE

Several parts of this study have appeared in previously published articles. I thank the publishers of these pieces for the opportunity they provided to test ideas.

Many individuals contributed to the preparation of this study, some directly and some through their work in the world. Instead of recounting them as individuals, I prefer to salute the magnificent contributions of the organizations that contribute so much to the well-being of children: the United Nations Children's Fund, the International Committee for the Red Cross, Save the Children, Defense for Children International, the Children's Defense Fund, and others.

This study is dedicated to all children, and especially to Greg and Jeff. Every day their very being reminds me that looking after our children is the same as looking after our future. Children give meaning and vision to our lives, and I am grateful to them for that.

I want to give special thanks to Joan, and to my Mom and Dad, for having looked after me.

The Politics
of
Children's Survival

Chapter One

PATTERNS OF MORTALITY

The central concern of this study is the outrageously high rate at which children die worldwide, and the hopeful prospects for reducing that rate. The health of children is important in itself, and it is a sensitive indicator of the quality of life in society. Certainly the quality of the lives of children provides a good sign of a community's prospects for the future.

Most research on children's mortality has been undertaken by clinically oriented medical practitioners or public health professionals concerned with finding remedies within existing social systems. A major purpose here is to see how social context affects children's mortality. We ask not only what technical interventions might be undertaken within meager public health budgets, but also why those budgets are so meager. What are the social and political roots of the high levels of children's mortality throughout the world?

This study is concerned with policy as well as politics. The argument here is that the problem of children's mortality, which is symptomatic of under-development, arises out of widespread powerlessness. The remedies therefore should center on strategies of empowerment. Feeding people, for example, is no way to end hunger, but helping people to set up their own food pro-duction systems usually is a sound strategy whose effects can be expected to last long after the development agents leave. The most meaningful remedies are those whose benefits persist long after the intervention has ended.

Enormous advances have been made in child survival since the turn of the century, but the rate of progress is slowing down. It is becoming increasingly clear that the effectiveness of technical remedies is affected by the social, economic, and political contexts in which they are embedded. It also has become clear that programs for child survival must draw the full engagement of both local people at the village level and governmental leaders at all levels if they are to succeed. Thus it would be useful to reexamine and systematize the processes by which child survival programs are planned, to take full account of the social as well as the technical dimensions, and to involve all concerned parties in an integrated way.

FRAMEWORK

Urban Jonsson, the director of the United Nations Children's Fund (UNICEF) office in Tanzania, has proposed an approach to analyzing children's mortality:

The conceptual framework is developed as a response to the prime question "why do young children die?" ... Diarrhoea is a more direct cause than lack of clean water. ... Diarrhoea is itself caused by other processes in the environment and society, maybe lack of proper sanitary facilities or practices. But these also are caused by other factors. ...

Deaths of children are caused by processes that may operate at different levels of society, from individual and household levels to national and international levels. ... The level of society is therefore a second important dimension of the conceptual framework.

... The immediate causes of deaths of young children are primarily malnutrition and diseases. ... A large number of children die in connection with birth or immediately afterwards. ... In a given context it is possible to identify specifically which immediate causes have led to the death of an individual child or to a high child death rate in a community. These immediate causes could be, e.g., diarrhoeal disease in combination with low energy intake. ... Actions could be taken to reduce the child death rate by promoting oral rehydration therapy and food supplementation. However, actions at this ... level must often be repeated in order to have a sustained effect. If long-term improvements are to be secured, ... [we must] ask why do children get diarrhoea and why do they not get enough food?

... Dietary inadequacies are caused by a general low supply of food, ... or by too little time to prepare food or to feed children. ... Causes at this level of analysis are called underlying causes. ...

... Underlying causes reflect an unequal distribution of income, availability of services and production opportunities. ... The reasons for maldistribution of commodities and services within geographic areas or even within households must be analyzed. ... These causes are called basic causes. The production, distribution and consumption of commodities and services depend on the socioeconomic structure of society.[1]

Immediate, underlying, and *basic* correspond at least roughly to *individual, household,* and *societal* levels, the organizing concepts of the following chapters.

Individual factors include biomedical aspects of both the mother's and the child's conditions, specifically their disease and nutritional status. This study is primarily about the social rather than the individual factors in child survival. The term *social* is used here in a broad way, to include political, economic, sociological, cultural, and other similar sorts of dimensions. Sometimes the term *socioeconomic* is used to encompass these dimensions.

The social or socioeconomic factors are distinguished here into two groups: *household* and *societal*. Thus the causes of children's mortality are here divided between the individual and the socioeconomic. Socioeconomic factors are again divided between the household and the societal.

Household factors include household income, parents' education, access to health services, water supply, and sanitation, race, and fertility patterns. Social factors at the household level can be described as *micro*social factors, by analogy with the term *microeconomics*.

The term *societal* indicates that the reference is to *macro*social factors, factors that are much more under the influence of governments than of individuals or households. Societal factors include considerations such as the nature of the economic system and the extent to which there are civil rights. Macro policy is important because it shapes the conditions and incentives under which individual and household decisions are made.

Access to services and amenities such as health care and water supplies can be assessed from the point of view of the household. The *provision* of such services is a societal issue, dependent on such things as national budgets and national priorities. At the household level we are concerned with the *consequences* of malnutrition, poverty, and inadequate health care services. At the societal level we inquire into the *sources* of malnutrition, poverty, and inadequate health care services.

This chapter describes the overall patterns of children's mortality. The immediately following chapters describe the individual and household factors associated with children's mortality, and the programmatic responses associated with these factors. Chapter 2 is on individual factors and Chapter 3 is on household factors. Chapter 4, on the child survival and development movement, describes the major programs that have been developed to address the child survival problem, especially growth monitoring, oral rehydration therapy, the promotion of breastfeeding, and immunization. These chapters cover material that will be familiar to those working on the child survival problem.

In subsequent chapters we examine child survival in relation to larger societal factors, relationships that so far have received little attention. Chapter 5 sets the stage by reviewing some of the major criticisms of conventional approaches to child survival, criticisms that center on the tendency to favor technical interventions and to neglect social factors. Chapters 6 through 10 examine food, poverty, war, repression, and population in relation to child survival.

The focus then turns to strategies for child survival that are sensitive to the social factors. In Chapter 11 we explore alternative designs of social systems. Chapter 12 examines the idea of viewing children as a form of human capital. Chapter 13 addresses the problem of motivating those who are politically powerful to support child survival work. Chapter 14 suggests rethinking the meaning of national development. Chapter 15 considers the challenge of planning for children's survival in concrete, site-specific situations. Finally, Chapter 16 examines the potentials of national and international law and institutions for improving children's prospects.

Before getting too deeply into the factors that help to explain children's mortality, it is important to have a rather pure description of its patterns, one that is not mixed up with explanations for the patterns. Thus the remainder of this chapter provides an overview of patterns of children's mortality.

MEASURES OF CHILDREN'S MORTALITY

The most commonly used indicator is the *infant mortality rate* (IMR), which is the number of children who die before their first birthday for every thousand born alive in a particular country or other geographic entity.

In some studies *child mortality* refers to the deaths of children between their first and fifth birthdays. The child mortality rate is the number of deaths of children in this age bracket divided by the number of living children in that age bracket. At times this bracket is described as referring to children aged 1–4, but it might be described more clearly as the age bracket 1–4.99.

Since the infant mortality rate and the child mortality rate use different denominators, the two cannot be easily combined. To overcome this problem, UNICEF is promoting use of what it calls the *under-five mortality rate* (U5MR), the number of deaths of children under five for every thousand born alive. This is the same as what is described throughout this study as the *children's mortality rate*. Our concern is with children's mortality, the deaths of children from birth to their fifth birthdays.

The U.S. Agency for International Development (USAID) sometimes reports mortality rates as percentages (deaths per 100 rather than deaths per 1,000).

Infants' and children's mortality rates, populations, and annual number of births are published regularly in UNICEF's annual *The State of the World's Children*.[2] The number of deaths of infants is also indicated, obtained by multiplying the infant mortality rate by the number of (thousands of) births. Similarly, the number of children's deaths (which includes infant deaths) is calculated by multiplying the children's mortality rate (U5MR) by the number of (thousands of) births. In Tanzania in 1985, for example, the infant mortality rate was 111 and the children's mortality rate was 183. There were 1,144,000 births. Thus there were about 126,984 infant deaths and about 209,352 children's deaths in Tanzania in 1985.

As in all social data, there are errors in children's mortality data. There is one particularly systematic source of error:

The death of a child during its first few weeks of life may be hidden from view for cultural reasons. In many traditional societies, a child must survive for a certain period of time after birth before it is acknowledged as a "life." Naming ceremonies and other rituals marking the arrival of a new life are purposely delayed by those accustomed to high rates of infant mortality. The fatalistic attitudes that prevent parents from seeking help also make them unlikely to report the death of a newborn infant.[3]

There are other similar problems. In the Soviet Union the practice has been to count a very low birth-weight infant as a live birth only if it lives for a full week. Also, it has been the practice in some Soviet health services to conceal infant deaths because of embarrassment regarding the quality of care.[4]

The motivations for understating deaths appear to outnumber and outweigh any possible motivations for exaggerating the number. Thus it is likely that overall child mortality rates are regularly underestimated.

GLOBAL PATTERNS

What do we know about the patterns of children's mortality? The search here is for intrinsic patterns, not for patterns of association with other variables. Associations will be discussed in the following chapters.

In the late 1980s over 14 million children under five died each year, more than 40,000 a day. Children's deaths accounted for about one-third of all deaths worldwide, and in the less developed countries they accounted for over half of all deaths. In North Africa children accounted for more than two-thirds of all deaths. In northern Europe and in the United States children accounted for 2 to 3 percent of all deaths.[5]

Child survival rates are closely related to life expectancies. Where life expectancies are higher, it is not so much because people actually live longer as it is because more children survive to maturity. There are wide discrepancies among countries in average life expectancies at birth, but there are much smaller differences among them in their average life expectancies at, say, 15 years of age.

Table 1.1 shows some of the major trends in children's mortality. In 1980 the world infant mortality rate was 82 per 1,000 live births, and the children's mortality rate was 125 for every 1,000 live births. About 15.4 million children died in 1980. The figures were lower in developed countries, higher in developing countries. All of these figures were expected to decline over time, except that the number of children's deaths in Africa is forecast to be higher by the year 2000. Africa now accounts for less than 30 percent of all children's deaths, but it is expected to account for more than 40 percent by the end of the century.

Estimates of past and future infant mortality rates for various regions are shown in Table 1.2.

Infant mortality rates have been dropping steadily in most of the world, declining from an average of 142 in 1950–55 to an average of 89 in 1975–80.[6] The world's infant mortality rate was 155 per 1,000 in 1950 and 71 in 1985.[7] The death rate of children between one and five years old fell by half

Table 1.1
Infant and Child Mortality Estimates and Projections

	1950			1980			2000		
	IMR	U5MR	U5D	IMR	U5MR	U5D	IMR	U5MR	U5D
World	163	251	24.8	82	125	15.4	53	78	10.9
Developed countries	64	84	1.6	18	22	0.4	11	12	0.2
Developing countries	188	295	23.2	92	142	15.0	59	87	10.7
Regions									
Africa	197	332	3.8	119	193	4.3	79	122	4.4
West Asia	218	334	0.7	90	131	0.5	45	58	0.3
South Asia	187	320	9.9	110	173	7.9	70	102	4.7
East Asia	199	273	7.3	37	55	1.2	22	27	0.6
Central and South America	132	201	1.5	67	94	1.1	42	58	0.7

Source: United Nations Children's Fund, Executive Board, 1987 Session, *Medium-Term Plan for the Period 1986–1990*, E/ICEF/1987/3, (New York: United Nations Economic and Social Council, 5 March 1987), p. 5.
IMR = infant mortality rate (the probability of dying before the age of one year expressed per 1,000 live births);
U5MR = under-five mortality rate (the probability of dying before the age of five years expressed per 1,000 live births);
U5D = number of infants' and children's deaths (in millions).

Table 1.2
Estimated Infant Mortality Rates by Region

REGION	PERIOD				
	1950 to 1955	1975 to 1980	1980 to 1985	1995 to 2000	2020 to 2025
Developed Regions	56	19	16	11	7
Developing Regions	180	96	88	62	33
Africa	191	124	112	83	45
Latin America	125	70	62	44	27
North America	29	14	11	7	6
East Asia	182	39	36	22	11
South Asia	180	115	103	72	34
Europe	62	19	15	10	7
Oceania	67	36	31	18	9
USSR	73	28	25	17	9
WORLD	156	85	78	56	30

Source: United Nations, *World Population Prospects (Estimates and Projections) as Assessed in 1984* (New York: United Nations, Department of International Economic and Social Affairs, 1986).

between 1950 and 1980.[8] Children's mortality rates have been declining more slowly in the 1980s. The overall number of children's death is expected to fall from its late 1980s level of about 14 million to about 11 million by the end of the century.

Total under–5 mortality figures for recent years are estimated as follows:[9]

1983	15,033,000
1985	14,529,000
1986	14,288,000
1987	15,625,000
1988	14,874,000

The trend in the 1980s suggests the decline in under–5 mortality worldwide may not be steady and decisive.

Africa has the highest children's mortality *rates*, but the *numbers* of children dying are greater in South Asia. In 1985–87 more children died each year in India and Pakistan than in all 46 nations of Africa put together: "In 1986, more children have died in Bangladesh than in Ethiopia, more in Mexico than in the Sudan, more in Indonesia than in all eight drought-stricken countries of the Sahel." The numbers are higher in Asia because the populations are so much larger. However, even the rate at which children die is almost as high in South Asia as it is in Africa.[10]

Table 1.3
Infant Mortality in the Soviet Union

YEAR	URBAN	RURAL	OVERALL
1970	23.3	26.2	24.7
1980	23.5	32.5	27.3
1981	22.8	32.7	26.9
1982	22.2	30.7	25.7
1983	21.7	30.6	25.3
1984	21.9	31.8	25.9
1985	21.7	32.0	26.0
1986	n.a.	n.a.	25.1

Source: *Argumenty i fakty*, 16–22 May 1987, p. 8, as reported in Michael Ryan, "Infant Mortality in the Soviet Union," *British Medical Journal*, 296 (19 March 1988), 850–51.

About two-thirds of children's deaths—almost 10 million per year—are deaths of infants. About a third—nearly 5 million per year—are deaths of children between their first and fifth birthdays.[11] In developing countries a larger proportion of the deaths are of children between their first and fifth birthdays. In developed countries a much larger proportion of children's deaths are accounted for by infants' deaths. Of the children in developing countries who die in their first year, about half die during the first 28 days, the neonatal period.

These data do not describe the high levels of morbidity and general misery associated with these deaths. UNICEF reported that 1981, when 17 million children died, was "another year of 'silent emergency': of 40,000 children quietly dying each day; of 100 million children going to sleep hungry at night; of ten million children quietly becoming disabled in mind or body."[12]

Published infant mortality rates for the Soviet Union are shown in Table 1.3. These rates are high for an industrialized country. What is extraordinary, however, is that there have been some increases in the rate in recent years. Earlier data from the Soviet Union showed a significant rise in the early 1970s.[13] In 1988, when the overall Soviet infant mortality rate was about 25, the highest regional rate was about 60, in the Karakalpak Autonomous Republic.[14]

Children's mortality data for the United States are readily available in several sources.[15] In 1910 the infant mortality rate in the United States was 124. The rate dropped steadily from 47 in 1940 to 10.9 in 1983, but then the speed of decline diminished rapidly. In the late 1960s William Ryan commented:

Our infant mortality rate is . . . a national disgrace. . . . Relative to other nations, our infant mortality rate does not look good and, in comparison, our performance on this score is rapidly *worsening*. At one time the United States ranked sixth among all nations of the world in this crucial measure of effective health care. (One might well wonder why, in view of our outstanding affluence, we should have any excuse for not ranking *first*, and by a wide margin.) Today, out of a total of fifty-seven nations, we stand only fifteenth.[16]

According to a 1989 report of the U.S. Congress, "in contrast to the dramatic decline in the rate of infant mortality between 1950 and 1980, progress on reducing infant deaths has slowed to almost a halt in recent years."[17] The infant mortality rate has been going down faster in many other nations, with the result that the U.S. standing in the rankings has deteriorated further. In 1983 the United States ranked seventeenth among the nations of the world.[18]

The deterioration continues. In 1988 data the U.S. infant mortality rate declined to 10.0, but 21 other countries had even lower rates:[19]

Japan	5.2
Iceland	5.4
Finland	5.8
Sweden	5.9
Switzerland	6.8
Taiwan	6.9
Hong Kong	7.7
Netherlands	7.7
Canada	7.9
Luxembourg	7.9
France	8.0
Denmark	8.4
Norway	8.5
Germany, West	8.6
Ireland	8.7
Spain	9.0
Germany, East	9.2
Singapore	9.4
United Kingdom	9.5
Belgium	9.7
Australia	9.8
United States	10.0

Some geographical areas in the United States have very high rates:

The nonwhite infant mortality in our nation's capital exceeds that in Cuba and Jamaica, both significantly poorer countries. Statewide data mask more severe infant death problems in some city neighborhoods. For example, two Baltimore census tracts show infant death rates as high as 59.5 per 1,000 live births. This exceeds the 1981 infant death rates in Costa Rica, Panama, Guyana and Trinidad and Tobago, and is more than double the rates in the Soviet Union.[20]

It is misleading to compare the worst in one country with the average in another; nevertheless, the point is telling.

Some observers explain the lagging performance of the United States by reference to its mix of races, and the fact that blacks persistently have an infant mortality rate about twice that of whites. But that can't be the whole story:

It has been argued that in the Scandinavian countries and Japan, where infant-mortality and low-birth-weight rates are lowest, the population is ethnically homogeneous. Yet even if one considers the infant-mortality and low-birth-weight rates for white Americans only, the Scandinavians and the Japanese are still ahead.[21]

COMPARATIVE MORTALITY

The current global figure of over 14 million children's deaths each year obviously is a large number, but perhaps that number can be made more meaningful by comparing it with other mortality figures.

Table 1.4 lists selected catastrophes of the twentieth century. I have added to the original compilation by USAID an additional entry indicating that children's mortality currently runs well over 14 million a year. I have also added a column *Annualized Deaths*, to provide a rough estimate of the yearly casualty rate of these catastrophes. Clearly, the original tabulation omitted the largest catastrophe. And this one continues year after year.

Let us examine the comparisons with warfare in greater detail. There have been an estimated 101,550,000 fatalities in wars between 1700 and 1987.[22] That yields an average of 353,833 fatalities per year, far less than the current figure of more than 14 million children's deaths each year.

The effects of warfare averaged over a long time are relatively modest, but warfare is episodic, with some periods far more intense than others. The most lethal war in all of human history was World War II. There were about 15 million battle deaths over a period of almost 6 years, for a rate of about 2.5 million deaths a year. If we add in civilian deaths, the rate comes up to about 8.6 million deaths a year—when children's deaths were running at well over 25 million per year. Thus this most intense war in history resulted in a lower death rate, over a very limited period, than results from children's mortality year in and year out.

The deaths of children have been far more numerous than deaths from warfare. As James Grant of UNICEF points out, the number of children who die unnecessarily each year "is the equivalent of 120 Hiroshimas. If there

Table 1.4
Selected Twentieth-Century Catastrophes

YEAR	PLACE	CATASTROPHE	TOTAL DEATHS (millions)	ANNUALIZED DEATHS (millions)
1975-79	Kampuchea	Pol Pot Regime	2	0.4
1967	Nigeria	Biafra Civil War	1	1
1958-61	China	Great Leap Forward/ Famine	30	7.5
1947	India	Independence	1	1
1937-45	Worldwide	World War II	15	1.67
1943	Bangladesh	Famine	2	2
1942	India	Famine	2	2
1939	China	Flood	1	1
1932-34	Soviet Union	Forced Collectivization/ Famine	5	1.67
1928	China	Drought	3	3
1921	Soviet Union	Drought	2	2
1920	India	Bubonic Plague	2	2
1918-19	Worldwide	Spanish Influenza	20	10
1914-18	Worldwide	World War I	9	1.8
1914	East Europe	Typhus	3	3
1988	WORLDWIDE	CHILDREN'S MORTALITY	14.87	14.87

Source: United States Agency for International Development, *Development and the National Interest: U.S. Economic Assistance into the 21st Century* (Washington, D.C.: USAID, 1989), p. 15.

were a Hiroshima occurring every third day, incinerating 100,000 children—the world would be up in arms! But somehow we accept this—we take it for granted."[23]

Counting late additions, at the end of 1987 there were 58,156 names on the Vietnam War Memorial in Washington, D.C. That is less than the number of children under 5 who die every 2 days throughout the world. A memorial for those children who die worldwide would be more than 250 times as long as the Vietnam memorial, and a new one would be needed every year.

In the United States, with 40,000 infants dying each year, "unless we act today, in the next 13 years we will lose more American infants than we have lost soldiers in all the wars fought by the nation in this century."[24]

This study focuses on the challenge of improving the life chances of small children. In dwelling on this issue, we should not be lulled into thinking this is a high priority everywhere. Just about everyone would like to save children, but people like many other things, too, and saving children is not always viewed as important. This is evident from the family level to the international level. In some cultures, pregnant women drink large quantities of alcoholic beverages. They know this will reduce the birth weight of the child, with all the risks that that entails, but they also know that low birth weight reduces the risk to the mother in the delivery process. Reducing the risk to the mother may be a higher priority. Similarly, "if a family's goal is to have as many surviving children as possible, high levels of fertility will be preferred, even through their children's survival chances are jeopardized."[25]

In many nations it is evident from the budget allocations for maternal and child health that children's mortality is not a high priority. While advocates of children's welfare may urge that others should share their concern, realism demands that we recognize that children's survival is only one issue among many in a very complicated world. Indeed, we cannot begin to understand why the problem looms as large as it does if we do not acknowledge that people have many other concerns as well.

EXPLANATIONS

Some studies imply that there is a single truth about the causes of children's deaths, and that therefore it is possible to find out how the different causes operate in some precise way. Some analysts try to assign specific correlation coefficients in relating global variables, as if they represent plausible empirical generalizations. But patterns vary a great deal from place to place and time to time. Correlation coefficients and regression analyses may correctly describe the data at one particular site, but it cannot be assumed that the same relationships hold elsewhere or that the data provide reasonable estimators for a basic underlying truth. This point is less important with regard to immediate causes because, at the clinical/biological level, most children do function in more or less the same way. As we move to consideration of household and societal factors, however, there is far more variability in the world under study. Thus it is important to get away from the idea that there is a single truth about how and why children die. The best we can do in a conceptual framework or in an overview of current knowledge is to say what kinds of things matter and describe the general ways in which they function.

Even if the patterns were very regular, we should see that finding statistical association is not the same as gaining understanding. If we show that children's mortality rates are highly correlated with, say, poverty levels, poverty is said to "explain" children's mortality in the sense that it accounts for a large share of the variance. With this sort of statistical "explanation," can we say that we really understand? Or if we report a hundred vignettes of how babies die in different circumstances, do we then understand children's mortality?

We should not cultivate illusions regarding what can be known scientifically about the causes of children's mortality. More important, we should not exaggerate what needs to be known before we can begin struggling with the question of what should be done about it. How do we know when we have an adequate understanding of the problem? The perspective taken here is that we understand children's mortality when we as a society know what can be done about the problem, and we either do it or acknowledge why we don't do it. Understanding is not a mathematical achievement; it is a matter of grasping the issues. A good explanation is one that provides guidance about what to do.

There are common factors accounting for children's mortality throughout the world, and certain kinds of generally applicable remedies can be identified. Child survival can be enhanced with oral rehydration therapy, immunization, and various other kinds of programmatic interventions. But health and welfare workers know that usually they deal only with symptoms, trying to clean up messes caused by forces much deeper than their tools can reach. They know these forces are societal, having to do with the systematic ways in which people relate to one another. This study tries to bring the societal sources of children's mortality more plainly into view, and thus strengthen our prospects for coming to grips with them.

NOTES

1. Government of the United Republic of Tanzania and United Nations Children's Fund (UNICEF), *Analysis of the Situation of Children and Women*, vol. 1 (Dar es Salaam: UNICEF, 1985), 68–80.

2. Comparable data are published in the World Health Organization's *World Health Statistics Annual*, in the World Bank's annual *World Development Report*, in the *World Population Data Sheet* released each year by the private Population Reference Bureau of Washington, D.C., and in several other secondary sources. According to Christopher J. L. Murray, "A Critical Review of International Mortality Data," *Social Science & Medicine*, 25, no. 7 (1987), 773–81, the best primary sources for quantitative analyses are the United Nations' *World Population Trends and Policies Monitoring Report* and the U.S. Bureau of the Census' *World Population*.

3. Katrina Galway, Brent Wolff, and Richard Sturgis, *Child Survival: Risks and the Road to Health* (Columbia, MD: Institute for Resource Development/Westinghouse/USAID, 1987), p. 17.

4. Michael Ryan, "Infant Mortality in the Soviet Union," *British Medical Journal*, 296 (19 March 1988), 850–51.

5. Jon E. Rohde, "Why the Other Half Dies: The Science and Politics of Child Mortality in the Third World," *Assignment Children*, 61/62, no. 1 (1983), 35–67.

6. United Nations Secretariat, "Infant Mortality: World Estimates and Projections, 1950–2025," *Population Bulletin of the United Nations*, no. 14 (1982), 31–53.

7. World Health Organization, *World Health Statistics Annual* (Geneva: WHO, 1988), p. 16.

8. James P. Grant, *The State of the World's Children 1987* (New York: Oxford University Press, 1987), p. 13.

9. James P. Grant, *The State of the World's Children 1986* (New York: Oxford University Press, 1986), Table 1, "Basic Indicators."

10. Grant, *The State of the World's Children 1987*, p. 7.

11. Ibid., p. 126.

12. James P. Grant, *The State of the World's Children 1981–1982* (New York: United Nations Children's Fund, 1982), p. 1.

13. Ryan, "Infant Mortality in the Soviet Union." Also see J. Dutton, "Changes

in Soviet Mortality Patterns, 1959–1977," *Population and Development Review*, 5 (1979), 267–91; C. Davis and M. Feshback, "Rising Infant Mortality in the U.S.S.R. in the 1970s," *International Population Reports*, series P–95, no. 74 (1980).

14. Esther B. Fein, "In Soviet Asia Backwater, Infancy's a Rite of Survival," *New York Times*, August 14, 1989, pp. A1, A6.

15. Dana Hughes, Kay Johnson, Sara Rosenbaum, Janet Simons, and Elizabeth Butler, *The Health of America's Children: Maternal and Child Health Data Book* (Washington, D.C.: Children's Defense Fund, 1987); *Historical Statistics of the United States, Colonial Times to 1970, Part 1* (Washington, D.C.: Bureau of the Census, U.S. Department of Commerce, 1975), p. 57.

16. William Ryan, *Blaming the Victim*, rev. ed. (New York: Vintage Books, 1976), pp. 161–62.

17. U.S. House of Representatives, Select Committee on Children, Youth, and Families, *U.S. Children and Their Families: Current Conditions and Recent Trends, 1989* (Washington, D.C.: U.S. Government Printing Office, 1989), p. 170.

18. Ruth Leger Sivard, *World Military and Social Expenditures 1986* (Washington, D.C.: World Priorities, 1986), p. 37.

19. *1988 World Population Data Sheet* (Washington, D.C.: Population Reference Bureau, 1988). The data vary among different sources, and the rankings vary as well.

20. Children's Defense Fund, *American Children in Poverty* (Washington, D.C.: CDF, 1984).

21. Stephen Budiansky, "A Measure of Failure," *Atlantic Monthly*, January 1986, pp. 32–35.

22. Ruth Leger Sivard, *World Military and Social Expenditures 1987–88* (Washington, D.C.: World Priorities, 1987), p. 28. These data were prepared by William Eckhardt. According to J. David Singer and Melvin Small, *The Wages of War, 1816–1965: A Statistical Handbook* (New York: John Wiley, 1972), there were almost 30 million casualties incurred by combatants in major wars between 1816 and 1965. This yields an average of about 200,000 deaths per year, still far lower than the estimated number of children's deaths each year.

23. James P. Grant, "Hunger and Malnutrition: A Hiroshima Every 3 Days...," *A Shift in the Wind*, no. 2 (August 1978), pp. 4–5.

24. National Commission to Prevent Infant Mortality, *Death Before Life: The Tragedy of Infant Mortality* (Washington, D.C.: NCPIM, 1988), p. 8.

25. Galway, et al., *Child Survival*, p. 44.

Chapter Two

INDIVIDUAL FACTORS

The immediate causes of children's mortality tend to differ, depending on the age of the child. The major distinctions are as follows.

The *perinatal period* is from 28 weeks of gestation to birth (or in some definitions, to the seventh day of life). Deaths in this period are primarily determined by the condition of the mother. Deaths of the fetus prior to birth or at birth (stillbirths) are not included in infants' or children's mortality data.

The *neonatal period* is from birth to 28 days. Deaths in this period are determined more by the condition of the mother than of the child. Immediate causes are low birth weight due to prematurity or intrauterine malnutrition, intrauterine asphyxia and infections, birth trauma, and neonatal infections. The first week is sometimes described as the *early neonatal period*.

The *postneonatal period* is from 28 days to one year. During this period breast milk is the primary source of nutrients. The immunity passed on to the child by the mother starts to disappear toward the end of the period. Supplementary feeding (weaning) may start toward the end of this period. The child begins exploring the environment, and thus is exposed to a variety of dangers.

Infancy is the period from birth to the first birthday.

Early childhood—the toddler age group—is the period from the first birthday to the fifth birthday. In early childhood the immediate causes of death are most often a combination of disease and malnutrition. After weaning has been completed (breast-feeding has ended) the most common cause of child deaths is disease.

In this study *children* includes both infants and those in early childhood.

These different time periods are given more or less arbitrary limits; there actually are no sharp thresholds in biological terms.

Not only the aggregate number but also the age distribution and the causes of children's deaths are very different in rich and in poor countries. Table

Table 2.1
Causes of Infant Death, 1984

CAUSE OF DEATH	MORTALITY RATE (deaths per 1000 live births)	
	UNITED STATES	ECUADOR
Infectious and Parasitic Diseases	0.197	10.422
Nutritonal Deficiencies	0.005	2.132
Diseases of the Nervous System	0.194	0.821
Diseases of the Respiratory System	0.360	9.481
Congenital Anomalies	2.330	1.836
Certain Conditions Originating in the Perinatal Period	5.092	11.776
Signs, Symptoms, and Ill-Defined Conditions	1.601	4.797
Accidents	0.228	0.502
ALL CAUSES	10.787	43.421

Source: *World Health Statistics Annual 1987* (Geneva: World Health Organization, 1987), pp. 418, 421.

2.1 shows the major causes of infant death in terms of the ninth revision of the International Classification of Diseases used by the World Health Organization (WHO).[1] These data for the United States and for Ecuador suggest the differences in the patterns for richer and poorer countries. A major distinguishing feature is the far higher incidence of deaths due to infectious diseases in poorer countries. In the United States infectious and parasitic diseases accounted for 0.197 points of the overall infant mortality rate, while in Ecuador they accounted for 10.422 points.

Table 2.2 indicates the distribution of immediate causes of children's deaths for 1986.

Following live birth, the risk of death is highest in the early neonatal period, and declines steadily as the child gets older. For countries with low infant mortality rates the rate of neonatal death exceeds that for postneonatal death. In countries with high infant mortality rates the postneonatal death rate tends to exceed the neonatal death rate. (The risk of death declines month by

Table 2.2
Estimated Annual Deaths of Children under 5 by Cause, 1986

CAUSE	NUMBER (millions)	PROPORTION (percentage)
Diarrhea	5.0	35.4
Malaria	3.0	21.3
Measles	2.1	14.9
Neonatal Tetanus	0.8	5.7
Pertussis (Whooping Cough)	0.6	4.3
Other Acute Respiratory Infections	1.3	9.2
Other	1.3	9.2
ESTIMATED TOTAL	14.1	100.0

Source: James P. Grant, *The State of the World's Children 1987* (New York: Oxford University Press, 1987), p. 111.

month, but the postneonatal death rate accumulates cases over an 11-month period.)

In richer countries most children's deaths are due to difficulties in the birth process, congenital anomalies, and accidents.[2] Over 2,000 deaths of infants in the United States in 1984 were attributed to their mothers' smoking.[3] Unexplained crib death, labeled as sudden infant death syndrome (SIDS), is a major concern. In Table 2.1, out of the 1.601 rate under the broad category "Signs, Symptoms and Ill-Defined Conditions," 1.429 is accounted for by SIDS. According to these WHO data, SIDS accounted for 5,245 out of a total of 39,580 infant deaths in the United States in 1984. Thus more than 13 percent of the U.S. infant mortality rate was attributed to SIDS.

In poorer countries, disease and malnutrition of the mother or the child are the major immediate causes of children's mortality.

The overall patterns of children's mortality prevalent in richer countries are likely to emerge in the poorer countries with the advent of economic growth.[4] Mortality rates in the older age groups tend to drop most quickly, while the neonatal mortality rates are most resistant to reduction.

Because of their much higher children's mortality rates, this study focuses on the problems that prevail in poorer countries.

DISEASE

Birth outcomes can be strongly affected by disease and malnutrition of the mother during pregnancy. Several different kinds of diseases can lead to fetal death or to disease or defects in the child, and thus to infant death. Maternal diseases are a factor mainly in neonatal deaths. Postneonatal deaths are associated more with diseases and malnutrition of the children themselves.

Table 2.3
Children's Mortality Due to Acute Respiratory Infection

	MORTALITY RATE DUE TO			
	ARI		ALL CAUSES	
	0-1 years	1-5 years	0-1 years	1-5 years
	(deaths/1000)			
Brazil and Bolivia	40	6	92	9
Papua New Guinea	30	4	72	16
Nepal--Mid Hills	43	20	200	90
Nepal--Mountains	330	160	490	300
U.S. and Canada	1.5	0.08	11	0.6

Source: Kirk R. Smith, *Biofuels, Air Pollution and Health: A Global Review* (New York: Plenum, 1987), p. 239.

Acute Respiratory Infection

In terms of the ninth revision of the International Classification of Diseases, deaths from tuberculosis, diphtheria, pertussis, measles, otitis media, upper respiratory tract diseases, other respiratory tract diseases, acute bronchitis and bronchiolitis, pneumonia, influenza, and pleurisy are related to acute respiratory infection (ARI).[5] Of these, measles, diphtheria, pertussis, and tuberculosis are vaccine-preventable.[6]

Of the many different diseases included in ARI, acute lower respiratory tract infections—primarily pneumonia and bronchiolitis—are the major types of ARI responsible for childhood mortality.[7]

With regard to morbidity, the magnitude of the ARI problem is about the same in richer as in poorer countries, but the rates of children's mortality attributed to ARI are far higher—perhaps 30 times higher—in poorer countries:

For example, in Peru, with regard to influenza and pneumonia only, the level of mortality is 37 times higher in infants and 43 times higher in children 1–4 years than in Canada or the United States. In the Philippines these rates are 24 to 73 times higher respectively for infants and children 1–4 years than in Australia.[8]

Table 2.3 indicates the extent to which children's mortality is due to ARI in several parts of the world.

By some estimates ARI accounts for about 4 million children's deaths each year, about 27 percent of the total. Thus this group of diseases is second only to diarrhea in causing children's deaths.[9] Pertussis (whooping cough) alone kills about 600,000 children a year, a rate that would be considerably higher in the absence of immunization programs.

AIDS

Acquired immune deficiency syndrome—AIDS—spreads in only three ways: sexual contact, blood, and from infected mother to child. Spread of the virus from an infected mother to her child can occur before, during, or shortly after birth. HIV can be passed to the unborn child in the womb, or it can be passed to the baby at the moment of birth. In one case breast milk was reported to contain the virus, but WHO experts doubt that HIV-contaminated breast milk could be a major transmission route to children.[10]

About half the infants born to infected mothers are infected with the virus. Most AIDS in children is due to virus infection in the mother. The former director of the WHO's Global Programme on AIDS speculated:

In areas where ten per cent or more of pregnant women are infected with the AIDS virus, infant mortality from this cause alone may exceed the infant mortality rate from all causes in industrialized countries. As a result, in those areas the projected gains in infant and child health anticipated through child survival initiatives may be cancelled tragically by AIDS.[11]

Among mothers attending prenatal clinics in Kampala, Uganda, the incidence of HIV infection has already reached 13 percent.[12] The incidence of AIDS in children is still small, but the fear is that it will grow very rapidly, in rich as well as in poor countries. "Zambia alone is expected to be caring for 6,000 infants with AIDS this year."[13] Studies in Zaire and Rwanda indicate the vulnerability of infants:

Blood tests on 4,710 healthy people in Kinshasa recently showed a peak prevalence at under one year of age and among young adults 16–29. In Kinshasa, in other words, infants and the most sexually active age groups are jointly the most infected with HIV. And in Rwanda, roughly 20 percent of AIDS victims are now children.[14]

Many of the HIV-positive children in Rwanda were infected by blood transfusions.[15] Almost all infants born with the virus die within the year.

The problem affects developed countries as well:

As of October 5, 1987, there were 42,354 cases of Acquired Immune Deficiency Syndrome (AIDS) in the United States. According to the federal Centers for Disease Control (CDC), 584 of these cases (1.4 percent) have been documented in children less than 13 years old. Two thirds of them have died.

By 1991, an estimated 10,000–20,000 American children will be sick or die from AIDS.[16]

An estimated 5,000 AIDS-infected babies were born in the United States in 1988.[17]

AIDS may also have indirect effects on children's mortality. Unfounded fears of AIDS transmission from unsterilized hypodermic needles might lead to reduced participation in immunization programs for other life-threatening diseases.

Similarly, the unfounded fear that breast-feeding could be a means of transmitting the virus may impede efforts to promote breast-feeding. Many immunization programs are now replacing reusable needles with disposable needles to minimize the risks of infection through immunization.

To the extent that AIDS becomes so widespread as to slow national social and economic development, it may further limit the capacity of nations to undertake child survival programs. In some African countries a quarter of the patients have AIDS or AIDS-related diseases. The health care costs of AIDS, either out of national budgets or out of international development assistance, could result in heavy cuts in the budgets for children's health care.[18]

AIDS still does not account for a large proportion of children's deaths, but the disease represents a serious threat to children in the future.

Diarrhea

Diarrhea is the single largest cause of children's mortality, leading to about 5 million deaths of children under 5 each year. Diarrhea includes a broad variety of specific types of illnesses caused by several different kinds of bacterial, viral, and parasitic pathogens in the intestine. It is not single, isolated bouts of diarrhea, but the effect of repeated episodes on poorly nourished children, which weakens them so badly that eventually one episode becomes their last. Most children's deaths from diarrhea are due to watery, dehydrating diarrhea.[19]

Malaria

Malaria is transmitted among humans by anopheline mosquitos in many tropical areas of the world. It occurs most commonly in sub-Saharan Africa and in New Guinea. Although it had declined for a time in response to control measures, it is resurgent in much of Asia and parts of Latin America. In areas where the parasite is always present in the population at some level, it can be the most deadly single disease, infecting virtually all children and accounting for up to 10 percent of children's deaths.

Malaria (and, to a lesser extent, other animal parasites) contributes to child mortality in four different ways:

The infection may kill the child even if the child was otherwise in a relatively healthy state. This is here called a *direct* cause of mortality. Parasites may contribute to the complex of malnutrition and infection that increases the risk of death and thus be *indirect* causes of mortality. Third, parasitic infection in the mother may lead to abortion or infection and death of the fetus in the uterus, a *prenatal* effect. Finally, parasitic disease may so disable a mother that she is unable to look after the child properly, so that its chance of survival is reduced. The extreme example of such a *generation delayed* effect occurs when the mother dies of parasitic disease.[20]

The prenatal effect may lead not only to fetal failure but also to neonatal death. However, the disease itself does not pass through the placenta.

Malaria has a specially marked effect on women:

Pregnant women are at heightened risk from malaria infection. For reasons that are not clearly understood, women lose whatever partial immunity they may have against the parasite during early pregnancy. Immunologically, they revert to the status of young children. This phenomenon is most pronounced during a first pregnancy and diminishes with each successive pregnancy. Upon the birth of the child or shortly thereafter, the women regain their ability to resist the disease. But severe malarial infection during the exposed period can cause stillbirth, fetal growth retardation, or premature delivery.[21]

Measles

Measles alone, characterized by rash, fever, conjunctivitis, and cough, is not very deadly. But together with its common complications—pneumonia, diarrhea, undernutrition, and systemic infection—measles killed about 1.86 million in 1988.[22] Undernutrition is recognized as the major cause of measles-associated mortality. The case mortality rates vary a great deal, in some situations running higher than 25 percent.[23]

Neonatal Tetanus

In 1988 neonatal tetanus claimed about 818,000 lives.[24] It is caused by infection of the newborn infant, usually at the umbilical stump, with tetanus organisms. It usually develops in the first or second week, and is fatal in 70–90 percent of cases. In some cases the infant mortality rate from neonatal tetanus alone can be as high as 25 or 30 per 1,000 live births.

Neonatal tetanus is more prevalent where there are large animals, as in horse- and cattle-raising areas, than in farming and urban areas. Male infants are at greater risk than females, partly because tetanus infection can result from circumcision during the first week of life. Methods of care of the umbilical cord have a great influence on the risk of incurring the tetanus infection.

Immunization of the mother with two doses of tetanus toxoid before delivery

Table 2.4
Major Nutrient Deficiencies

DISEASE	NUTRIENT LACKING
PROTEIN-CALORIE MALNUTRITION	
Kwashiorkor	Protein
Marasmus	Protein and calories
Mid-to-moderate PCM	Protein and calories
VITAMIN-DEFICIENCY DISEASES	
Xerophthalmia	Vitamin A
Beriberi	Vitamin B1
Ariboflavinosis	Vitamin B2
Pellagra	Niacin
Scurvy	Vitamin C
Rickets	Vitamin D
MINERAL-DEFICIENCY DISEASES	
Anemia	Iron
Goiter	Iodine
Rickets and osteomalacia	Calcium

Source: James E. Austin, *Confronting Urban Malnutrition: The Design of Nutrition Programs* (Baltimore: Johns Hopkins University Press/World Bank, 1980), p. 11.

is highly effective in preventing neonatal tetanus. The quality of the training of birth attendants is also an important factor.[25]

MALNUTRITION

The major nutrient deficiencies worldwide are listed in Table 2.4. According to WHO, the most important deficiency diseases are the following:

a. *protein-calorie malnutrition (PCM)*, because of its high mortality rate, its wide prevalence, and the irreversible physical and sometimes mental damage it may cause

b. *xerophthalmia*, because of its contribution to the mortality of malnourished children, its relatively wide prevalence, and the permanent blindness it causes

c. *nutritional anemias*, because of their wide distribution, their contribution to mortality from many other conditions, and their effects on working capacity

d. *endemic goiter*, because of its wide distribution.[26]

Xerophthalmia results primarily from vitamin A deficiency, anemia from iron deficiency, and goiter from iodine deficiency.

Eye diseases of various forms are the most common consequences of vitamin A deficiency. While vitamin A deficiency alone is not likely to result in death, it does have mortality implications, as explained in Chapter 6, in the section "Malnutrition/Disease Interactions."

Iodine deficiency can lead to goiter, cretinism, deaf-mutism, and neuro-motor impairment. (While goiter is closely associated with inadequate iodine intake, it can arise from other sources as well.) Iodine deficiency in pregnant women can lead to increased fetal and neonatal mortality. By one rough estimate, iodine deficiency may account for more than 15 deaths out of 1,000 live births in at-risk areas in Asia. It also accounts for a broad variety of reproductive failures leading to infertility and miscarriages.[27] Iodine deficiency is a major factor in physical and mental underdevelopment of children in some areas, but there is no indication that it makes a substantial contribution to worldwide child mortality.

Iron-deficiency anemia can lead to increased fetal and neonatal mortality, but its contribution to overall child mortality rates is not clear.

Extreme deficiencies in vitamin A, iron, or iodine may sometimes be a factor, but the form of nutritional deficiency most commonly associated with children's deaths is protein-energy malnutrition (PEM), sometimes described as protein-calorie malnutrition (PCM). Usually the problem is not the lack of specific nutrients but simply inadequate food intake.

Neonatal deaths may be due to the mother's protein-energy malnutrition, while postneonatal deaths are more likely to be due to inadequacy in the child's own food intake.

The most widespread form of malnutrition throughout the world is PEM. It is so prevalent that in the absence of other specifications, references to malnutrition are understood to indicate PEM. Kwashiorkor and marasmus are intense forms of PEM.

PEM is usually due to a lack of energy foods, not a lack of protein intake. The symptoms of protein deficit often observed in cases of severe malnutrition result from the fact that the protein that is obtained is diverted to fulfilling immediate energy needs, and thus is not available for the growth, mainte-nance, and tissue repair functions it normally fulfills. If energy supplies are adequate, the protein remains available for its body building and maintenance functions, a phenomenon described as *protein sparing*.[28]

The role of food and nutrition in children's survival is discussed further in Chapter 6.

LOW BIRTH WEIGHT

Low birth weight (LBW) is defined as a weight of less than 2,500 grams, about 5.5 pounds. LBW is a major factor in perinatal mortality, and results in higher mortality and morbidity rates during later periods as well. It is best understood not as a cause in itself but as an intervening variable. LBW is a sensitive indicator of malnutrition and disease in the mother, and a good predictor of increased mortality risk in the child.

A careful review of studies of the determinants of LBW found that:

Factors with well-established direct causal impacts on intrauterine growth include infant sex, racial/ethnic origin, maternal height, pre-pregnancy weight, paternal weight and height, maternal birth weight, parity, history of prior low-birth-weight infants, gestational weight gain and caloric intake, general morbidity and episodic illness, malaria, cigarette smoking, alcohol consumption, and tobacco chewing. In developing countries the major determinants of IUGR [intrauterine growth retardation] are Black or Indian racial origin, poor gestational nutrition, low pre-pregnancy weight, short maternal stature, and malaria. In developed countries, the most important single factor, by far, is cigarette smoking, followed by poor gestational nutrition, and low pre-pregnancy weight.[29]

The major modifiable factor in intrauterine growth retardation in developed countries is cigarette smoking.[30]

Most LBW results from intrauterine growth retardation, but some results from prematurity. The health status of a pregnant woman, and thus of her fetus, is indicated by her weight gain during pregnancy. A low weight gain due to inadequate nutrition combined with hard physical work is likely to be associated with LBW of the child.

In 1986 there were about 20.3 million LBW infants worldwide.[31] In Africa about 14 percent, and in South Asia about 31 percent, are LBW. In 1985 in the United States, 253,554 infants—about 6.8 percent of all births—had LBW. In the United States 12.4 percent of black babies have LBW.[32]

In the United States, LBW babies are 40 times more likely to die in the first month of life than are babies of normal weight. LBW babies who survive are twice as likely to suffer handicaps such as cerebral palsy, chronic lung problems, epilepsy, delayed speech, blindness, deafness, and mental retardation.[33]

NOTES

1. World Health Organization, *Manual of the International Classification of Diseases, Injuries, and Cause of Death, Ninth Revision (1975)* (Geneva: WHO, 1977).

2. On accident mortality worldwide, see *World Health Statistics Quarterly*, 39, no. 3 (1986).

3. "Smoking-Attributable Mortality and Years of Potential Life Lost—United States, 1984," *Morbidity and Mortality Weekly Report*, 36, no. 42 (October 30, 1987), 693–97.

4. Historical trends in infant mortality patterns are analyzed in Thomas McKeown, *Medicine in Modern Society: Medical Planning Based on Evaluation of Medical Achievement* (New York: Hafner, 1966).

5. Jerzy Leowski, "Mortality from Acute Respiratory Infections in Children Under

5 Years of Age: Global Estimates," *World Health Statistics*, 39, no. 2 (1986), 138–44.

6. See *ARI News*, published by Appropriate Health Resources & Technologies Action Group, Ltd. (AHRTAG), 1 London Bridge Street, London SE1 9SG, UK. The various forms of ARI are described in *Acute Respiratory Infections in Children* (Washington, D.C.: Pan American Health Organization, 1983).

7. Stanley O. Foster, "Immunizable and Respiratory Diseases and Child Mortality," in W. Henry Mosley and Lincoln C. Chen, eds., *Child Survival: Strategies for Research* (Cambridge: Cambridge University Press, 1984), pp. 119–40.

8. Leowski, "Mortality from Acute Respiratory Infections," p. 142. Here 1–4 years means from first to fifth birthdays.

9. Katrina Galway, Brent Wolff, and Richard Sturgis, *Child Survival: Risks and the Road to Health* (Columbia, MD: Institute for Resource Development/Westinghouse/USAID, 1987), p. 22. In Leowski's analysis, "the figure of 4 million ARI-related deaths per year in children under 5 may well be an underestimate." According to Carl Taylor, "Chance to Cut Death Rate Dramatically," *UNICEF Intercom*, no. 50 (October 1988), pp. 1–2, pneumonia alone accounts for about 5 million children's deaths each year.

10. AIDS and the Third World, rev. ed. (Alexandria, Va.: The Panos Institute, 1987), p. 38.

11. Jonathan M. Mann, "A Global Challenge," *World Health*, March 1988, pp. 4–8.

12. Samuel I. Okware, "AIDS Control in Uganda," *World Health*, March 1988, p. 21.

13. David Sassoon, "AIDS: Its Impacts on Mothers and Children," *Action for Children*, 2, no. 1 (1987), 1, 10.

14. *AIDS and The Third World*, p. 37.

15. Ibid., p. 44.

16. National Commission to Prevent Infant Mortality, *Perinatal AIDS* (Washington, D.C.: NCPIM, 1988).

17. "5,000 AIDS-Infected Babies Expected This Year," *Sunday Star-Bulletin and Advertiser* (Honolulu), November 13, 1988, p. A–25.

18. *AIDS and The Third World*, pp. 37–40; "AIDS in the Third World: A Growing Threat to Development," *Hunger Report* (Select Committee on Hunger, U.S. House of Representatives), VIII/87 (September 29, 1987), 1–2.

19. See the quarterly *Dialogue on Diarrhoea: The International Newsletter on the Control of Diarrhoeal Diseases*, published by Appropriate Health Resources & Technologies Action Group, Ltd. (AHRTAG), 1 London Bridge Street, London SE1 9SG, UK.

20. David J. Bradley and Anne Keymer, "Parasitic Diseases: Measurement and Mortality Impact," in W. Henry Mosley and Lincoln C. Chenn, *Child Survival* (Cambridge: Cambridge University Press, 1984), pp. 163–87.

21. Galway, et al., *Child Survival*, p. 28.

22. "Progress in Global Coverage," *Expanded Program on Immunization Update*, March 1988, as reported in *World Immunization News*, 4, no. 5 (September–October 1988), 32.

23. Foster, "Immunizable and Respiratory Diseases," pp. 128–33.

24. "Progress in Global Coverage," p. 32.

25. Foster, "Immunizable and Respiratory Diseases," p. 123.

26. James E. Austin, *Confronting Urban Malnutrition: The Design of Nutrition Programs* (Baltimore: Johns Hopkins University Press/World Bank, 1980), p. 10.

27. Eric Dulberg, "A Model for Predicting the Prevalence of Developmental IDDs from Goiter Data—Preliminary Report," *IDD Newsletter* (International Council for Control of Iodine Deficiency Disorders), 1, no. 1 (August 1985), 6.

28. D. S. McLaren, "The Great Protein Fiasco," *Lancet* (1974), 2, 93–96.

29. M. S. Kramer, "Determinants of Low Birth Weight: Methodological Assessment and Meta-Analysis," *Bulletin of the World Health Organization*, 65, no. 5 (1987), 663–737.

30. Ibid., p. 724.

31. "The Incidence of Low Birth Weight: An Update," *Weekly Epidemiological Record, WHO*, no. 27 (6 July 1984). Cross-national data on the percentage of infant births with LBW are included in the nutrition table in UNICEF's *The State of the World's Children*.

32. C. Arden Miller, "Infant Mortality in the U.S.," *Scientific American*, 253, no. 1 (July 1985), 31–37. Also see James W. Buehler, Joel C. Kleinmann, Carol J. R. Hogue, Lilo T. Strauss, and Jack C. Smith, "Birth Weight-Specific Infant Mortality, United States, 1960 and 1980" and other studies in *Public Health Reports*, 102, no. 2 (March–April 1987).

33. National Commission to Prevent Infant Mortality, *Death Before Life: The Tragedy of Infant Mortality, Appendix* (Washington, D.C.: NCPIM, 1988), p. 23.

Chapter Three

HOUSEHOLD FACTORS

Many different household-level factors, such as income, education, and occupation, are associated with children's mortality rates. They affect children's mortality through their influence on the more immediate individual-level causes, but the linkage mechanisms are not well understood. Assessment of the causal roles of household factors is especially difficult because of the interrelationships among the factors themselves. Also, patterns of association that are strong in some countries may be weak or quite different in others. The policy implications of observed associations are not direct.

A very thorough review, *Socio-Economic Differentials in Child Mortality in Developing Countries*, has been prepared by the Department of International Economic and Social Affairs of the United Nations.[1] In each of the following sections, the findings of this review are summarized in the first few paragraphs. Observations in subsequent paragraphs are based on other sources, which are acknowledged here.

MATERNAL EDUCATION

Maternal education is clearly and strongly associated with children's mortality, in that a child's probability of dying is inversely related to the mother's years of schooling. Maternal education is one of the strongest socioeconomic factors associated with children's survival.

Several different mechanisms may be at work. For example, the importance of the mother's education could result from the ability of a better-educated woman to attract a husband who earns more. Education may be important in terms of specific knowledge of basic preventive and curative procedures. Formal education may facilitate the use of available health care facilities, either because it undermines women's belief in traditional remedies or because educated women can afford to use health care facilities.

Table 3.1
Infant Mortality Rates and Mother's Education, United States, 1980

MOTHER'S EDUCATION (years)	INFANT MORTALITY RATE (deaths per 1000 live births)		
	Blacks	Whites	All Races
0-8	25.6	15.1	17.2
9-11	22.5	13.7	16.3
12	18.1	8.9	10.6
13-15	16.2	7.4	8.8
16 and more	13.6	6.7	7.3

Source: Carol J. R. Hogue, James W. Buehler, Lilo T. Strauss, and Jack C. Smith, "Overview of the National Infant Mortality Surveillance (NIMS) Project—Design, Methods, Results," *Public Health Reports*, 102, no. 2 (March–April 1987), 126–38, esp. 133.

The major effect may be that educated women are less fatalistic, better able to deal with the modern world, and more aware of simple hygienic measures. More highly educated women may allocate more food to their children. They are likely to reject traditional taboos against the eating of some high-protein foods.

Higher levels of education lead to better opportunities for employment or other income-earning activities. Increasing the share of time devoted to income earning may be disadvantageous to the child because the mother then has less time to devote to the child, but it can be advantageous because of the increase in income.

Educated women may be physically healthier because as girls they were in school, and to some extent were spared the physical demands of agricultural and household work.

The linkage between maternal education and infant mortality has been demonstrated in the United States. As indicated in Table 3.1, in the United States the National Infant Mortality Surveillance project showed very clearly that infant mortality is lower with higher levels of maternal education. The pattern holds for both blacks and whites, but the effect of education on mortality levels seems to be stronger for whites.

The association between maternal education and children's survival may be directly causal, perhaps because women learn better child care techniques, or both may be rooted in common factors such as higher income/wealth levels.

John Caldwell suggests that the more fundamental issue may be women's autonomy rather than education.[2] It has been shown that when women have

Table 3.2
Effect of Parents' Schooling on Child Mortality

SCHOOLING OF	LIVING IN	
	URBAN AREAS	RURAL AREAS
Mother	- 3.9 %	- 3.5 %
Father	- 3.6 %	- 1.2 %

Source: United Nations, Department of International Economic and Social Affairs, *Socio-Economic Differentials in Child Mortality in Developing Countries*, ST/ESA/Ser. A/97 (New York: United Nations, 1985), p. 288.

higher status in the society, the children's survival rates are higher, especially for girls.[3]

PATERNAL EDUCATION

The father's education is also associated with children's mortality risk, but usually less strongly than the mother's education. Paternal education seems to affect children's mortality more through its role in determining economic status than in directly affecting child care skills. However, more highly educated fathers may initiate changes in the family's hygiene and food preparation practices.

Table 3.2 shows the average effect of parents' education on children's mortality for the 15 countries covered in the U.N. review. This table is based not on examination of education alone but of education together with a number of other variables, in multivariate analyses. The table shows that for each additional year of mother's education, children's mortality rates are likely to be lower by 3.9 percent in urban areas and 3.5 percent in rural areas. (In simple bivariate analyses, each additional year of mother's education corresponded to an average reduction of children's mortality rates of 6.8 percent.) For each additional year of father's education, children's mortality rates are likely to be lower by 3.6 percent in urban areas and 1.2 percent in rural areas. The smaller effect of the father's education in rural areas may reflect the fact that higher education levels do not lead to higher income levels in rural areas as much as they do in urban areas.

Since the populations in developing countries are predominantly rural, the effect of the father's education for the country as a whole tends to be considerably weaker than the effect of the mother's education.

ETHNICITY AND RELIGION

Systematic differences have been observed in the children's mortality rates among different ethnic or religious groups. For example, in the United States blacks have a higher infant mortality rate than that for whites, and in India, Christian women have low, and Muslim women have high, infant mortality rates. Such differences are generally accounted for in terms of systematic differences in other variables such as education or economic status.

While differences among religious groups usually can be accounted for in terms of other socioeconomic variables, it appears that ethnicity may have some independent effect. For example, people of Chinese extraction in many different settings appear to have unusually low child mortality rates.

MOTHER'S CHILDHOOD RESIDENCE AND LIFETIME MIGRATION STATUS

A mother's current health and general status are determined in part by her life history. In the few studies that have been done on place of origin and patterns of migration, the only consistent finding is that children of women from rural areas tend to have higher mortality rates than children of women from urban areas.

FATHER'S OCCUPATION

The nature of the father's occupation affects children's mortality rates primarily through its role in determining the family's economic status. Consistently, lower mortality levels are found for children of professional and white-collar workers than for children of fathers in agricultural and production occupations. The difference is greater in urban areas than in rural areas. Apparently the occupation as such, apart from difference in income levels, has no significant effect on children's mortality.

Although not considered in the U.N. review, land tenure—closely associated with occupation—can be a significant factor. In the state of Rio Grande do Sul in Brazil it was found that

young children in areas with large ranches, livestock-raising, and a high proportion of agricultural wage-earners presented a higher mortality and had a poorer nutritional status than children in areas with small properties, crop agriculture, and self-employed family workers. Children of landowners showed least malnutrition and the smaller risk of death compared to children of laborers.[4]

In a study of nutritional blindness in Bangladesh, it was found that almost 80 percent of blind children came from landless households.[5]

In Kenya, households with larger farms had a lower prevalence of stunting than households of smallholders.[6]

Similarly, in Malawi, Sri Lanka, and many other less developed countries, the highest infant mortalities are in areas dominated by large plantations. The Solomon Islands may be an exception to this pattern; its plantations appear to operate in a less exploitative fashion than those in most less developed countries.

ECONOMIC ACTIVITY OF THE MOTHER

There are two major factors relating women's economic activity to children's mortality. On the one hand, the increased income that is generated can lead to improved nutrition and health care. On the other hand, income-earning activities can result in reduction of the time available for child care. Working women are likely to breast-feed for a shorter time. In some cases the mother's health may deteriorate because of bad working conditions, making her incapable of providing good child care.

The research shows that, in most countries, children whose mothers are involved in income-earning activities generally have slightly higher mortality rates than those whose mothers are not income earners. However, in several African countries the children of employees were at lower risk. In Asian countries the children of employees were at higher risk—possibly because female participation in the labor force is associated with severe economic stress within the household.

INCOME AND WEALTH

Household income and wealth affect children's mortality largely through their effects on children's consumption of goods and services that affect their health, including food, shelter, clothing, sanitary facilities, use of health care services, and adult supervision. There have been very few studies of allocations within the household to goods and services for children.

In general, households with higher incomes have lower levels of children's mortality, presumably because children in such households enjoy more health-enhancing goods and services. However, there can be some countervailing influences. For example, in some cases higher income may be obtained from extra hours of work, which means less time spent in child care. Because of this sort of linkage, an increase in the mother's income conceivably could have more adverse effects than an increase in the father's income.

In at least one study, however, it was found that income to the mother had more positive effects than income to the father. It was shown that an increment in the mother's income had roughly five times as large an effect in reducing mortality as a proportional (not equal) increase in the father's income. In the culture of the region under study, mothers were expected to earn most of the funds necessary for childrearing, but it seems plausible that, in general, income earned by the mother will have a greater effect in reducing children's mortality than income earned by the father.

Older children can produce income that can result in better life chances for them and their siblings. But employment can also lead to serious deterioration in the working child's health.

The power structure of the family is important because children may not be free to allocate resources to themselves. The health and survival of all family members usually are high in the rank order of the parents' priorities, but sometimes other considerations intervene. The allocation of resources may depend in part upon the perceived value of children to the family. Discriminatory behavior, usually in the form of differential treatment of male and female infants, may depend on the anticipated future productivity of the child. Discrimination in child care by sex is likely to depend on the perceived employment opportunities for women, the status of women, and societal norms.

The research in developing countries consistently shows a negative relationship between infant mortality and income at the household level. The studies differ only in the degree to which income accounts for the variation in mortality, in comparison with other explanatory factors.

MARITAL STATUS AND HOUSEHOLD STRUCTURE

Factors such as whether the mother is single, married, or divorced; the legal status of the union; polygamous versus monogamous union; marital frequency; and the presence of other adults and other children in the household can be associated with children's mortality rates.

It is often found that children born to unmarried women ("illegitimate" births) have a higher risk of mortality. Much of that can be attributed to the fact that illegitimate infants are more likely to be of low birth weight, they are more likely to be born to teenage mothers, and usually they are born to women without previous births.

Children of currently married women have lower mortality rates than children born to widowed and divorced mothers. This may be partly because currently married women have higher socioeconomic status and higher education levels.

Children of consensual unions—those lacking official legal sanction—often have higher mortality rates than children of legal unions, but the evidence does not show a consistent pattern. One factor here may be that consensual unions occur more frequently among people of lower socioeconomic status.

Children of polygamous unions tend to show higher mortality rates than children of monogamous unions.

In general, there appears to be a strong, direct association between stable family relationships and low levels of child mortality.

CHARACTERISTICS OF HOUSING, INCLUDING TOILET AND WATER SUPPLY FACILITIES

The effect of housing conditions on health presumably works largely through the conditions' impact on sanitation, thus affecting the incidence of infectious diseases. The quality of housing is highly correlated with other factors, such as income, class, status, and urban/rural residence, so it is difficult to isolate the effects of specific household amenities.

Large differentials in child mortality are observed with respect to housing materials, lavatory facilities, water supply, and electricity: the lowest mortality levels are associated with the most modern amenities. However, when other socioeconomic characteristics of the household are taken into account, very little of the variance in child mortality rates can be associated specifically with household amenities alone. Moreover, no systematic urban/rural differences in the effects on mortality of dwelling characteristics are found. To quote the United Nations review directly:

The results appear somewhat puzzling. Housing characteristics are expected to exert a relatively direct impact on mortality because these conditions are closely related to the risk of exposure to infectious agents (germs, vectors etc.) and the extent to which residents are protected from cold, heat, wind, rain and so on. One would expect that, if these variables are important for child mortality, much of their impact would be retained when other socioeconomic variables are introduced. This does not prove to be the case.[7]

Contrary to the conclusions of the U.N. review, several studies provide strong evidence that adequate water supply, in both quantity and quality, and good sanitation facilities are important for limiting disease and, thus, mortality. It is particularly important in controlling diarrhea.[8] A study in Sri Lanka showed that the nature of the water supply was the most significant environmental factor of those studied in accounting for infant mortality rates.[9]

Other socioeconomic factors appear to have far greater effects than the simple presence or absence of household amenities. Leonard Sagan addresses the puzzle thus:

the provision of access to clean water is widely considered to be a major factor in explaining mortality decline. Yet the matter is far from proven. For example, when clean water is introduced into a highly contaminated environment where filth, illiteracy, and infectious diseases are highly prevalent, the anticipated improvement in mortality rates is frequently disappointing. . . . To reduce the level of contamination in the home requires not only a clean water source, but also the use of soap and water, clean hands, personal hygiene, safe disposal of feces, and finally, the conviction that these measures are important, are useful, and will make a difference. Critical to such behavior is education, without which a clean water supply is generally useless.[10]

Water supply and sanitation are partly household factors, in that parents and children must follow the appropriate behaviors (such as hand washing), and partly societal factors, in that governments have responsibility for helping to provide adequate supplies of clean water and other sanitation facilities. This responsibility would include the provision of educational programs to encourage appropriate behaviors.

RURAL-URBAN RESIDENCE

There is a common assumption that cities offer greater advantages because of their greater employment opportunities, more extensive and more modern health facilities, and highly educated populations. But these considerations are compromised by pockets of urban poverty that are often enlarged by the steady migration of people from rural areas into the cities.

On balance, urban dwellers do tend to have lower child mortality rates. The research findings suggest that it is the socioeconomic characteristics of the urban population, rather than life in the city itself, which explain this. "When these socio-economic factors are controlled, the urban advantage generally evaporates; and an underlying urban hazard sometimes appears."

There is a consistent urban bias in the provision of health services, but:

In view of the persistently weak findings about the importance of urban-based curative services for general mortality conditions, it is perhaps not surprising that they do not seem to account for an urban superiority in child mortality conditions. The findings of this study clearly show that the urban mortality advantage is attributable more to characteristics associated with the higher socio-economic status of its population than to the specificities of the health sector.[11]

In the United States, infant mortality rates are highest in the urban areas.[12]

REGION OF RESIDENCE

There are variations by region in children's mortality rates in most countries. For example, the southern regions of the Sudan have much higher levels of children's mortality than the northern regions, even after controlling for a variety of other factors. Regional variations are largely due to differences in socioeconomic factors, but differences in climate may be a factor, particularly in accounting for variations in disease environment. Socioeconomic factors account for a great deal of the variation in child mortality rates from region to region, but some aspects of the environment may also contribute to differentials by region. It appears that regional inequalities in mortality are greatest in countries with the largest regional differences in ecology and climate. One study suggested there may be an optimum atmospheric temperature range for child survival.

HEALTH CARE

Access to modern health care services by mothers and children is sometimes thought to be particularly important in reducing mortality. This assumption has been challenged by those who argue that too much emphasis is still being placed on short-term, vertically organized public health interventions and modern medical institutions at the expense of social and economic development. It is not a single episode of diarrhea that kills, but the fact that children are weakened by chronic malnutrition and must continually battle disease. Curing an episode and returning the child to the same environment is not likely to have much lasting impact.

Does access to utilization of health facilities assure significant reductions in child mortality? There is evidence that village-based primary health care systems can have a significant effect, but in some cases there is only a very weak association between the provision of health care services and reductions in children's mortality.

The research indicates that access to and utilization of health care services are positively related to improved child survival rates. The effect may be mediated by education, in that more highly educated parents are more likely to take advantage of available health services.

The U.N. review of the impacts of health care facilities would have been strengthened if it had made a more systematic distinction between access to and actual use of such facilities.

Where health services are available, they are likely to emphasize curative care in hospital settings rather than preventive work through primary health care programs. In the mid-1970s it was estimated that in Ghana, hospital care received 85 percent of national health expenditures and served 10 percent of the population, while primary health care received 15 percent of national health expenditures and served 90 percent of the population.[12] "The World Bank has estimated that on average two-thirds of government health expenditures in developing countries go to teaching hospitals and medical training."[13] The U.N. review acknowledged this urban bias, but apparently it did not distinguish between the impacts of urban-curative and rural-preventive health services.

The U.N. review did not focus on it, but it is important to recognize that prenatal care is an important factor affecting the risks of infant mortality. As the data in Table 3.3 show, in the United States, infant mortality rates are far lower where there is prenatal care than where there is none. Infants born to mothers who obtained prenatal care beginning in the first trimester have lower mortality rates than those for whom prenatal care began later.

CONCLUSION

The U.N. review concluded that the mother's education was the most powerful of the variables studied in accounting for children's mortality. In urban areas, the effect of the father's education was comparable in strength with that of the mother's education. Ethnic variation in child mortality within countries also proved to be quite strong.

The other variables showed relatively weak effects. For example, while the distinction between rural and urban residence was expected to be important,

Table 3.3
Infant Mortality Rates and Prenatal Care, United States, 1980

MONTH PRENATAL CARE BEGAN	INFANT MORTALITY RATE (deaths per 1000 live births)		
	Blacks	Whites	All Races
1-3	17.3	8.5	9.7
4-6	17.6	11.0	12.6
7-9	16.4	10.8	12.4
None	67.7	38.3	48.7

Source: Carol J. R. Hogue, James W. Buehler, Lilo T. Strauss, and Jack C. Smith, "Overview of the National Infant Mortality Surveillance (NIMS) Project—Design, Methods, Results," *Public Health Reports*, 102, no. 2 (March–April 1987), 126–38, esp. 133.

it showed little independent effect after other socioeconomic factors were taken into account. It appears that urban children's mortality is substantially lower than rural children's mortality mainly because of the higher social status of urban residents. The urban bias in public services in itself does not seem to have much impact on child survival. This finding is consistent with the view that health care systems which emphasize large hospitals and expensive curative strategies are not well adapted to the needs of developing countries.

Economic status is associated with children's mortality, but not as strongly as expected. After controlling other variables, doubling of household (or a parent's) income corresponds to a reduction of mortality between 1 and 9 percent. The U.N. review observes: "Thus, the income coefficients appear to offer very little support for pursuing health advance through an income policy."[14]

Amenities such as piped water and flush lavatories, in themselves, appeared to have only moderate effects on children's mortality. Piped water had virtually no systematic effect. The availability of a flush lavatory reduced mortality by about 10 percent in the four countries for which data were available. Overall:

the results suggest that even the sum of "direct" mortality effects of doubling everyone's income, providing every household with a flush lavatory and piped water, and turning every agricultural labourer into a professional/white collar worker would be less than the "direct" effect of providing 10 years of school for each woman.... The very considerable impact of mother's education and ethnicity points above all to the potential importance of child care practices in determining levels of child mortality. ... The resources available to the household are also important, but their role is hardly overwhelming.... The spread of good hygienic practices... among even the poorer classes in developing countries has very likely served to offset much of the material disadvantages these groups suffer.

The fact that these non-economic factors evidently play such a major role in child mortality should be reassuring to policy-makers, since they are probably not subject to the same inertial forces as are the economic factors.[15]

Issues of technique, such as child care practices and personal hygiene, are relatively more important than the sheer volume of inputs reflected in variables such as income, housing facilities, and residence in urban areas. It is not simply the amount of resources but the way in which the available resources are used that is critically important.

The U.N. study said that "the variables studied here do not have effects that vary systematically with features of the national setting,"[16] but the basis for this is not evident. The study concentrated on household-level variables, and did not systematically assess associations of children's mortality with national-level variables.

NOTES

1. United Nations, Department of International Economic and Social Affairs, Socio-Economic Differentials in Child Mortality in Developing Countries, ST/ESA/Ser. A/97 (New York: United Nations, 1985).

2. John C. Caldwell, "Routes to Low Mortality in Poor Countries," Population and Development Review, 12, no. 2 (June 1986), 171–220.

3. Carol P. MacCormack, "Health and the Social Power of Women," Social Science & Medicine, 26, no. 7 (1988), 677–83.

4. Cesar G. Victora and J. Patrick Vaughan, "Land Tenure Patterns and Child Health in Southern Brazil: The Relationship Between Agricultural Production, Malnutrition and Child Mortality," International Journal of Health Services, 15, no. 2 (1985), 253–74. Also see Cesar G. Victora, J. Patrick Vaughan, Betty Kirkwood, Jose Carlos Martines, and Lucio B. Barcelos, "Child Malnutrition and Land Ownership in Southern Brazil," Ecology of Food and Nutrition, 18 (1986), 265–75.

5. N. Cohen, M. A. Jalil, H. Rahman, M. A. Matin, J. Sprague, J. Islam, J. Davison, E. Leemuhis de Regt, and M. Mitra, "Landholding, Wealth and Risk of Blinding Malnutrition in Rural Bangladeshi Households," Social Science & Medicine, 21, no. 11 (1985), 1269–72.

6. J. Haaga, J. Mason, F. Z. Omoro, V. Quinn, A. Rafferty, K. Test, and L. Wasonga, "Child Malnutrition in Rural Kenya: A Geographic and Agricultural Classification," Ecology of Food and Nutrition, 18 (1986), 297–307.

7. United Nations, Department of International Economic and Social Affairs, Socio-Economic Differentials, p. 242.

8. John Briscoe, "A Role for Water Supply and Sanitation in the Child Survival Revolution," PAHO Bulletin, 21, no. 2 (1987), 93–105; S. A. Esrey, R. G. Feacham, and J. M. Hughes, "Interventions for the Control of Diarrhoeal Diseases Among Young Children: Improving Water Supplies and Excreta Disposal Facilities," WHO Bulletin, 63, no. 4 (1985), 757–72.

9. M. Patel, "Effects of Health Service and Environmental Factors on Infant Mortality: The Case of Sri Lanka," Journal of Epidemiology and Community Health, 34 (1980), 76–82.

10. Leonard A. Sagan, *The Health of Nations: True Causes of Sickness and Well-Being* (New York: Basic Books, 1987), p. 36.

11. United Nations, Department of International Economic and Social Affairs, *Socio-Economic Differentials*, p. 255.

12. National Commission to Prevent Infant Mortality, *Death Before Life: The Tragedy of Infant Mortality* (Washington, D.C.: NCPIM, 1988), p. 8.

13. Katrina Galway, Brent Wolff, and Richard Sturgis, *Child Survival: Risks and the Road to Health* (Columbia, Md.: Institute for Resource Development/Westinghouse/USAID, 1987), p. 51.

14. United Nations, Department of International Economic and Social Affairs, *Socio-Economic Differentials*, p. 289.

15. Ibid., pp. 289–90.

16. Ibid., pp. 290–91. On the great importance of education in accounting for modernization, see A. Inkeles and D. Smith, *Becoming Modern: Individual Change in Six Developing Countries* (Cambridge, Mass.: Harvard University Press, 1974).

Chapter Four

THE CHILD SURVIVAL AND DEVELOPMENT MOVEMENT

There has been considerable interest in the problem of children's mortality at least since the industrial revolution, but the modern child survival and development movement has its roots in initiatives taken in the late 1970s. In May 1977 the Thirtieth World Health Assembly resolved that the main social goal of governments and the World Health Organization (WHO) in the coming decades would be the attainment of "health for all by the year 2000." In 1978 the International Conference on Primary Health Care was held in Alma Ata, U.S.S.R., sponsored by WHO and the United Nations Children's Fund (UNICEF). The resulting Declaration of Alma Ata said that the goal of health for all by the year 2000 was to be achieved through the strengthening of primary health care. It set guidelines and goals for primary health care work for the remainder of the century.

One of the twelve major indicators for monitoring global progress specified the objective that "the infant mortality rate for all identifiable subgroups is below 50 per 1000 live births."[1] It was acknowledged that "some countries may wish to set more stringent targets for their own national strategy." It was in this context that several agencies launched worldwide child survival activities, including UNICEF, WHO, the U.S. Agency for International Development (USAID), and several private voluntary organizations.

INSTITUTIONAL SETTING

At the international level UNICEF is recognized as the lead agency for child survival and development. Born out of the need to care for the many thousands of children who faced famine and disease as a result of World War II, UNICEF was formally created in December 1946 by the U.N. General Assembly. Originally expected to serve only temporarily, in recognition of the continuing needs the General Assembly extended its life in 1950.

Through the years UNICEF participated in many activities in behalf of children. In 1947–50 it helped to ship milk and other vital supplies to several countries. In 1948 it participated in a worldwide vaccination campaign to fight tuberculosis. In 1953 it began its program of penicillin vaccinations to combat yaws. In the late 1950s UNICEF joined the worldwide effort to eradicate malaria. In the early 1970s the emphasis was on programs for supplying village drinking water. In 1979 UNICEF led the public education campaigns of the International Year of the Child.[2]

It was in 1983 that UNICEF launched its drive to save the lives of millions of children. It now works with governments all over the world to help formulate national programs for child survival and development. UNICEF field offices have a great deal of autonomy in this effort, but they have backup support from headquarters in New York. Where it is feasible, a baseline study is prepared locally, usually with a title of the form *Situation Analysis of Women and Children in (Country)*. This becomes the basis for the planning effort. The formal written plan for national action includes provisions regarding UNICEF assistance. It becomes the basis for a signed agreement between the government and UNICEF.

WHO has not organized its contribution to the effort in terms of designated child survival programs. Only its program on maternal and child health is specifically oriented to children. Several other WHO programs, such as those on acute respiratory infection, diarrheal diseases, and nutrition, have particular relevance for children.

Several of WHO's program objectives make explicit reference to children. Under "Protection and Promotion of the Health of Specific Population Groups," WHO's target says that by 1995 "in developing countries maternal, infant and child mortality will show a marked reduction."

One of the targets with respect to diarrhea is more concrete, asking that "in 1995 the number of deaths from childhood diarrhoea in developing countries will be reduced by 50 percent or 3.4 million"—meaning a reduction by these amounts in comparison with what would be expected in 1995 in the absence of a diarrhea disease control program.

With respect to nutrition, the WHO targets ask that by 1995 "among infants and young children, wasting from acute malnutrition will no longer be a problem of public health significance in any region of the world, while stunted growth will show declining trends."

WHO's Expanded Programme on Immunization was initiated in 1973, and has been carried out in close cooperation with UNICEF.[3] WHO program objectives for 1990–95 ask that by 1995 neonatal tetanus will have been eliminated and measles and polio will have been sharply reduced.

WHO takes major responsibility for dealing with acute respiratory infection (ARI). By the end of 1987, ARI control programs had begun in 17 countries, and a number of others were well advanced in their national program planning. Emphasis has been placed on the training of health care workers in the management of ARI. In August 1987 WHO's ARI program was placed under common management with its Diarrhoeal Diseases Control program to enable them to share experience and expertise. Both programs depend on a case management approach through the primary health care system.[4] WHO objectives for 1990–95 with respect to ARI are set in terms of inputs such as the initiation of comprehensive ARI programs and the evaluation of recommended control methods, rather than in terms of outputs such as the number of ARI-related deaths averted.

WHO calls for reductions in the incidence of malnutrition and various diseases, but no specific goals are set for corresponding reductions in children's mortality.[5]

UNICEF and WHO have described the ways in which their roles complement one another: "WHO's strength lies in providing technical and scientific information and in its experience in health education; UNICEF's strength lies in imparting this knowledge to people and in mobilizing them to action based on it."[6]

USAID has a child survival program, with about $150 million being devoted to child survival in fiscal year 1986. Its main focus is on immunization and oral rehydration therapy, but it is also concerned with the provision of nutrition services and with birth spacing. The agency places special emphasis on 22 large countries where mortality rates are especially high.

USAID supports several organizations that provide technical assistance for the design, management, and evaluation of their child survival programs. These include PRITECH (Technology for Primary Health Care), HEALTH-COM (Communication for Child Survival), REACH (Resources for Child Health) and PRICOR (Primary Health Care Operations Research). USAID also works with a number of other governmental agencies and private voluntary organizations.[7]

UNICEF, WHO, and USAID are the leading international actors in the child survival movement. Other international organizations—such as the Food and Agriculture Organization of the United Nations, the Pan American Health Organization, and the U.N. High Commissioner for Refugees—also play important contributory roles. Numerous private voluntary organizations—such as Save the Children, World Vision, and Catholic Relief Services—also act internationally. In addition there are countless governmental and nongovernmental agencies within nations that are involved in efforts for child survival and development. Furthermore, there is an intricate web of coordination and cooperation among these many different bodies.

In its child survival and development effort described in the 1982–83 edition of *The State of the World's Children*, UNICEF emphasized four low-cost programmatic remedies. They were identified by the acronym *GOBI*, for *G*rowth monitoring, *O*ral rehydration, *B*reast-feeding, and *I*mmunization. These four are reviewed below.

The variety of programs was later expanded and the acronym became

GOBI-FFF, adding *F*ood supplements, *F*amily planning, and *F*emale education.[8] While such programs are undertaken by many agencies throughout the world, they have never taken hold as major elements of the child survival movement. Compared with GOBI, FFF did not have as much appeal:

Although these were equally regarded as critical to the overall improvement of child health, they did not pass as easily all [UNICEF Executive Director James] Grant's tests of low cost, political acceptability, and potential for popular acclaim; they were not, in his view, as "do-able." "Do-ability" was an all important consideration. The essential consideration for do-ability was that the word could be made to spread, the demand come forward, and enough of a country's social apparatus would assert itself to achieve the target.[9]

A major new initiative was launched in the United States with the establishment of the National Commission to Prevent Infant Mortality in 1987. In the United States the problems are primarily with newborns rather than with children between their first and fifth birthdays. Thus the commission's focus is on low birth weight, health insurance, and prenatal care, rather than on the sort of interventions promoted in the developing countries.

GROWTH MONITORING

Growth monitoring refers to systematic measuring and charting of the heights and weights of children to assess their health status. Such monitoring may be used to measure the health effects of specific interventions, such as sanitation or nutrition programs. The more fundamental use of growth monitoring in child survival programs is to alert health workers or parents to problems that might otherwise be missed. "For example, a mother may not notice a gradual onset of low-grade infections in a child who is being weaned but may be able to relate such a development to diminution in the rate of growth as depicted on a growth chart."[10]

Systematic growth monitoring programs have been adopted in many parts of the third world. It was a major part of the national nutrition program in Indonesia even before its widespread promotion by UNICEF:

By 1982, two million mothers in 15,000 Indonesian villages had been given KMS—*Kartu Menuju Sehat*, meaning: "towards good health cards." Once a month, they attended a meeting at their local weighing post where their toddlers were put in a simple harness and hung from a market scale. The nutrition cadres—volunteers with some training—plotted a mark on a rainbow coloured chart for the child's weight opposite the child's age. The line joining the marks month by month showed immediately whether the child was on or off the road to health.[11]

Much emphasis has been placed on comparing height and weight measures with standards such as those developed by the U.S. National Center for

Health Services, the U.S. Centers for Disease Control, and the WHO. For the purpose of alerting mothers to possible problems, however, increasing emphasis is placed on the individual child's own growth trajectory over time. Whether the child is large or small, faltering growth usually signals a problem that requires attention.

ORAL REHYDRATION

Oral rehydration therapy (ORT) is based on the use of a solution that the body will absorb even when it rejects most other forms of food or drink. Often the oral rehydration solution is simply small amounts of sugar and salt dissolved in water, but other mixes are used as well. The simple sugar-and-salt solution has been effective in preventing deaths from diarrhea in many different circumstances.[12]

By the late 1980s the solution was mass-produced in 47 developing countries, and 90 countries had national programs to promote the use of ORT. UNICEF estimates that ORT may be preventing more than 600,000 deaths a year. The global ORT effort is being coordinated by WHO's Diarrhoeal Disease Control Programme.[13]

BREAST-FEEDING

Breast-feeding has many advantages, not only increasing the survival chances of the child but also reducing the likelihood that the child will get sick. Breast-feeding also inhibits conception:

Promoting breast-feeding... is one of the most effective low-cost ways of increasing the survival chances of infants in poor communities. At the same time the hormonal changes produced in the mother's body by the act of breast-feeding also have a contraceptive effect. Although not totally dependable from an individual mother's point of view, breast-feeding still prevents more conceptions than family planning programmes.[14]

Several programs have been undertaken to promote breast-feeding, most prominently the worldwide campaign against the promotion of manufactured formulas, which climaxed in the passage of the International Code of Marketing for Breast-milk Substitutes by the World Health Assembly in 1981. A small private group, the International Nutrition Communication Service, has developed successful models for modifying maternity hospitals to support breast-feeding. The Bangkok Breast-feeding Promotion Project provided training and support for improved hospital practices. Similar projects have been undertaken in Honduras and Brazil.[15]

IMMUNIZATION

Immunization campaigns are undertaken against six major communicable diseases: diphtheria, measles, pertussis (whooping cough), polio, tetanus, and tuberculosis. In 1973 WHO decided to make routine immunization available to children worldwide, through its Expanded Programme on Immunization. In 1977 the World Health Assembly declared a goal of universal child immunization by 1990.

UNICEF assisted national immunization drives with vaccines, kerosene refrigerators, cold boxes, and training for vaccination teams, but with the advent of the GOBI idea, UNICEF became much more involved. UNICEF's executive director, James Grant, successfully motivated many national leaders to launch large-scale immunization campaigns, and helped to organize the campaigns. Major campaigns have been undertaken in Brazil, Burkina Faso, Colombia, El Salvador, and many other countries, and coverage rates have gone up substantially.[16]

In some cases armed combat has been suspended to allow the immunization of children. In El Salvador:

The nation's immunization days made headlines in 1985 as government and guerrillas stopped fighting for three "days of tranquility" so that teams from the Ministry of Health and the International Red Cross could vaccinate nearly a quarter of a million children.

The guns fell silent again. . . . On 6 April 1986, at over 1,600 vaccination posts set up across the country, 237,000 children were innoculated against five diseases and 58,000 mothers were given injections against tetanus.[17]

Combat was suspended in El Salvador once again in January 1987 to allow the immunization of children.

Similar "days of tranquility" were established in Lebanon in September, October, and November of 1987:

Not only did Lebanon's various factions refrain from fighting during the days of tranquility, but they also turned their military organizations to peaceful purposes. Transport and communication networks were put in the service of the campaign. Radios and walkie-talkies usually employed to direct bombs to targets or to coordinate militia movements, carried requests for vaccine replenishment and other life-saving messages.[18]

In 1985 in Uganda, UNICEF persuaded both sides in the civil war to allow the nationwide immunization program to go on despite the conflict.[19]

Nicaragua has been very successful in its immunization efforts, inoculating 95 percent of its infants against tuberculosis and 85 percent against polio. According to Nicaragua's health minister, despite the war, "at times we have depended on the army to transport vaccines, or actually to vaccinate."[20]

As a result of the worldwide effort of UNICEF, WHO, and many other national and international agencies, in 1988 it was reported that:

Two thirds of the developing world's children are now receiving a first dose of DPT vaccine and 50 percent are completing the full course of three injections. Half are also being immunized against polio and 39 percent against measles. The result is the saving of approximately 1.4 million young lives each year.[21]

It has been estimated that immunization coverage in developing countries in 1990 could reach almost 75 percent for DPT and almost 70 percent for measles.

NOTES

1. World Health Organization, *World Health Statistics Annual 1986* (Geneva: WHO, 1986), p. vii.

2. *UNICEF at 40*, a special issue of *UNICEF News*, iss. 123 (1986); and Maggie Black, *The Children and the Nations: The Story of Unicef* (New York: UNICEF, 1986).

3. Black, *The Children and the Nations*, pp. 481–89.

4. "The WHO ARI Programme," *ARI News*, no. 11 (August 1988), p. 7.

5. World Health Organization, *Eighth General Programme of Work Covering the Period 1990–1995* (Geneva: WHO, 1987).

6. "UNICEF-WHO Joint Committee on Health Policy," *World Health Forum*, 8, no. 2 (1987), 268–69.

7. U.S. Agency for International Development, *Child Survival: A Second Report to Congress on the AID Program* (Washington, D.C.: USAID, 1988).

8. Richard Cash, Gerald T. Keusch, and Joel Lamstein, eds., *Child Health and Survival: The UNICEF GOBI-FFF Program* (London: Croom Helm, 1987).

9. Black, *The Children and the Nations*, p. 476.

10. James R. Hebert, "Growth Monitoring: The 'G' in GOBI-FFF," in Richard Cash, Gerald Keusch, and Joel Lamstein, eds., *Child Health and Survival* (London: Croom Helm, 1987), pp. 11–20.

11. Black, *The Children and the Nations*, p. 471.

12. Norbert Hirschhorn, "Oral Rehydration Therapy: The Programme and the Promise," in Richard Cash, Gerald Keusch, and Joel Lamstein, eds., *Child Health and Survival* (London: Croom Helm, 1987), pp. 21–46.

13. James P. Grant, *The State of the World's Children 1988* (New York: Oxford University Press, 1988), p. 20.

14. James P. Grant, *The State of the World's Children 1987* (New York: Oxford University Press, 1987), p. 10.

15. Marian Frank Zeitlin, "Breast-Feeding as a Component of the Child Survival Strategy: The 'B' in GOBI-FFF," in Richard Cash, Gerald Keusch, and Joel Lamstein, eds., *Child Health and Survival* (London: Croom Helm, 1987), pp. 47–62.

16. Black, *The Children and the Nations*, pp. 475–90; *Universal Child Immunization by 1990*, a special issue of *Assignment Children*, 69/72 (1985). Also see *World*

Immunization News, published by Task Force for Child Survival, Carter Presidential Center, One Copenhill, Atlanta, Ga. 30307, telephone (404) 420-5120.

17. Grant, *The State of the World's Children 1987*, p. 52.

18. "Tranquility Comes to Lebanon in UNICEF Immunization Drive," *Action Children*, 2, no. 4 (1987), 1, 10; Richard Reid, "Immunization in Lebanon: 'Grand Alliance' in Action," *World Immunization News*, 4, no. 2 (March–April 1988), 7–8.

19. Cole Dodge, "Corridors of Peace in Uganda," *Assignment Children*, 69/72 (1985), 345–46.

20. Madeline Eisner, "Nicaragua to Halve Infant Mortality," *UNICEF Intercom*, no. 50 (October 1988), 18, 21.

21. Grant, *The State of the World's Children 1988*, p. 4.

Chapter Five

CRITICISM OF CHILD SURVIVAL PROGRAMS

Action as ambitious as the worldwide movement for child survival and development naturally draws many supporters, but it also draws many critics. Some are more constructive than others, and some are better balanced than others. All help us to gain a better understanding of the nature of the challenge. We begin by reviewing concerns relating to the specific GOBI-FFF programs and then move on to more general concerns.

GROWTH MONITORING

Growth monitoring can be useful, but frequently there are practical problems in obtaining and using scales, making blank charts available, and training people to use the scales and the charts. Interpreting the charts can be difficult. Some growth monitoring programs have been ritualistic, with growth monitoring becoming an end in itself and not triggering appropriate follow-up actions. Health workers or parents may not know what to do, or they may know and still not do it for a variety of reasons. Several concerns have emerged about growth monitoring:

the regular weighing of children does not, in itself, achieve anything useful. Indeed it may make heavy demands on the time and other resources of parents and the welfare services that support them. . . . staff in child health programmes are bound to have difficulty in stimulating mothers to spend time ensuring that their children are weighed regularly. . . . Despite the continued stress, in international literature, on the importance of using growth records to assess the velocity of a child's weight gain, field workers tend to concentrate on the actual weights of children as they are seen. . . . All too often *changes* in weight are not available to health workers and they have to rely on the information conveyed by a single weight figure at a particular point in time. The attendance rate of children from deprived backgrounds at weighing centres is frequently low, especially when they are under three years of age. Yet if growth monitoring really is going to lead to a reduction in children's suffering and mortality, it is the younger ones who need to be kept under the closest surveillance.

Field workers who do utilise growth charts are often unable to offer any useful intervention for the child who shows serious growth problems.[1]

The benefits of growth monitoring are very indirect:

Unlike immunisation, which represent a discrete complete action at each stage, growth monitoring is a process which entails calling into action other processes if it is to be successful. For health workers and mothers who expect more immediate gratification which comes from giving or receiving "medicine," growth monitoring may be viewed as an unfulfilling activity.

Of all the activities stressed by UNICEF in *GOBI*, growth monitoring requires the highest level of instruction and participation. Without the active involvement of mothers, health workers and children, growth monitoring will, and usually does, function the most poorly of the four *GOBI* components.[2]

The 1987 edition of UNICEF's *The State of the World's Children* said that growth monitoring is "possibly the most essential step towards the eradication of child malnutrition of our times." The 1988 edition does not mention growth monitoring. The 1989 edition acknowledges that "very few nations have taken advantage of the growth monitoring technique on a national level," but argues that it has been successful where it has been tried.

Growth monitoring can be useful, but only as one component of child care programs that also involve education of both health workers and parents, and provide appropriate nutrition and other health interventions when they are needed. These programs must be tailored to particular local circumstances.

ORAL REHYDRATION

Oral rehydration therapy (ORT) is useful only for dehydrating diarrheas, not for dysenteric or chronic diarrheas. In many cases people are taught how to use ORT, but do not use it because it does not conform to their understanding of the character of diarrhea. Concerns have been expressed regarding the ways in which ORT and other child survival techniques make demands on the mother's time:

Although they can have important benefits in terms of child survival and child development, the time costs of utilizing ORT, growth monitoring and improved weaning practices appear to be considerable while the potential time and money savings to women from these technologies seem to be quite limited. The main effect of ORT is to prevent death and perhaps to slightly reduce duration of disease, but there is no evidence that ORT reduces the incidence of diarrhea.[3]

ORT deals only with symptoms, and does not address the causes of diarrhea. It does nothing to decontaminate local water supplies or to improve local sanitation, for example.

One key issue regarding effectiveness is the possibility that ORT may only postpone death, saving children who succumb a short time later to other illnesses. In Honduras, "diarrhea death rates fell during an ORT campaign but no change in overall death rates could be detected."[4]

There is some confusion regarding the effectiveness of the simple solution of salt and water in comparison with alternatives such as the "full" WHO formula, which also includes bicarbonate and potassium. Some of the frequently cited successes have been based on use of the WHO formula rather than the simple solution that is widely advocated.

BREAST-FEEDING

When the International Code of Marketing for Breast-Milk Substitutes was passed by the World Health Assembly in May 1981, many activists who had fought the formula manufacturers closed their files, thinking they had won.[5] Unfortunately, the manufacturers have continued their campaigns to sell infant formula. The resistance against the manufacturers by private voluntary organizations has resumed.[6]

Nevertheless, the major international organizations involved in the child survival movement have not mounted an extensive campaign to promote breast-feeding. Despite the "B" in GOBI and the vigorous advocacy for breast-feeding in their publications, they have undertaken remarkably little programmatic action to support it. Apparently they have not looked into the extent to which breast-feeding might reduce the incidence or impact of acute respiratory infections (ARI) and other deadly diseases.

IMMUNIZATION

Immunization against measles, pertussis, tetanus, poliomyelitis, diphtheria, and tuberculosis has been described as one of the most effective forms of preventive primary health care. Nevertheless, these diseases persist. Why?

Historically, the decline of major infectious diseases in Europe and North America actually predated the introduction of antibiotics and vaccines. The massive improvements were due not to immunization programs but to improvements in the standard of living.[7] Similarly, "infant ARI mortality fell in the presently developed countries well before the development of antibiotics. Indeed, the rates, even though much smaller than those in developing countries, have continued to decrease faster."[8] The eradication of smallpox in the 1970s occurred more than 150 years after the introduction of the vaccine. We should be cautious about placing too much faith in immunization programs. Extensive investment in immunization campaigns may draw resources away from other important health and development programs.

Immunization programs are centrally controlled and administered in a top-down fashion. Thus they run contrary to the fundamental principles of community-based primary health care called for at Alma Ata in 1978. As one critic of the program for universal child immunization in India by 1990 put it, such programs

are inhibiting community self-reliance and social control over medical technology by making people once again dependent on Western countries for funds, vaccines, and equipment. . . . Even if it were possible to save some children by providing them protection against the diseases, these children would be condemned to live a life of virtual "living death" under the hostile ecological conditions that prevail so extensively in different parts of the country.[9]

There are real questions to be raised about the effectiveness of immunization campaigns in reducing children's mortality. In India it has been estimated that only 8 out of 100 child deaths are due to the diseases for which immunizations are given.[10] Also, children saved from one of the immunizable diseases may be taken by malnutrition and the many other lethal diseases that threaten them:

When vaccination against smallpox became available in the early part of the nineteenth century, smallpox deaths, which occurred most commonly among children, fell precipitously. However, the overall death rate was relatively unaffected as deaths from gastrointestinal and other diseases subsequently rose. One cause of death was replaced by another, as would be expected if there had been no change in the immune defense of the population.[11]

"Success" in the immunization literature is usually based on numbers of programs started and rates of coverage achieved rather than on lives saved. Many agencies have a tendency to describe their achievements in terms of inputs, effort expended, but these should not be confused with outputs, the health results achieved.

COMPREHENSIVE VS. SELECTIVE PRIMARY HEALTH CARE

These concerns related to specific child survival programs fit squarely into the debate between those who advocate comprehensive and those who advocate selective primary health care. Susan Rifkin and Gill Walt frame the distinction this way:

we see "primary health care" as being concerned with a developmental process by which people improve both their lives and their life-styles. Good health is a key factor to this process. We see "selective primary health care" as being concerned with medical interventions aimed at improving the health status of the most individuals at the lowest cost.[12]

With some qualifications, the GOBI-FFF interventions are rather pure forms of selective primary health care. The question is, are technical interventions such as immunization programs really useful? The critics argue that selective primary health care:

(1) negated the concept of community participation with programmes planned from the "bottom up"; (2) gave allocations only to people with priority diseases leaving the rest to suffer; (3) reinforced authoritarian attitudes; (4) had a fragile scientific basis; and (5) had a questionable moral and ethical value in which foreign and elite interests overruled those of the majority of the people.[13]

Some critics say the selective approach has attracted a strong following, especially among foreign donor agencies, because selective primary health care

produces recordable results, encourages the private sector to be involved in health service delivery to large populations, appeals to donors because of the "cost-effective" arguments, promotes use of advanced technologies which benefit multinationals and maintains the financial and institutional *status quo*.[14]

The research emphasis in health is on finding technological means for overcoming diseases at the clinical level. But this does no good for the children of poor countries who die of very ordinary, very well understood diseases and of malnutrition. The need is not so much for technical invention as for social invention. Conventional science-oriented research strategies are particularly pernicious because their search for universals systematically blinds them to the requirements of specific local contexts. The scientific approach to the formulation of health care interventions is biased in favor of top-down, imposed technological interventions such as immunization, and biased against interventions that require a great deal of adaptation to local circumstances, such as strategies for engaging community participation. The scientific approach measures success in terms of aggregate numbers of services delivered, and tends to be insensitive to the articulation of satisfaction or dissatisfaction in local dialects. Local voices do not participate in the evaluation process.

The child survival interventions really are selective, and the selections are difficult to understand. A portion of the ARI mortality can now be prevented by immunization for diphtheria, measles, tuberculosis and pertussis, but "these diseases seem to contribute less than a quarter of overall ARI morbidity ... and there is at present no effective immunization for the other agents that cause ARI."[15]

Through the mid-1980s UNICEF's "child survival and development revolution" centered on the seven action fronts enumerated in the GOBI-FFF acronym. But GOBI is not mentioned at all in the 1988 or 1989 edition of UNICEF's *The State of the World's Children*. In the late 1980s most of

UNICEF's and USAID's resources and efforts focused on the "twin engines" of immunization and ORT. Thus their selective primary health care has become even more selective, with the result sometimes described as "monofocality" or "bifocality." In *The State of the World's Children 1989* the emphasis became trifocal, focusing on immunization, ORT, and birth spacing. There is real concern that emphasizing just one or two or three program elements may tend to displace other important primary health care activities since, after all, emphasizing one means deemphasizing others. UNICEF's response has been that immunization and ORT can open the way for the full spectrum of health care activities. This is yet to be demonstrated.

There are many technical issues in child survival and development: what interventions work? under what conditions? how well? for how long? with what side effects? Individuals and organizations develop vested interests in particular sorts of analyses and particular sorts of remedies. Sometimes, instead of choosing among alternatives, the solution is simply to let different approaches coexist. They confront one another only when they must draw from the same pool of resources.

One major issue is the question of going to scale.[16] Some approaches may work well in the clinic or in a village or two, but there may be no sensible way to make them work at a provincial, national, or global scale. A small growth monitoring or feeding program may work well, perhaps with health workers and funding from an international agency, but how would that experience help in solving the hunger problem in countries of many millions of people? Immunization programs still fall far short of the targeted levels of coverage. Other sorts of programs, most of which have not been pushed nearly as vigorously as immunization, reach few people and their scope of coverage grows slowly. Why? The question is not a technical one. It can be addressed only at the societal level, in terms of social organization and social priorities.

CONSERVATISM

The focus on the micro or household level has led to a very conservative orientation in nutrition and other child survival programs:

The analysis of malnutrition causality focused primarily on attributes of the malnourished and their families, not on the social, economic and political order around them. Similarly, the standard nutrition interventions advanced by nutrition planners such as food subsidies or supplements, nutrition education and health care are interventions targeted to the malnourished; they do little to manipulate broader social, economic and political relationships in a manner favorable to people who are poor, dependent and powerless.[17]

Conservatism is reinforced by the persistent tendency to view socioeconomic factors as functioning primarily at the household level rather than the societal level. The U.N. review of *Socio-Economic Differentials in Child Mortality in Developing Countries*, summarized in Chapter 3, showed very plainly that the major concern has been household-level rather than societal variables. This micro orientation creates a strong bias in favor of adjustments by individuals and households rather than by the social structures in which they find themselves.

Factors such as education, income, and occupation do vary from household to household, but it is important to appreciate that they are largely determined by the social contexts in which people are embedded. When half or more of a nation's population are listed as being engaged in agriculture, that does not mean all these people freely chose that occupation over, say, being university professors. Race is an individual or household-level factor in biological terms, but it draws its importance from its impacts at the societal level. Studies of socioeconomic factors associated with children's mortality tend to crowd their attention onto the individual and the household, thus in effect absolving the society-as-a-whole from any distinct responsibility for children's mortality.

The result is not simply conservatism but also its close ally, blaming the victims:

The causes of malnutrition are found primarily among the malnourished, and not in the social order in which they live. Since it is the characteristic of the malnourished and their families which function as the determinants of malnutrition, changes are required only for those suffering nutritional deficiencies and not for the rest of society. There has been no serious examination of the alternative hypothesis that the persistency of widespread malnutrition is largely a reflection of social and political organization, institutional and economic arrangements, and choices of development strategies. Malnutrition is reduced to the status of a technical problem.[18]

The poor are charged with ignorance and inappropriate behavior, and are asked to change their life-styles to better adjust to the circumstances in which they are embedded. For example, they are asked to adjust to the realities of contaminated water by treating diarrhea, rather than being coached in methods for demanding improved waterworks from their local governments. Despite the enormous burdens the poor already face, they are asked to sit through lectures providing answers to questions they never asked. The promoters of these programs are not called upon to change their life-styles, or to learn anything, or to accept any share of responsibility for existing conditions. Local people are asked to make adaptations that the advocates would never consider making themselves.

Many of the most important questions relating to child survival work are related to cultural relativism and cultural sensitivity. Why do child survival programs typically treat people as objects? Why aren't people's views taken more fully into account? Why aren't people more fully engaged in the formulation and the implementation of child survival programs?

At times modern high-technology medicine and health care systems are used—often imposed—where they are quite inappropriate. A common man-ifestation of this is the construction of large, modern, resource-consuming hospitals in urban centers, leaving inadequate resources for the provision of primary health care services in rural areas.

Also, *we* who provide programs tend to assume that *they* who receive programs—the targets of our campaigns—understand malnutrition, diseases, and children's mortality in much the same ways *we* do. Where differences in understanding are noted, the reflexive response is to assume *they* are wrong, and perhaps foolish or superstitious. Very regularly, the prescribed remedy is that *they* should be administered some education, which means getting *them* to see things as *we* see them. The idea that *we* might benefit from some education regarding *their* way of understanding is rarely enter-tained.[19]

Not only household-level factors but also macro, societal factors must be taken into account. Specific technical interventions may have demonstrable effectiveness under some conditions, but there is still a danger:

the difficulty is that by identifying specific techniques and strongly promoting them, they divert attention and resources from the process of development to the highlighting of specific programmes with exaggerated and often unpredictable outcomes. Indeed, seeking interventions and "instant" successes, planners put in danger the long and slow process that leads to sustained improvements in people's lives. They create a climate of short-term expediency instead of long-term change. . . . It is the develop-mental processes that need further exploration and research strengthening capabilities within countries, not injecting techniques into them.[20]

We should be fully aware of the implications of doing Band-Aid work where major surgery is needed. In turn-of-the-century England, advocating the ed-ucation of mothers as a means of promoting children's welfare "was an easier path to follow than a direct attack on the low wages and poor housing that were the root cause."[21] The nutrition program launched in the Philippines in the mid-1970s may have looked good, but it takes on a different coloring if it is seen as a largely symbolic cover for the failure of land reform. In much the same way the development of high-yield varieties of grains through the green revolution "was, in fact, an alternative to agrarian reform, which implies redistribution of power; it was a means of increasing food production without upsetting entrenched interests."[22] Child survival programs may sometimes amount to pacification programs, inducing accommodation to circumstances that should in fact be changed.

For some agencies and ministries, as presently constituted, we cannot rea-sonably expect anything other than conservative, technically oriented work focused on micro-level issues. But many of these organizations are more conservative than is required by the constraints they face. Some use their programs to push particular ideological perspectives. USAID, for example, presses for the privatization of health care and other social services under its child survival programs, as it does in many other programs. USAID and UNICEF annual reports are public relations pieces, reporting no failures and sometimes suggesting they deserve credit where none is due.[23]

The discovery that factors such as maternal education and poverty are important in determining the level of children's mortality should in turn raise new questions: Why do women have such low levels of education in so many countries? Why are so many people in poverty? Why are amenities such as clean water and health care services in short supply in so many places? After all, schools and health services are not natural resources available only in fixed and given quantities. Their availability is largely the result of deliberate human decisions. These are decisions at the macro or societal level, not the micro or household level. The "settings" on many important variables are determined much more by governments than by households.

It is tempting to respond to problems of malnutrition with new programs for nutrition intervention and food production. But the food situation is shaped far more by the character of the economy and by government policies than by specific nutrition programs and projects. Governments' macroeconomic policies affecting such things as the prices of exports and imports and the level of unemployment have a very strong influence in determining the extent of malnutrition and of child survival. Nutrition interventions—even those which work—may distract attention from more fundamental issues:

When aid agencies operate as though lack of food were the basic problem, their efforts (e.g., food supplements, the Green Revolution) clearly do save the lives of some people. But the social structure that perpetuates malnutrition among a large percentage of the population, year after year, generation after generation, remains untouched.[24]

Good nutrition does not come from nutrition programs, and good health does not come from health care services. The advocates of comprehensive public health care recognize

that health is influenced not only by health services but by a multitude of environmental, social and economic factors. These factors include income, education, housing, food production, sanitation, and motivations among others. The management of health needs to include not only the management of health services but also the management of agriculture, schooling, irrigation and markets for produce. . . . health is not merely a disease problem but a development problem. . . . It is not enough to keep responsibility for health in the health ministry alone.[25]

Health services may help, but they are not the source of good health. Immunization and oral rehydration programs may increase child survival rates, but they do not address the social situation and the government policy-making that set the patterns of mortality. It is important to look beyond specific projects and programs to see how social structures affect the interests of children.

NOTES

1. David Nabarro and Paul Chinnock, "Growth Monitoring—Inappropriate Promotion of an Appropriate Technology," *Social Science & Medicine*, 26, no. 9 (1988), 941–48.

2. James R. Hebert, "Growth Monitoring: The 'G' in GOBI-FFF," in Richard Cash, Gerald T. Keusch, and Joel Lamstein, eds., *Child Health and Survival: The UNICEF GOBI-FFF Program* (London: Croom Helm, 1987), pp. 11–20. Critical analyses may also be found in Nicky Cape, "Growth Charts: Help or Hindrance?" *Health Policy and Planning*, 3, no. 2 (June 1988), 167–70, and Nancy Gerein, "Is Growth Monitoring Worthwhile?" *Health Policy and Planning*, 3, no. 3 (September 1988), 181–94. Also see *Indian Journal of Pediatrics*, 55, no. 1, supp. (January–February 1988), for numerous articles from the symposium "Growth Monitoring and Promotion: An International Perspective"; and Mahshid Lofti, "Growth Monitoring: A Brief Literature Review of Current Knowledge," *Food and Nutrition Bulletin*, 10, no. 4 (December 1988), 3–10.

3. Joanne Leslie, Margaret Lycette, and Mayra Buvinic, "Weathering Economic Crises: The Crucial Role of Women in Health," in David E. Bell and Michael R. Reich, eds., *Health, Nutrition, and Economic Crises: Approaches to Policy in the Third World* (Dover, Mass.: Auburn House, 1988), pp. 307–48, see 340.

4. Norbert Hirschhorn, "Oral Rehydration Therapy: The Programme and the Promise," in Richard Cash, Gerald Keusch, and Joel Lamstein, eds., *Child Health and Survival* (London: Croom Helms, 1987), pp. 21–46, see 28.

5. The breast vs. bottle controversy up to the mid-1980s is summarized in Maggie Black, *The Children and the Nations: The Story of UNICEF* (New York: UNICEF, 1986), pp. 429–37, 474–75.

6. One of the major organizations involved is Action for Corporate Accountability, 3255 Hennepin Avenue South, Minneapolis, Minn. 55408. The telephone number is (612) 823–1571.

7. Thomas McKeown, *The Modern Rise of Population* (New York: Academic Press, 1976).

8. Kirk R. Smith, *Biofuels, Air Pollution and Health: A Global Review* (New York: Plenum Press, 1987), p. 240.

9. Debabar Banerji, "Hidden Menace in the Universal Child Immunization Program," *IFDA Dossier*, no. 61 (September/October 1987), 55–62; and in *International Journal of Health Services*, 18, no. 2 (1988), 293–99. A different sort of critique is in Walene James, *Immunization: The Reality Behind the Myth* (South Hadley, Mass.: Bergin & Garvey, 1988).

10. Ritu Priya, "India: The Medico-Friend Circle on Child Health," *IFDA Dossier*, 69 (January/February 1989), 15–23.

11. Leonard A. Sagan, *The Health of Nations: True Causes of Sickness and Well-Being* (New York: Basic Books, 1987), p. 68.

12. Susan B. Rifkin and Gill Walt, "Why Health Improves: Defining the Issues

Concerning 'Comprehensive Primary Health Care' and 'Selective Primary Health Care,' " *Social Science & Medicine*, 23, no. 6 (1986), 559–66.

13. Banerji, "Hidden Menace," as summarized in Susan Rifkin and Gill Walt, "Why Health Improves," *Social Science & Medicine*, 23, no. 6 (1986), 559–66.

14. J. P. Unger and J. Killingsworth, "Selective Primary Health Care: A Critical Review of Methods and Results," *Social Science & Medicine*, 22 (1986), 1001, as summarized in Susan Rifkin and Gill Walt, "Why Health Improves," *Social Science & Medicine*, 23, no. 6 (1986), 559–66.

15. Smith, *Biofuels, Air Pollution, and Health*, p. 240.

16. Pierre E. Mandl, ed., *Going to Scale for Child Survival and Development*, spec. iss. of UNICEF's *Assignment Children* 65/68 (1984).

17. John Osgood Field, "Multisectoral Nutrition Planning: A Post-Mortem," *Food Policy*, 12, no. 1 (February 1987), 15–28.

18. Peter Hakim and Giorgio Solimano, "Nutrition and National Development: Establishing the Connection," *Food Policy*, 1, no. 3 (1976), 107–15.

19. There are exceptions, such as Mitchell G. Weiss, "Cultural Models of Diarrheal Illness: Conceptual Frameworks and Review," *Social Science & Medicine*, 27, no. 1 (1988), 5–16.

20. Rifkin and Walt, "Why Health Improves."

21. Tony Waterston, "War Is Good for Babies and Other Young Children," *Lancet*, no. 8536 (April 4, 1987), 780.

22. Susan George, "Foreword," in Nicole Ball, ed., *World Hunger: A Guide to the Economic and Political Dimensions* (Santa Barbara, Calif.: ABC-Clio, 1981), p. xix.

23. For example, USAID's *Child Survival: A Second Report to Congress on the AID Program* says that "infant and child mortality is declining in almost every country where AID works," implying a causal connection, when in fact it is declining almost everywhere even without USAID involvement.

24. Sylvia Noble Tesh, *Hidden Arguments: Political Ideology and Disease Prevention Policy* (New Brunswick, N.J.: Rutgers University Press, 1988), p. 64.

25. Rifkin and Walt, "Why Health Improves."

Chapter Six

FOOD

As explained in Chapter 2, there are several varieties of malnutrition, but the most important in relation to children's survival is protein-energy malnutrition. The discussion here refers to that, and not to any of the specific nutrient deficiencies.

Field assessment of nutrition status is commonly based on anthropometric (body) measures. Measurements are made of the heights and weights of children, and the results are compared with appropriate norms:

A typical nutrition survey will report three categories of malnutrition classified according to the Gomez scale of expected weight for age. Third degree malnutrition, the severe category, is reserved for individuals whose weight is less than 60 percent of the expected weight for that age. Between 60 and 75 percent is the moderate category, or second degree malnutrition. First degree, or mild, malnutrition is reported for individuals between 75 and 90 percent of expected weight, and 90 to 110 percent is considered normal. Such weight-for-age statistics are used to interpret current nutritional status, while height-for-age statistics are taken as indicators of more chronic nutritional problems. Heights less than 90 percent of height-for-age standards indicate stunting associated with long-standing food deficits.[1]

With many technical variations, the extent of malnutrition is commonly assessed in terms of the extent to which children's growth falls short of the relevant standard.

Where field measurements cannot be made, the extent of malnutrition can be estimated on the basis of estimates of the overall food supplies, population size, and the distribution of food within the population. This is how the major international organizations form their estimates.

The Food and Agriculture Organization of the United Nations (FAO) estimates that in 1979–81, depending on the criterion used, there were between 335 million and 494 million people in developing countries who were un-

Table 6.1
Childhood Malnutrition in Developing Regions, 1980

AREA	NUMBER (millions)	PROPORTION (percentage)
Africa	20.6	35.1
Near East	10.6	24.6
Asia	99.1	48.3
Latin America and Caribbean	11.6	21.1

These figures show estimates of the number and the proportion of children aged 6 to 60 months who were below 80 percent of the median standard weights for their ages.
Source: J. Haaga, C. Kenrick, K. Test, and J. Mason, "An Estimate of the Prevalence of Child Malnutrition in Developing Countries," World Health Statistics Quarterly, 38(3), 1985, Table 1, p. 343.

dernourished.[2] The World Bank estimates that in 1980 about 340 million people did not get enough energy to prevent stunted growth and serious health risks. About 730 million did not get enough energy to sustain an active working life.[3]

According to a report in May 1989 by the president of the World Food Council, the number of hungry people in the world increased by 15 million between 1970 and 1980. In the first half of the 1980s, however, the number increased by 40 million, to a total of 512 million.[4]

Many of the malnourished are children: "In the developing world today, it is estimated that nearly 40 percent of all children under 5 suffer from acute or chronic protein-calorie malnutrition. In absolute numbers this translates into 141 million children in 1980."[5] It has been estimated that there are about 20 million people in the United States who are chronically malnourished.[6]

Estimates of the geographical distribution of malnourished children are indicated in Table 6.1. Contrary to the common belief that the problem is most widespread in Africa, there are almost five times as many malnourished children in Asia as in Africa.

Estimates of the numbers of people malnourished in any given area are greatly affected by the measures and criteria used, and choices on these vary a great deal. Thus it is far more difficult to interpret and compare data on malnutrition than data on children's mortality.

CAUSES OF MALNUTRITION

Inadequate food supply in the household is a major factor in causing malnutrition. Often, however, the types of food and the methods of feeding are also important. Weaning foods and feeding patterns are critical. At times children are given inappropriate foods, such as tea. Some beliefs regarding appropriate foods and feeding patterns can result in deficient diets for pregnant or lactating women, or for children.[7]

Some foods, such as rice and maize, have inadequate nutrient density, which means that small children cannot take in large quantities at one sitting. Children who depend on bulky carbohydrates must be fed frequently during the day or they will not get enough.

The supply of food in the household may be adequate, but its distribution within the family may be skewed against small children and in favor of the male head of household.[8] Of course, this is not a significant problem where household food supplies are abundant.

Feeding with breast milk substitutes clearly illustrates how malnutrition can arise from provision of the wrong kind of food. The promotion of infant formula is especially pernicious in third world countries where sanitation is poor, literacy levels are low, and people are poor. The result has been that infants fed with formula have had much higher infant mortality rates than breast-fed infants. The health effects of formula feeding have been less severe in developed countries, but it is clear that morbidity levels are higher among formula-fed infants even in developed countries. Recent studies have shown that formula-fed infants are more likely to get cancer. Leonard Sagan points out:

The highest death rates in premodern societies are among infants and toddlers whose survival is less dependent on available food supplies than on the culturally determined practices of breast feeding and weaning.... Millions of babies have died from inadequate nutrition where an adequate food supply was no farther than the mother's breast.[9]

Thus malnutrition does not necessarily mean that household food supplies are inadequate. Often it is more a matter of food *behavior* than of food *supply*.

Even with appropriate food intake, malnutrition can result from disease, particularly diarrhea or parasitic diseases. There may be enough good food coming in, but it may in effect run right out, or it may be diverted to the nutrition of parasites. As indicated below in the section "Malnutrition/Disease Interactions," infection often leads to malnutrition. Disease often increases the body's food requirements. Usually it is not malnutrition alone, but the combination of malnutrition and disease, that leads to death.

MALNUTRITION, MORTALITY, AND MORBIDITY

There is a strong association between protein-energy malnutrition and children's mortality, at least where the malnutrition is severe. As Table 6.2 shows,

Table 6.2
Nutritional Deficiency as Associated Cause of Death

UNDERLYING CAUSE OF DEATH	NUTRITIONAL DEFICIENCY AS ASSOCIATED CAUSE (%)
All causes	47
Infective and Parasitic Diseases	61
Diarrheal diseases	61
Measles	62
Other	59
Diseases of Respiratory System	32
Other Causes	33

This table indicates the extent to which nutritional deficiency was an associated cause of death of children under 5 years of age in 13 Latin American projects. Neonatal deaths are excluded.

Source: Ruth Puffer and Carlos V. Serrano, Patterns of Mortality in Childhood (Washington, D.C.: Pan American Health Organization, 1973).

studies in Latin America suggest that in almost half (47 percent) of children's deaths malnutrition is a significant underlying cause. In Indonesia, "nutritional deficiency has been identified as an associated cause in 16 percent of the deaths of children aged 1–4."[10]

In rural Punjab, India, it was found that "on average, child mortality doubled with each 10 percent decline below 80 percent of the Harvard weight median. Children above the 80 percent level had mortality rates as good as those for children in four southern European countries."[11]

A study of children in a rural area of Bangladesh showed that several different anthropometric measures (weight-for-age, weight-for-height, height-for-age, arm circumference-for-age, and arm circumference-for-height) all were effective in predicting mortality over the two years following the measurements. According to all of the indicators, severely malnourished children were at much higher risk of dying.[12]

By one estimate, approximately 60 percent of all children's deaths are associated with malnutrition.[13] But the linkage between malnutrition and mortality is not always evident. In the late 1970s and early 1980s the infant mortality rate in Sri Lanka declined while the nutritional status of the bottom fifth of the population also declined.[14] Kerala has the lowest infant mortality rate of all the states of India, but it is also among the lowest in per capita intake of nutrients.[15]

There is no generally accepted procedure for determining the extent to which deaths are due specifically to malnutrition. This is one reason why the major international health-data-gathering agencies—WHO, FAO, and UNI-

CEF—do not provide estimates of the numbers of people who die from malnutrition each year.

Children who are severely malnourished in terms of anthropometric measures certainly are more likely to die prematurely. But the great majority of children who are categorized as malnourished are only mildly or moderately malnourished, and their prospects are not so grim.[16] In the United States, for example, there is not much of a linkage between malnutrition and children's mortality because the malnutrition is rarely severe.

MALNUTRITION/DISEASE INTERACTIONS

Thus there is not always a strong linkage between malnutrition and mortality. Even more surprising, perhaps, is the fact that there is not always a strong tie between malnutrition and disease. In a 1988 overview of a series of empirical studies, the researchers "do not find a significant positive impact of nutrition on health status." Apart from the possibility of measurement error, the lack of association might be explained in several ways:

This surprising result may reflect one or more of the following factors: (1) increased nutrient intakes partly go to increase productivity rather than to improve indicators of health . . . ; (2) within limits, human metabolism adjusts in response to nutrient intakes, with little impact on health indicators . . . ; (3) there is tremendous intrapersonal variation in nutrient intakes over time.[17]

At extreme levels of undernutrition or overnutrition, health surely will be impaired. But within very broad limits the human body is capable of adapting to the level of nutrition it receives. That is one reason why it is difficult to establish nutrient requirements with great confidence.[18]

There is interaction between malnutrition and disease.[19] Malnutrition increases the likelihood of onset of a wide variety of diseases, but most particularly infectious diseases. Conversely, disease increases the likelihood of malnutrition:

frequent illness accompanied by anorexia may be the major factor contributing to clinical malnutrition in children. It is not all caused by food deprivation by unknowing or non-caring parents, as many simplistically presume. Food in the last analysis is certainly the ultimate deficiency, but effective prevention of measles, tuberculosis, and pertussis, early treatment of pneumonia and diarrhea, and reduction of malnutrition before birth are highly efficacious technological approaches to reducing malnutrition.[20]

When the initial infection does not itself prove fatal, parasitic diseases such as malaria lead to increased mortality indirectly, especially through their influence on nutrition:

Many effects of parasites result by way of nutritional impairment, and it has proved very difficult to separate out the roles of individual parasites in the multifactorial causation of malnutrition in human populations. . . . Parasitism and nutrition are inextricably linked for at least two reasons. First, many parasites are acquired as a direct result of the feeding behavior of the host; and second, the host by definition provides all the nutrients for the parasites it harbors. . . . Whether infection or inadequate nutrition is the initiator, children suffering from the combination enter a positive feedback loop whereby their probability of survival is progressively decreased by the mutual reinforcement of malnutrition and infection.[21]

There are many diseases to which children are more vulnerable when they are malnourished. In Costa Rica, children with severe protein-energy malnutrition were 19 times more likely to develop pneumonia than normal children.[22]

In addition to increasing the likelihood of onset of various diseases, malnutrition intensifies the disease. This increases the likelihood that death will result. Case mortality rates differ, depending on how well or poorly nourished the individuals are. For example, most well-nourished children who get measles get through it successfully, but poorly nourished children are likely to die from it. In a study of Philippine hospital cases of patients with acute respiratory infection (ARI), only 0.6 percent of those who were normally nourished died, but 2.3 percent of those who were mildly malnourished and 7.7 percent of those who were seriously malnourished died from the ARI.[23] In a study in Costa Rica, mortality from ARI was 12 times higher in malnourished infants than in those of normal weight.[24] Case mortality rates for pneumonia, which run about 0.4 percent in the United States, range from 5 to 20 percent in developing countries.[25]

Children are more vulnerable to ARI when they are malnourished, but vitamin A deficiency is an especially important factor. Because vitamin A deficiency causes physical changes in the linings of the lungs and digestive tract that favor bacterial infection, children with vitamin A deficiency are more likely to contract ARI. They also are more likely to die from it. As Figure 6.1 shows, in a study done in Indonesia, children who were so deficient in vitamin A as to show symptoms of eye disease had a much higher mortality rate from respiratory infections than those with no symptoms of eye disease.[26]

In examining malnutrition-disease interactions it is important to distinguish between the onset of infection and the subsequent disease. Infection refers to the presence of organisms in the body, whether or not they produce significant damage or symptoms. Disease, however, refers to a pathological response, such as tissue destruction or other symptoms. An individual may carry the organisms associated with cholera, tuberculosis, or AIDS, and thus be infected, but may not have the disease.

The distinction is important. While the incidence of infection is largely due to exposure, and thus to environmental factors, the response is largely determined by the health status of the infected individual. Sanitation measures may help in controlling the incidence of infection, but apparently they are

Figure 6.1
Xerophthalmia's Effect on Infection Mortality

RESPIRATORY INFECTION

	ABSENT	PRESENT
EYES NORMAL	5.1	9.6
EYES DISEASED	38.3	93.8

Numbers in cells indicate mortality rates in terms of deaths per 1,000 cases.
Source: A. Sommer, I. Tarwotjo, G. Hussaini, and D. Susanto, "Increased Mortality in Children with Mild Vitamin A Deficiency," *Lancet*, September 10, 1983, pp. 585–88.

not so significant in determining disease outcomes. Historically "the decline in infectious disease deaths appears to have preceded, rather than followed, improvements in sanitation and to have occurred long before the decline in infection."[27]

From 1900 to 1930 the incidence of measles remained constant, but deaths from measles declined sharply, apparently because personal resistance to the disease increased. The case mortality rates for children with measles is far higher in poor countries than in rich countries because of the differences in their ability to cope with the infection.

In addition to malnutrition-disease interactions, there are many disease-disease interactions, all too complex to explore here. Stanley Foster points out that in dealing with measles, health planners face three conflicting hypotheses:

1. Measles immunization will increase child survival in proportion to measles deaths prevented.
2. Measles immunization will, because of its synergistic impact with other major causes of under–5 mortality, increase survival in excess of measles deaths prevented.
3. Measles immunization will not increase child survival because deaths prevented through immunization will be replaced by deaths from other causes.[28]

Similar questions could be raised in relation to many other sorts of child survival activities. In third world situations, selective interventions that reduce deaths from specific diseases may result in increased deaths from other diseases, thus producing no net gain.

Malnutrition and disease are so closely coupled that it should never be assumed that malnutrition acts alone in causing children's deaths.

THE IDENTIFICATION PROBLEM

So far we have accepted the idea that anthropometric measures are useful for identifying malnutrition. But if we are concerned with distinguishing among different causes of ill health, there are serious questions to be raised. W. Henry Mosley and Lincoln Chen suggest that the anthropometric approach to assessing malnutrition should be reconsidered:

Customarily, growth faltering in a cohort of children is called "malnutrition," and this, in turn, leads to the inference that it is simply the consequence of dietary deficiency. There is now abundant evidence that growth faltering is due to many factors and that it may be more appropriately considered a nonspecific indicator of health status. . . . There is a growing body of evidence that "malnutrition" among young children is as much dependent on maternal health factors and infections as it is on the nutrient deficiency. It is thus more appropriate to consider the levels of physical stunting and wasting in cohorts of children as nonspecific indicators of health status (as is the case with the level of mortality) rather than as a specific indicator of dietary deficiency.[29]

There is evidence that children grow better when their caregivers are warm and loving than when they are cold disciplinarians,[30] which certainly supports the view that growth is more an indicator of overall health status than of malnutrition in particular.

Too often anthropometric measures are taken to be indicators of malnutrition in particular rather than of health status in general. Unfortunately, there is no other practical means for assessing malnutrition in the field. Malnutrition is still a rather vague construct,[31] and without a widely accepted means for operationalizing that construct, we hardly know what it means. Malnutrition is not nearly so unambiguous as death.

The effectiveness of nutrition interventions is usually measured in terms of nutrition status assessed on the basis of anthropometric measures. A review of the effects of nutrition interventions on the growth of children showed that overall, "anthropometric improvement was surprisingly small."[32] As the authors speculate, part of the reason may have been that there is often considerable leakage of food away from the targeted individuals, with the result that their dietary intake actually does not improve very much. However, a more fundamental reason may be that food supply was not really a major problem to begin with, and the observed growth retardation could have been addressed more effectively with other kinds of programs, perhaps emphasizing immunizations or sanitation. The nutrition interventions not only may have reached the wrong individuals, but also may have been altogether the wrong instrument.

Thus the Mosley-Chen perspective has important policy implications. Where low-weight children have been found, they have been labeled as malnourished, and the response typically has been to introduce some sort of nutrition intervention. The reinterpretation of the weight or height data as being shaped by more than nutrition should lead to consideration of a much broader range of remedies.

UNICEF now recognizes that "most malnutrition is not caused by shortages of food in the house" and that "most feeding programmes fail to have any significant effect on children's nutritional status."[33] This may be why UNICEF now places relatively low priority on food supplementation.

Since good anthropometric measures are not available everywhere, especially in less developed countries, some organizations use infant mortality rates to estimate the extent of malnutrition.[34] There is a correlation between infant mortality and malnutrition, so that in the absence of better measures, the first may provide a reasonably good estimate of the second. But there are anomalies. Perhaps the hunger organizations that use infant mortality rates to operationalize their interests should acknowledge that they are working on the broader child survival problem and are interested in supporting the full range of child survival strategies.

FOOD PRODUCTION AND DISPOSITION

Many areas have abundant food supplies and chronic malnutrition at the same time. In Zimbabwe, for example, "maize stocks remain large, but maize buyers are few. And even with bumper grain crops 500,000 people in Matableland, the Ndebele region in southwestern Zimbabwe, are experiencing food shortages. Up to half the children in this prospering nation may be suffering from malnutrition."[35] And in Tanzania, "Iringa Region is one of the most important producers of food for export to other parts of Tanzania. It has also been noted that many of the areas and villages in Iringa with high food production have among the highest levels of malnutrition."[36] In Brazil, "two-thirds of the population is malnourished despite the country's ranking as the world's second-largest food exporter."[37]

The green revolution is said to have been responsible for "moving India from having the largest food deficit in the world to producing enough grain to feed all of its people."[38] It is true that India can now be described as self-sufficient in the sense that it no longer is a regular importer of large amounts of grain. India's market demand for grain is being met. But that does not mean that needs are being met. Malnutrition persists. Moreover, in many parts of India the new high-yield varieties have displaced coarse grains and pulses that have been important in the diets of the poor. India's boast is based on a misleading twist of words which falsely suggests that India is in fact feeding all its people.

The coexistence of abundance and hunger is most striking in the United States, where millions of Americans are chronically malnourished despite the fact that the country produces enormous surpluses of food.

It may be useful to increase food production in poor countries for a variety of reasons, but it should not be assumed that doing so will necessarily help to alleviate malnutrition. Questions need to be raised about the disposition of new food supplies, whether from increasing production or from imports. Some may go to exports, some to livestock feed, and some to middle and upper classes, leaving little for the poor, who need it most. The patterns are easily illustrated.

Exports

Rice production in Thailand increased 31 percent from 1970 to 1980, but exports increased 263 percent. In combination with a population increase, this level of exportation led to a decline in per capita rice availability of 18.5 percent over the period. The energy intake per capita per day reached a peak of 1,662 calories in 1968 and fell to 1,384 in 1977. The food balance sheets for Thailand do not indicate any compensation from other food items. Thailand increased its rice production, but increased its rice exports even more, and thus the amount remaining for domestic consumption actually decreased.

In 1985 developed market economies sold $28.8 billion worth of food to developing countries and territories, but $36.2 billion worth was sold in the opposite direction.[39] The net result was that over $7 billion worth of food flowed from poorer countries to richer countries. On balance the poor feed the rich.[40]

Feed

With economic growth, the use of cereals for livestock feed tends to increase faster than the use of cereals for human consumption. Grain imports into less developed countries are largely for feed rather than for direct human consumption.[41] Since commercially raised animal foods are consumed more by the rich than by the poor, the use of staples as feed is a mechanism that moves food toward the rich, siphoning supplies away from those who need it most. In Mexico, "the 20 million poorest people in the country now consume less grain than is fed to the animals producing meat, milk, and eggs for the rich."[42]

Income Class

Where there is a problem of food supply, a distinction should be made between availability and access. There may be plenty of food available in the local market, but if you don't have money, you don't have access to it. Even in famine situations, usually the community suffers not because of the simple absence of food but because the price of the food that is available escalates out of reach. Malnutrition is more the result of poverty than of absolute shortages of food.[43]

In the absence of special measures, there is no reason to believe that the distribution of new food supplies will be skewed any differently than the distribution of existing food supplies. The green revolution has increased grain supplies in many countries but has not resulted in corresponding reductions of malnutrition because the poor remain unable to make a claim on the new supplies. The new supplies tend to go to those who are already advantaged.

Many observers have applauded the fact that in recent years, contrary to Malthus' prediction, the rate of growth of food production has been greater than the rate of population growth in every area of the world except Africa. They suggest that this is a favorable trend pointing toward the end of malnutrition in much of the world. But since food is distributed primarily on the basis of purchasing power, not need, increases in consumption are likely to be enjoyed by those who are already adequately nourished. Average intake levels may increase but do little to alleviate malnutrition.

It has been suggested that overall economic growth is likely to be effective in alleviating malnutrition because it increases income levels. One study says that "a rise in per capita income increases the demand for food and tends to raise dietary energy levels."[44] Certainly increasing average incomes will increase average consumption levels, but that says nothing about the consumption levels of those who are most at risk of malnutrition. The benefits of economic growth tend to concentrate in the upper ranks of society. With increasing national income the supply of food may move away from poorer classes toward richer classes. The size of the pie as a whole may be increasing, but if it moves away from the poor at a rapid rate, that growth does them little good.

In the Philippines, for example, despite the fact that the gross national product per capita increased in the first half of the 1970s, the number of people in poverty increased. Between 1970 and 1974 there was a slight increase in the total amount of cereals used, largely due to increased consumption of cheaper corn products. However, consumption of meat, poultry, eggs, dairy products, fish, fruit, and vegetables fell sharply during the same period. For the lowest income class, consumption levels declined in every food category except root crops.[45]

In a study of the impact of rapid agricultural development on nutrition undertaken in Mexico:

It was found that the average food intake rose significantly, but this change was the result of the economic impact of the higher income group. Approximately 30 percent of the population, comprising the poorest peasants, showed no improvement in food intake so the prevalence of malnutrition in the area was virtually unchanged.[46]

During periods of rapid economic growth in India, Mexico, and the Philippines, there has been only slow growth in calorie intake. The same pattern holds true in the world overall:

Broadly, available income per person in LDCs rose by about 75 per cent from 1950 to 1970; daily calorie intake per head rose by under 20 per cent, as against at least 40 percent to be expected if growth had been equally distributed; and most of those extra calories were in the more expensive forms of food. So the main gainers from growth have been those who do not need much extra simple, cheap food; not the hungry, not the poor.[47]

As demonstrated by the green revolution, growth in the agriculture sector can bypass the poor in both the disposition of the food products themselves and in the disposition of the wealth that is generated from their sale.[48]

Thus agricultural growth and food imports do not necessarily help to reduce hunger. New supplies are not likely to reduce malnutrition if the poor remain poor and thus remain unable to make a claim on the new supplies. The advantaged can outbid the poor and use the new resources for their own purposes.

POLICY OBJECTIVES

It is important to make distinctions of the sort developed here because confusion of "the food problem," "the hunger problem," "the malnutrition problem," "the self-sufficiency problem," "the child survival problem," and "the poverty problem" is likely to lead to inappropriate policies. "The problem" is different things to different people.

Ministries of agriculture and private bodies concerned with food, such as the International Food Policy Research Institute in Washington, D.C., pursue many different objectives, but the alleviation of malnutrition is not always of highest priority. For example, dissertations completed or under way at the Food Research Institute at Stanford University include titles such as "New Directions in Indonesia's Feed Livestock Industry" and "Alternative Techniques for Shrimp Production and Their Interactions." None of the 39 titles show an explicit concern with malnutrition.[49]

The World Food Institute at Iowa State University publishes a yearly report on *World Food Trade and U.S. Agriculture*. Its account of current issues in food trade discusses such things as subsidies and exchange rates, but widespread chronic undernutrition is not raised as a major issue.[50]

Aquaculture was once thought to have enormous potential for helping to solve the problem of malnutrition worldwide. Searching the aquaculture literature, however, one finds many studies about the nutrition of fish but none about the nutrition of people. The interest is in the commodity value of the product, not its nutritive value, and certainly not its potential for helping to deal with malnutrition.[51]

In one food policy study we are told that "maize is the second most important food crop in Thailand," but quickly learn that this says little about its contribution to the national diet: "More than one third of the annual production is consumed domestically as animal feed and the rest is exported (contributing substantially to foreign exchange earnings)."[52]

Products such as sugar, pineapple, tea, coffee, cocoa, shrimp, and beef, destined for the rich, may be described as foods by national policymakers, but they do little for the direct nutrition of the poor. Production of such items often displaces the production of staples that are important in the diets of the poor. Thus, increasing some kinds of food supplies can result in increased malnutrition.

The most common food policy objectives of developing countries are (1) assuring adequate and stable food consumption for the population as a whole, (2) assuring consumer welfare through the provision of cheap food, (3) assuring the welfare of food producers, (4) generating revenue for the government, (5) generating and conserving foreign exchange, (6) assuring food self-sufficiency, (7) stabilizing domestic food prices, and (8) increasing domestic food production.[53] Often policymakers pursue objectives such as working to increase overall food supplies or increasing government revenue *rather than* alleviating malnutrition. The alleviation of malnutrition sometimes has low priority in the formulation of national food policies.

One study defines food security as "the ability of food deficit countries, or regions or households within these countries to meet target consumption levels on a year-to-year basis."[54] Although the casual reader might assume that the study was motivated by concern with the malnutrition problem, the editor explains that "chronic malnutrition that is caused by persistent poverty constitutes a long-term problem whose dimensions and solutions lie beyond the question of food security, which we conceive as a problem of short-term variability." Making a clear choice against attending to the malnutrition problem, he follows by saying, "Thus, we do not adopt the nutritional basis for our target consumption, but instead use the trend level of consumption as the target." This could mean asking "How can we continue to overeat?"

Our concern here is not with those who plainly pursue other objectives. The concern here is that many researchers and development agents suggest that their work will help alleviate malnutrition or reduce children's mortality, but never open that proposition to examination. For example, the United Nations University's Programme on Food, Nutrition, Biotechnology and Poverty has invested much of its resources in INFOODS, a project designed to prepare more precise nutrient analysis of different foods.[55] Why? Would anyone suggest that the major reason for malnutrition is that people don't know the nutrient content of their foods well enough? Who will the project benefit? How?

Consider the design of programs to alleviate malnutrition. It is often easier to move people from moderate to mild malnutrition or from mild nutrition to normal than to improve the condition of those who are seriously malnourished. This could lead to a form of triage, selecting against the most severe cases and bringing about little reduction in children's mortality. Policymakers should ask if that sort of success is acceptable.

National policymakers often fail to distinguish between the ways in which a food item might contribute to the national diet by increasing average consumption levels, and the ways in which it might help to alleviate malnutrition. The task is to increase consumption by those who are undernourished, especially those who are extremely undernourished. In terms of public policy, raising an individual's energy intake from 1,600 to 2,000 calories a day should be valued much more highly than raising an individual's intake from 2,600 to 3,000 calories a day.

Effective action in the alleviation of human suffering requires sound understanding and clarity of purpose. Increasing national food supplies may be a sensible objective for several reasons. But if an agency wants to increase food supplies *in order to* alleviate malnutrition, or if it wants to alleviate malnutrition *in order to* reduce children's mortality, then the linkages should be described and not just implicitly assumed. And the effectiveness of the chosen means to the end should be compared with other possible means. The green revolution may have been effective in increasing the production of certain grains in some countries, but that does not necessarily mean that it was effective in alleviating malnutrition in those countries. Even if it was effective to some degree, other means might have been far more effective.

The overall level of food supplies in a nation may affect the level of malnutrition, and the level of malnutrition is likely to affect the extent of children's mortality. But there are no simple one-to-one associations here. There are many other causal factors involved in malnutrition and in children's mortality, factors that vary from place to place and time to time.

Until we have much more and better research, we will have a great deal of uncertainty regarding how things work. But it could be very helpful very quickly if we pressed for greater clarity of purpose and more explicit accounts of why we do things the way we do. Far too many social programs are based on no visible analysis at all. What is it that food-related agencies and programs are really concerned with? Which are means, and which are ends?

Many governmental and nongovernmental agencies place a great deal of emphasis on increasing food supplies. Of course they may press for increasing food supplies for reasons such as supporting food producers or increasing exports. But if the intention is even in part to help alleviate malnutrition or to reduce children's mortality, that approach should be questioned. Malnutrition may result from inadequate food supplies, but it may also result from improper food behavior or from disease.

Where malnutrition does exist, it may or may not lead to premature death, depending on its severity and its linkages with disease in specific cases. Too narrow a focus on malnutrition can lead to the neglect of other important factors contributing to children's mortality.

Where there are problems with food supply, a clear distinction should be made between adequacy at the societal level and adequacy at the household level. In most countries the average food supply is more than sufficient to keep everyone well nourished. But many people are too poor to get access to the food that is available. Those who have greater purchasing power are able to claim larger shares than the poor. For all these reasons, increasing a nation's food supply is not likely to be an effective means for alleviating malnutrition or for reducing children's mortality. Lack of food at the global or national level is not the major cause of the high level of children's mortality worldwide.

NOTES

1. C. Peter Timmer, Walter P. Falcon, and Scott R. Pearson, *Food Policy Analysis* (Baltimore: Johns Hopkins University Press/World Bank, 1983), pp. 30–31.

2. Food and Agriculture Organization of the United Nations, *The Fifth World Food Survey* (Rome: FAO, 1985), p. 24.

3. World Bank, *Poverty and Hunger: Issues and Options for Food Security in Developing Countries* (Washington, D.C.: World Bank, 1986), p. 1.

4. "Number of Hungry Still Growing," *Development Forum*, 17, no. 4 (July–August 1989), 9.

5. Katrina Galway, Brent Wolff, and Richard Sturgis, *Child Survival: Risks and the Road to Health* (Columbia, Md.: Institute for Resource Development/Westinghouse/USAID, 1987), p. 34.

6. Physician Task Force on Hunger in America, *Hunger in America: The Growing Epidemic* (Boston: Harvard University School of Public Health, 1985); J. Larry Brown, "Hunger in the U.S.," *Scientific American*, 256, no. 2 (February 1987), 36–41. Contrary views are presented in several articles in *Insight*, 4, no. 26 (June 27, 1988), 8–15.

7. See, for example, C. S. Wilson, "Food Taboos of Childbirth: The Malay Example," *Ecology of Food and Nutrition*, 2 (1973), 267–74; C. Laderman, "Food Ideology and Eating Behavior: Contributions from Malay Studies," *Social Science & Medicine*, 19, no. 5 (1984), 547–59; K. A. Dettwyler, "Infant Feeding in Mali: Variations in Belief and Practice," *Social Science & Medicine*, 23 (1986), 651–64.

8. See the special issue, *Household Food Distribution*, of *Food and Nutrition Bulletin*, 5, no. 4 (December 1983). This journal regularly carries articles on the distribution of food within the household.

9. Leonard A. Sagan, *The Health of Nations: True Causes of Sickness and Well-Being* (New York: Basic Books, 1987), p. 45.

10. *Child Survival and Development in Indonesia 1985–1989* (Jakarta: Government of Indonesia and UNICEF, 1985), p. 1.

11. Arnfried A. Kielman and Colin McCord, "Weight-for-Age as an Index of Risk of Death in Children," *Lancet*, 1, no. 8076 (June 10, 1978), 1247–50.

12. Lincoln C. Chen, A. K. M. A. Chowdhury, and Sandra L. Huffman, "Anthropometric Assessment of Energy-Protein Malnutrition and Subsequent Risk of Mortality Among Preschool Aged Children," *American Journal of Clinical Nutrition*, 33, no. 8 (August 1980), 1836–45.

13. Roy L. Prosterman, *The Decline in Hunger-Related Deaths*, Hunger Project Papers no. 1 (San Francisco: The Hunger Project, 1984), p. 3. Also see Ann Ashworth, "International Differences in Infant Mortality and the Impact of Malnutrition: A Review," *Human Nutrition: Clinical Nutrition*, 36C (1982), 7–23.

14. S. W. R. de A. Samarasinghe, "Sri Lanka: A Case Study from the Third World," in David E. Bell and Michael R. Reich, eds., *Health, Nutrition, and Economic Crisis: Approaches to Policy in the Third World* (Dover, Mass.: Auburn House, 1988), pp. 39–80, esp. p. 75.

15. C. R. Soman, "Inter-Relationship Between Fertility, Mortality and Nutrition— The Kerala Experience," in P. V. Sukhatme, ed., *Newer Concepts in Nutrition and Their Implications for Policy* (Pune, India: Maharashtra Association for the Cultivation of Science, 1982); T. N. Krishnan, "Infant Mortality in Kerala State, India," *Assignment Children*, 65/68 (1984), 293–308. The average intake is low, but with nutrition programs providing a solid nutritional floor for the poor, apparently the distribution of food is much less skewed than it is elsewhere.

16. The linkage between mild and moderate (rather than severe) malnutrition and children's mortality is explored in Reynaldo Martorell and Teresa J. Ho, "Malnutrition, Morbidity, and Mortality," in W. Henry Mosley and Lincoln C. Chen, eds., *Child Survival: Strategies for Research* (Cambridge: Cambridge University Press, 1984), pp. 49–68.

17. Jere R. Behrman, Anil B. Deolalikar, and Barbara L. Wolfe, "Nutrients: Impacts and Determinants," *World Bank Economic Review*, 2, no. 3 (September 1988), 299–320.

18. Philip Payne, "Public Health and Functional Consequences of Seasonal Hunger and Malnutrition," in David E. Sahn, ed., *Causes and Implications of Seasonal Variability in Household Food Security* (Washington, D.C.: International Food Policy Research Institute, 1987); P. V. Sukhatme, ed., *Newer Concepts in Nutrition and Their Implications for Policy* (Pune, India: Maharashtra Association for the Cultivation of Science, 1982).

19. Nevin Scrimshaw, Carl E. Taylor, and John E. Gordon, *Interaction of Nutrition and Infection* (Geneva: World Health Organization, 1968); Gerald Keusch and Nevin S. Scrimshaw, "Control of Infection to Reduce Malnutrition," in Julia Walsh and Kenneth Warren, eds., *Strategies for Primary Health Care* (Chicago: University of Chicago Press, 1986).

20. Jon E. Rohde, "Why the Other Half Dies: The Science and Politics of Child Mortality in the Third World," *Assignment Children*, 61/62, no. 1 (1983), 51.

21. David J. Bradley and Anne Keymer, "Parasitic Diseases: Measurement and Mortality Impact," in W. Henry Mosley and Lincoln C. Chen, eds., *Child Survival* (Cambridge: Cambridge University Press, 1984), pp. 163–87.

22. Galway, et al., *Child Survival*, p. 23.

23. T. E. Tupasi, "Nutrition and Acute Respiratory Infection," in R. Douglas and E. Kerby-Eaton, eds., *Acute Respiratory Infections in Childhood, Proceedings of an International Workshop* (Adelaide, Australia: University of Adelaide, 1985), as reported in Galway, et al., *Child Survival*, p. 23.

24. J. W. James, "Longitudinal Study of the Morbidity of Diarrheal and Respiratory Infections," *American Journal of Clinical Nutrition*, 25 (1972), 690–94.

25. Galway, et al., *Child Survival*, p. 23.

26. Daniel D. Bankson and Robert M. Russell, "Vitamin A Deficiency and Immune Function: Effects on Morbidity and Mortality," in Richard Cash, Gerald T. Keusch, and Joel Lamstein, eds., *Child Health and Survival: The UNICEF GOBI-FFF Program* (London: Croom Helm, 1987), pp. 141–54.

27. Sagan, *The Health of Nations*, pp. 31–35.

28. Stanley O. Foster, "Immunizable and Respiratory Diseases and Child Mortality," in W. Henry Mosley and Lincoln C. Chen, eds., *Child Survival* (Cambridge: Cambridge University Press, 1984), pp. 119–40.

29. W. Henry Mosley and Lincoln C. Chen, "An Analytic Framework for the Study of Child Survival in Developing Countries," in W. Henry Mosley and Lincoln C. Chen, eds., *Child Survival* (Cambridge: Cambridge University Press, 1984), pp. 25–45.

30. Sagan, *The Health of Nations*, pp. 100–02.

31. See, for example, Sukhatme, *Newer Concepts in Nutrition*, pp. 223–34; *An Analysis of the Situation of Children in India* (New Delhi: UNICEF Regional Office for South Central Asia, 1984).

32. G. H. Beaton and H. Ghassemi, "Supplementary Feeding Programs for Young Children in Developing Countries," *American Journal of Clinical Nutrition*, 35 (1982), 864–916.

33. James P. Grant, *The State of the World's Children 1987* (New York: Oxford University Press, 1987), p. 65.

34. Cf. Prosterman, *The Decline in Hunger-Related Deaths*. Also see the critique of the Hunger Project's interpretation of infant mortality rate in Jack Clark and Jim Chapin, "It Doesn't Add Up," *Seeds*, December 1984, pp. 26–27.

35. Jack Shepherd, "Poised on the Brink," *The Atlantic*, 260, July 1987, pp. 26–31.

36. World Health Organization and United Nations Children's Fund, *Joint WHO/UNICEF Support for the Improvement of Nutrition in the United Republic of Tanzania, Annual Report 1986* (Dar es Salaam: WHO and UNICEF, 1986), p. 70.

37. Richard Martin, "Rich and Poor a Door Apart," *Insight*, August 17, 1987, p. 18.

38. Introduction to M. S. Swaminathan, *Sustainable Nutrition Security for Africa: Lessons from India*, Hunger Project Papers, no. 5 (San Francisco: The Hunger Project, 1986).

39. United Nations Conference on Trade and Development, *Handbook of International Trade and Development Statistics* (New York: United Nations, 1988), p. A8.

40. George Kent, *The Political Economy of Hunger: The Silent Holocaust* (New York: Praeger, 1984).

41. A. Schnittker and M. E. Abel, "Food Aid and Food Trade," *Society*, 17, no. 6 (1980), 19–25.

42. A. Chavez, "Food Distribution, Consumption, and Price Politics in Mexico,"

in *Food Price Policies and Nutrition in Latin America* (Tokyo: United Nations University, 1980).

43. Amartya K. Sen, *Poverty and Famines: An Essay on Entitlement and Deprivation* (New York: Oxford University Press, 1981); World Bank, *Poverty and Hunger: Issues and Options for Food Security in Developing Countries* (Washington, D.C.: World Bank, 1986).

44. L. Bachman and L. A. Paulino, *Rapid Food Production Growth in Selected Developing Countries: A Comparative Analysis of Underlying Trends, 1961–1976* (Washington, D.C.: International Food Policy Research Institute, 1979).

45. A. Ravenholt, *Malnutrition in the Philippines* (Hanover, N.H.: American Universities Field Staff International, 1982).

46. Mercedes Hernandez, Carlos Perez Hidalgo, Juan Ramirez Hernandez, Herlinda Madrigal, and Adolfo Chavez, "Effect of Economic Growth on Nutrition in a Tropical Community," *Ecology of Food and Nutrition*, 3 (1974), 283–91.

47. Michael Lipton, *Why Poor People Stay Poor: A Study of Urban Bias in World Development* (Cambridge, Mass.: Harvard University Press, 1977).

48. George Kent, "Aid, Trade, and Hunger," *Food and Nutrition Bulletin*, 7, no. 4 (December 1985), 73–79. The poor sometimes do benefit from agricultural development, but this effect tends to be weak. See Per Pinstrup-Andersen and Peter B. R. Hazell, "The Impact of the Green Revolution and Prospects for the Future," *Food Reviews International*, 1, no. 1 (1985), 1–25.

49. *Food Research Institute: Biennial Report 1988* (Stanford, Calif.: Food Research Institute, Stanford University, 1988), pp. 20, 22.

50. *World Food Trade and U.S. Agriculture: 1960–1987* (Ames: World Food Institute, Iowa State University, 1988).

51. George Kent, *Fish, Food, and Hunger: The Potential of Fisheries for Alleviating Malnutrition* (Boulder, Colo.: Westview Press, 1987).

52. Kumpol Puapanichya and Theodore Panayotou, "Output Supply and Input Demand in Rice and Upland Crop Production: The Quest for Higher Yields in Thailand," in Theodore Panayotou, ed., *Food Policy Analysis in Thailand* (Bangkok: Agricultural Development Council, 1985), pp. 23–99, see 27.

53. U.S. Department of Agriculture, *Food Policies in Developing Countries* (Washington, D.C.: USDA, 1983).

54. Alberto Valdés and Ammar Siamwalla, "Introduction," in Alberto Valdés, ed., *Food Security for Developing Countries* (Boulder, Colo.: Westview Press, 1981), p. 2. The same definition is used in Anthony H. Chisholm and Rodney Tyers, eds., *Food Security: Theory, Policy, and Perspectives from Asia and the Pacific Rim* (Lexington, Mass.: D. C. Heath, 1982).

55. Special INFOODS issue, *Food and Nutrition Bulletin*, 5 (1983); William M. Rand and Vernon R. Young, "Report of a Planning Conference Concerning an International Network of Food Data Systems (INFOODS)," *American Journal of Clinical Nutrition*, 39 (1984), 144–51; William M. Rand, "Food Composition Data: Problems and Plans," *Journal of the American Dietetic Association*, 85, no. 9 (September 1985), 1081–83.

Chapter Seven

POVERTY

Malnutrition and disease are the major immediate causes of children's mortality, and there are important underlying causes such as inadequate sanitation, but it is widely accepted that "these are symptoms of a single overriding disease—that of poverty."[1] Table 7.1 shows health indicators of nations by level of development, categorized on the basis of average gross national product per capita. In the mid-1980s developed nations had an average infant mortality rate of 12.8, while for the least developed nations the average rate was 141.2.

Table 7.2 categorizes nations differently, but the major distinguishing factor still is wealth level. Here again it is clear that infants' and children's mortality rates are very different in rich nations and poor nations, and these differences are systematically associated with a broad variety of causal and contributing factors.

THE SOURCES OF POVERTY

Poverty is a major factor leading to high levels of malnutrition and disease, and thus to high levels of children's mortality. However, we should not leave the issue there, as if it were now wholly explained. Why is there so much persistent poverty in the world?

Nations may be poor for several different reasons. Some, such as Afghanistan and the dry, landlocked nations of Africa, have very meager endowments of natural resources. Some have natural resources but lack the capacity for exploiting them, such as Albania and Myanmar (Burma). The most common pattern, however, is that nations produce large amounts of wealth, but do so in a way that results in a very skewed distribution of benefits, as in Brazil and Venezuela. On the whole there is

Table 7.1
Health Indicators by Level of Development

INDICATOR	LEAST DEVELOPED COUNTRIES	OTHER DEVELOPING COUNTRIES	DEVELOPED COUNTRIES
Number of countries	36	93	37
Total population (millions)	324	3,330	1,172
Infant mortality rate (per 1000 live births)	141.2	78.9	12.8
Life expectancy at birth (years)	47.9	61.5	72.4
Coverage rates (percentage)			
Safe water supply	34.7	57.2	95.8
Sanitation	16.8	29.1	76.6
Local health care	48.5	72.8	99.8
Attendance during pregnancy	33.3	47.8	99.4
Attendance at childbirth	36.7	44.5	99.4

Source: World Health Organization, *World Health Statistics Annual 1986* (Geneva: WHO, 1986), p. 45.

not much association between the natural resource endowments of nations and the quality of life they enjoy.

Most poverty "results from socio-economic development patterns which in most of the poorer countries have been characterized by a high degree of concentration of power, wealth and incomes in the hands of relatively small elites of national or foreign individuals or groups."[2]

But what causes this concentration? The ordinary, normal working of the market system creates wealth, but it also leads to poverty, and thus to high rates of mortality among children.

It is obvious that the market system prevents poor people from getting adequate food. But it is not so obvious that the market also helps to make and keep them poor. The market system increases the wealth and power of some while reducing the wealth and power of others. Poverty and malnutrition are the inevitable results.

Market system here means any social system in which economic outcomes are determined primarily by freely negotiated transactions between independent parties, uncoerced by government or other regulations. In contrast with the economists' theoretical markets, in which everyone has equal bargaining power, in real markets the parties usually are not of equal bargaining power.

The way in which the market system concentrates wealth and power in the hands of some and impoverishes others is very simple. The elementary transaction of the market system is the bargain, the negotiated exchange.

Table 7.2

Health and Wealth in Developing and Industrialized Countries, 1986

INDICATOR	DEVELOPING COUNTRIES	INDUSTRIALIZED COUNTRIES
Under-5 mortality rate	130	18
Infant mortality rate	85	15
Life expectancy (years)	60	73
GNP/capita (US dollars)	685	8,150
GNP/capita growth rate (%)	2.1	2.7
Population growth rate (%)	2.6	0.8
Public military expenditures		
(US dollars, billions, 1982)	153	521
(% of GNP, 1982)	5.2	5.3
Public education expenditures		
(US dollars, billions, 1982)	113	530
(% of GNP, 1982)	3.9	5.4
Public health expenditures, 1982		
(US dollars, billions, 1982)	50	477
(% of GNP, 1982)	1.7	4.8
Income inequality, 1970-1982	51	40
(% income to top 20% of households)		
Adult illiteracy, 1985		
(millions)	874	19
(%)	38	2
Enrollment at secondary level		
(millions, 1984)	173	87
(%, 1984)	36	87
Measles immunization		
(millions)	21.6	13.5
(%)	26	76
Polio immunization		
(millions)	30.9	11.7
(%)	37 %	66 %
DPT immunization		
(millions)	32.8	11
(%)	40 %	62 %
Tuberculosis (BCG) immunization		
(millions)	40.9	10.3
(%)	49	58
Anemia in children under 5		
(millions)	211.9	10.6
(%)	51	12
Anemia in pregnant women		
(millions)	63.6	2.5
(%)	59	14
Anemia in women, 15-49 years		
(millions)	305	32.7
(%)	47	11
Maternal mortality, 1983	494,000	6,000
Maternal care		
(millions)	53.8	17.6
(%)	48	98
Prenatal care coverage		
(millions)	85.5	17.8
(%)	68	100
Infant care coverage		
(millions)	62.5	17.5
(%)	62.5	100
Low birth weight babies		
(millions)	19	1.3
(%)	18	7
Safe water, 1985 (%)	57	96
Sanitation facilities, 1985 (%)	29	77
Daily per capita supply of calories, 1984	2,495	3,451
Daily per capita supply of protein, 1984 (grams)	60	103
Daily per capita supply of fat, 1984 (grams)	43	132

Source: James P. Grant, *The State of the World's Children 1987* (New York: Oxford University Press, 1987), p. 123.

One's bargaining strength depends on the quality of one's alternatives. Some people (or companies, or countries) are stronger than others because they have better options.

Those who have greater bargaining strength tend to gain more out of each transaction than do those who have lesser bargaining strength. Thus, over repeated transactions, stronger parties systematically enlarge their advantages over weaker parties. Bargainers do not move to an equilibrium at which the benefits are equally distributed but instead move apart, with the gap between them steadily widening. Asymmetrical exchange feeds on itself, making the situation more and more asymmetrical.

This pattern is clear in the growth of nations. If we chart their growth in terms of gross domestic product per capita, we find that those which start higher rise faster, while those which start lower rise more slowly. The pattern for developed nations as a group compared with that for developing nations as a group is shown in Figure 7.1.

As shown in Table 7.3, in the 1965–84 period the low-income economies had an average annual growth rate in GNP per capita of 2.8 percent; the lower-middle-income economies grew at 3.1 percent; the upper-middle-income economies grew at 3.3 percent; and the industrial market economies grew at 2.4 percent.

Expressed in these terms, it may appear that the growth rates were more or less comparable, with the industrial economies growing at a slightly lower rate than the low-income nations. However, these figures are percentages of very different baseline levels of GNP per capita. If we estimate the amounts of growth in 1984 by multiplying columns II and III in Table 7.3, we find in Column IV that the low-income economies had average per capita income gains of $7.28, while the industrial market economies had average per capita income gains of $274.32. The gains in industrial market economies were more than 37 times those in low-income nations!

Both parties benefit in the exchange process, but unequally. The rich get richer, and the poor get richer, but more slowly. We know that in voluntary transactions both parties must get some benefit, for any party that did not benefit could refuse to trade.

However, when the exchange process is accompanied by inflation, the real gains to both parties are diminished. The gains to the poorer, weaker party, being smaller, may as a result actually become negative. This is especially likely because inflation rates are much higher for poor nations than for rich nations. Thus, with the combination of trade plus inflation it is likely that the rich get richer and the poor get poorer. The apparent gains from trade for the poor are likely to be wiped out by inflation.

Poverty is endlessly re-created. It is a product of an ongoing process, not a static condition. If it were not, then surely, given all the development programs that have been undertaken, it would have been eradicated by now. Poverty is not re-created simply by population growth. The important forces

Figure 7.1
Gross Domestic Product per Capita, 1960–78

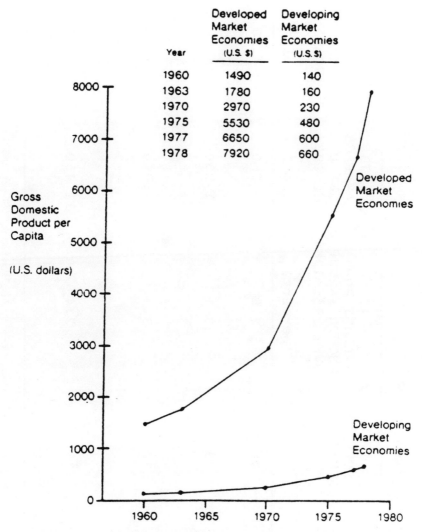

Year	Developed Market Economies (U.S. $)	Developing Market Economies (U.S. $)
1960	1490	140
1963	1780	160
1970	2970	230
1975	5530	480
1977	6650	600
1978	7920	660

Source: Yearbook of National Account Statistics, 1979, vol. 2 (New York: United Nations, 1980), p. 3.

are economic, but also political, social, and cultural. Those with low bargaining power are destined to remain marginalized because those with whom they relate have greater bargaining power. For example,

in Punjab and Haryana the trickle-down effect of the green revolution was partially visible in the improved daily wages for agricultural labor, which increased by 89 percent

Table 7.3
Gross National Product per Capita, 1965–84

GROUP	I NUMBER OF COUNTRIES	II AVERAGE ANNUAL GROWTH IN GNP/C OVER 1965–1984 (percent)	III AVERAGE GNP/C IN 1984 (dollars)	IV ESTIMATED AVERAGE INCREASE, 1984 (dollars)
Low-income economies	36	2.8	260	7.28
Lower middle-income economies	39	3.1	1,250	38.75
Upper middle-income economies	20	3.3	1,950	64.35
Industrial market economies	19	2.4	11,430	274.32

Source: World Development Report 1986 (New York: Oxford University Press/World Bank, 1986), pp. 180–181.

from 1961 to 1968. However, this seeming gain was totally offset by a rise in prices of about 93 percent over the same period in spite of the substantial increase in agricultural production.[3]

Poor peasant farmers who find ways to increase their crop production are soon faced with increasing demands from their landlords, suppliers, creditors, and tax agents. They are likely to be pressed back to their original situations. They are stuck in particular social structures.

ECONOMIC GROWTH

Economic growth alone is not likely to alleviate poverty and hunger, and thus improve child survival rates, at a sufficiently rapid rate in the less developed countries. Free markets simultaneously create and concentrate wealth. The concentration results from the systematic transfer of value from the bottom toward the top. The pie becomes larger, but it also shifts steadily away from the poor. Those at the top certainly benefit, but for those at the bottom the net result is not so predictable. Many economies grow, but with no corresponding reduction of the numbers of people in poverty.

The numbers of poor people can increase at the same time the gross national products increases. A World Bank economist observed:

It is now clear that more than a decade of rapid growth in underdeveloped countries has been of little or no benefit to perhaps a third of their population. Although the average per capita income of the Third World has increased by 50 percent since 1960, this growth has been very unequally distributed among countries, and socio-economic groups. Paradoxically, while growth policies have succeeded beyond the expectations of the first development decade, the very idea of aggregate growth as a social objective has increasingly been called into question.[4]

The World Bank now acknowledges that "because growth alone is not sufficient to alleviate poverty, programs and policies must be carefully designed to ensure that the benefits of growth reach the vast numbers of poor in developing countries."[5]

In the United States the proportion of the population under the poverty line has remained stuck at more than 10 percent for decades.[6] The richest 5 percent increased their incomes by 37.3 percent from 1977 to 1988, adjusted for inflation (in 1988 dollars), while the poorest 10 percent had their incomes decrease by 10.5 percent.[7] According to U. S. census data,

despite five years of economic recovery, the poverty rate in 1987—which was 13.6 percent—was higher than in any year of the 1970s, including the recession years of 1974 and 1975. . . . the gap between rich and poor families in 1987 hit its widest point since the Census Bureau first began collecting data in 1947.

This poverty hit blacks, Hispanics, and children the hardest: "Poverty rates for children of all races remained far above the levels of the 1970s. Some 20.6 percent of all children (under 18) were poor in 1987. . . . Some 13 million children were poor last year, compared to 11.5 million in 1980 and 9.9 million in 1978."[8]

Free markets create wealth, but they also create and sustain poverty. How else could we explain continuous poverty and hunger in the United States?

The benefits of economic growth are not evenly distributed; they tend to favor those who are already well off. No wonder it is those who are well off—whether individuals or nations—who speak most vigorously in favor of economic growth as an objective. Just as most ordinary people are not preoccupied with security in the way their leaders are, so they are not much concerned with issues of national economic growth. Even at a personal level, most people are not anxious to get rich, but simply want an adequate material basis for decent living.

In contrast, on the evidence of both their rhetoric and their actions, most governments are more concerned with national economic growth and balance of payments than with such things as poverty, malnutrition, and children's mortality. Political leaders say that economic growth and improved foreign exchange holdings are means to alleviate poverty and thus reduce malnutrition and children's deaths. The fact is that gains in economic resources usually are devoted to other purposes. The benefits of economic growth do trickle down, but in the absence of special measures that trickle is slow and meager.

A better way to understand the leaders' focus on increasing growth and foreign exchange holdings is that these are of great importance to their politically powerful constituencies. Political leaders have a much greater and more direct interest in increasing economic growth and foreign exchange holdings because these things make them more powerful. Alleviating malnutrition among those who are politically weak doesn't benefit the political leadership nearly as much. The class bias of economic growth's effects helps to explain the policy bias of national decision makers.

RECESSION

For many years following World War II the poorer countries of the world were drawn into the international economy by increasing the export orientation of their national economies. They also borrowed heavily, often under considerable pressure by international lenders. Then, beginning in the late 1970s, the structure weakened. The external debt of developing countries rose sharply. Commodity prices fell. Beginning in 1982, it was recognized that may poor countries would not be able to meet their loan repayment schedules.

During periods of economic recession, when poverty becomes more intense and more widespread, children's mortality rates are affected. According to UNICEF:

between 1950 and 1980 child death rates fell by 50 percent; average life expectancy rose by 30 percent; food production trebled, and school enrollment rates doubled. ... Such advances were made possible, in the main, by overall development and economic growth. But then, with the 1980s, came economic recession. ... In this decade, more than half the nations of Africa have seen their average real incomes fall by more than 15 percent. In Latin America, average earnings today are 9 percent lower than in 1980. In the developing world as a whole, 1986 has been the seventh consecutive year of negative or negligible growth in incomes. Only in the larger or more dynamic economies of south and east Asia has the momentum of economic development been maintained. ... The brunt of this blow has been borne by the poor.[9]

The declines in the 1980s were not only economic:

The average weight-for-age of young children, a vital indicator of normal growth, is falling in many of the countries for which figures are available. In the 37 poorest nations, spending per head on health has been reduced by 50 percent, and on education by 25 percent, over the last few years. And in almost half of the 103 developing countries from which recent information is available, the proportion of 6-to-11 year olds enrolled in primary school is now falling. ... In other words, it is children who are bearing the heaviest burden of debt and recession in the 1980s.[10]

The effect of economic decline on children's mortality has been documented in many different circumstances. In Toledo, Ohio, "while overall infant mortality had declined steadily from 1950 to 1970, post-neonatal mortality for the overall resident population showed a staggering increase between 1960 and 1970—years characterized in Toledo by adverse economic and social conditions."[11]

In Sri Lanka, following successive crop failures in 1973 and 1974 and subsequent increases in food prices, "post-neonatal mortality increased by an astounding 37 percent for the country as a whole and by almost 60 percent in the estate sector. In a single year, 1974, post-neonatal mortality increased by almost 150 percent in the estate sector."

In Bangladesh in the mid-1970s, poor harvests led to sharp increases in the price of rice, which in one region "provoked an increase in child mortality among the landless of almost 400 percent."

A study of patterns in Costa Rica from 1910 to 1981 showed that "in the years of economic contraction, infant mortality tends to reduce at a slower pace and in a few cases to increase."

The recession of the first half of the 1980s corresponded to slowdowns in the rate of decline in children's mortality in several developing countries, including Chile and the Philippines. In Brazil, Ghana, and Uruguay, infant mortality rates increased substantially.[12]

In the United States in the early 1980s, the number of people under the official poverty line increased, and there were signs of increasingly widespread malnutrition. These occurred partly as a result of economic conditions, and partly because of the anti-welfare ideology that pervaded the Reagan administration.

STRUCTURAL ADJUSTMENT

To deal with the economic pressures on them, many poor countries have had to make substantial policy adjustments. They have reduced their imports, devalued their currencies, and cut government expenditures, often under pressure from the lending agencies. In many cases the adjustments have resulted in higher unemployment and lower wages. The attempts to restore the basis for long-term economic growth have had real short-term costs.

In many countries the costs not only of recession but also of adjustment have been borne disproportionately by the poor:

It is the poor and the vulnerable who are suffering the most, and for two main reasons.

The first is that the poor have the least economic "fat" with which to absorb the blow of recession. . . .

The second reason is that the poor also have the least political "muscle" to ward off that blow. Services which are of concern to the richer and more powerful sections of society—such as the major hospitals, universities, national airlines, prestige development projects, and the military—have not borne a proportional share of the cuts in public spending. With some honourable exceptions, the services which have been radically pruned are health services, free primary education, and food and fuel subsidies—the services on which the poor are most dependent and which they have least opportunity to replace by any other, private, means. . . . Meanwhile, the proportion of national budgets devoted to the military is approximately 30 percent higher than total spending on health and education combined.[13]

Some structural changes made in response to economic stress have increased children's mortality rates. Policymakers may view this as an unfortunate but necessary price that has to be paid for gains on other dimensions. They would argue that structural adjustment to achieve steady economic growth would in the long run lead to reduced children's mortality along with other kinds of positive outcomes. This possibility is certainly implied in the fundamental observation that richer countries have lower children's mortality rates. Nevertheless, the short-term costs in terms of children's mortality are excessive.

And structural adjustment is sharply discriminatory; poor people rarely enjoy the benefits of the beguiling long run. Growth-oriented development policy, administered by those in power, is of greatest benefit to the powerful. The benefits that accrue to the poor, if they ever come about, are incidental in their programs.

The motivations behind structural adjustment center on economic growth, an objective that is biased in favor of the rich. Why is there no "structural adjustment" centered on reducing children's mortality, an objective biased in favor of the poor? How might adjustment programs be shaped if the highest priority were to be given to the sustained reduction of children's mortality rates, and economic growth were seen simply as one of many possible means to that end? Consider Mahbub ul-Haq's appeal:

We were taught to take care of our GNP, because this would take care of poverty. Let us reverse this and take care of poverty, because this will take care of the GNP. Let us worry about the content of GNP even more than its rate of increase.[14]

UNICEF has been pressing for "adjustment with a human face," adjustment policies that are not carried out at the expense of the poor. These "are not arguments for introducing more welfare programmes into stagnant economies."

They are part of a wider argument for a different approach to the whole adjustment process, an approach which would not only seek to protect the poorest and most vulnerable but also contribute to a quickening of economic growth of a kind which smaller and poorer producers could both contribute to and benefit from.[15]

RECESSION DOES NOT EXPLAIN POVERTY

The focus on economic recession and on adjustment policies should not distract us from more fundamental structural issues. A 1985 study by a group of physicians at Harvard University attributed malnutrition in the United States to the fact that the Reagan administration had cut back sharply on welfare programs.[16] It showed that there had been sharp recent increases in the number of Americans under the official poverty line. But the study did not go beyond concern with recent changes to ask why, for decades, under many different administrations, more than 10 percent of the U.S. population had been under the poverty line. Why have Americans come to regard this as normal? Why should there by any poverty at all in the richest country that has ever existed in all of human history? The Harvard group, focusing on the recession and the anti-poor policies of the Reagan administration, did not raise the question of why there should be any hunger at all in the United States. Recent recessions in the United States and worldwide account for recent incremental increases in poverty, but they don't account for chronic poverty.

In much the same way, the child survival movement has become very much concerned with the effects of economic recession on children's mortality, but it gives little attention to the ways in which basic social structures— in which recession is only a passing event—affect children's mortality. Studies of adjustment policies focus on recent incremental changes in economic conditions and health status. The prior conditions are accepted as immutable facts of nature, normal and proper, beyond explanation and beyond concern.

If "at root, the poor growth performance of the developing countries is caused by the economic slump of the industrialized world," why does it follow that "given their debt situation and poor external prospects, developing countries will have to undertake massive belt-tightening in the foreseeable future"?[17] Why should it be the poor countries that do the adjusting? Their belts are already tight. Moreover, if their suffering during the recession has been largely due to their linkages with the industrialized world, why should they be pressed to undertake adjustments that make them even more dependent upon and vulnerable to the developed world? The unfortunate fact is that "international economic forces tend to work out their effects in one-sided ways. The banks in rich countries that made unwise loans have suffered little; the adjustments have fallen in overwhelming measure on the people in poor countries."[18]

It is the poor countries that are called upon to do the adjusting because they are weak and vulnerable to the pressures of the more powerful developed countries. The structural adjustment policies of the international lending agencies in effect blame the victims; they do not consider that it might be the structure of the world economy itself that is in need of adjustment.

With such widespread and persistent poverty in the world, there must be something in prevailing social systems that endlessly re-creates poverty. There is something in the steady-state background that needs to be explained. Why are there large numbers of chronically poor and malnourished people all the time, in the United States and worldwide?

As UNICEF observes, "the poor have usually gained least in good times and suffered most in bad times."[19]

The fact that so much of today's staggering debt was irresponsibly lent and irresponsibly borrowed would matter less if the consequences of such folly were falling on its perpetrators. Yet now, when the party is over the the bills are coming in, it is the *poor* who are being asked to pay.

Today, the heaviest burden of a decade of frenzied borrowing is falling not only on the military or on those with foreign bank accounts or on those who conceived the years of waste, but on the poor who are having to do without necessities, on the unemployed who are seeing the erosion of all that they have worked for, on the women who do not have enough food to maintain their health, on the infants whose minds and bodies are not growing properly because of untreated illnesses and malnutrition, and on the children who are being denied their only opportunity ever to go to school.

In short, it is hardly too brutal an oversimplification to say that the rich got the loans and the poor got the debts.[20]

There is class bias in economic growth, in recession, and in countries' adjustments to recession. There is a ratcheting process that regularly works against the interests of the poor. The reason is simple: The poor, being politically weak, don't have their hands on the ratchet. Economic policies made by the strong respond first to the interests of the strong.

DEVIATION

Some households and some societies do unusually well or unusually poorly with respect to nutrition status or children's mortality rates. They deviate from what would be expected on the basis of their income levels alone. In Chapter I we saw that the United States has a worse infant mortality rate than several countries with much lower average income levels. China, Sri Lanka, and Costa Rica have had far better children's mortality rates than would be expected on the basis of their average income levels, at least in some phases of their recent histories. Some, such as Saudi Arabia, Iran, Libya, Iraq, and Algeria, have done far worse than would be expected on the basis of their income levels.[21]

There are many cases in which young children living in impoverished, socioeconomically depressed environments are better nourished than would be expected on the basis of their families' income levels. Children do well despite poverty if they are favored with attentive, affectionate mothering, close families, supportive neighbors and friends, and active communities with employment opportunities and well-developed social services.[22]

As shown in Chapter 3, many studies have demonstrated that education, especially women's education, can have a strong impact on children's mortality. In India, income per capita has little association with infant mortality, but female literacy is strongly related. Despite its middling income level, the state of Kerala, with the highest female literacy rate in India, had the lowest infant mortality rate.[23]

Leonard Sagan finds that "the statistical association between literacy and health is consistently stronger than that between health and income." He examined literacy and death rates among the states of the United States:

The data show the same thing—while the per capita income of each state has no statistical relationship with infant mortality rates (for 1980), education as measured by the percent of residents who complete high school is highly significant statistically in predicting the infant mortality in that state (the probability of such a strong relationship occurring by chance is one in a thousand).[24]

The fact that there is not a one-to-one association between income levels and children's mortality levels means there are possibilities for doing things to improve children's survival prospects even while people remain poor. But there are dangers to this observation. It may suggest that people ought to find ways to adapt to their poverty rather than find ways to transform that condition. It may suggest that poverty is somehow unimportant.

Worse, it is sometimes twisted to suggest that the poor *should not* have more money. Conservatives complain that when poor people get a bit of money, they squander it on beer or cigarettes or radios. The implication is that increasing the income of the poor won't help to improve their nutrition status.

Formal studies have shown that among the poor, "nutrition income elasticities are so low that income increments will not have much effect on nutrition."[25] Small changes in income will have little or no effect on the nutritional status of poor families. But there can be no doubt that richer families (or nations) are far less likely to be undernourished than poorer families (or nations). Income level is a very compelling determinant of nutrition status, disease vulnerability, and children's mortality.

Chapter 6 pointed out that malnutrition may result not only from inadequate food supplies but also from disease and from inappropriate food behaviors. When household food supplies are abundant, family members will be much less vulnerable to disease. And "errors" in food behavior are much less critical for those who are wealthy. Those who castigate the poor for spending their money on beer and snacks are much more understanding when the rich do the same sort of thing. The poor are expected to calculate the nutrient values of their food intake in far more sophisticated ways than middle-class people are ever expected to do.

Recognizing the possibility of deviance simply means recognizing that there are factors other than economics that influence human welfare, which is not surprising. But money should not be underestimated. It certainly is important in keeping children alive.

NOTES

1. Katrina Galway, Brent Wolff, and Richard Sturgis, *Child Survival: Risks and the Road to Health* (Columbia, Md.: Institute for Resource Development/Westinghouse/USAID, 1987) p. 7.

2. Food and Agriculture Organization of the United Nations, *Annual Report* (Rome: FAO, 1974).

3. D. N. Dhanagare, "The Green Revolution and Social Inequalities in Rural India," *Bulletin of Concerned Asian Scholars*, 20, no. 2 (April–June 1988), 2–13, see p. 4.

4. Hollis Chenery, "Redistribution with Growth," in Hollis Chenery et al., eds., *Redistribution with Growth* (London: Oxford University Press, 1974).

5. World Bank, *The World Bank Annual Report 1988* (Washington, D. C.: World Bank, 1988), p. 41.

6. *Economic Report of the President* (Washington, D. C.: U.S. Government Printing Office, 1988), Table B–30.

7. Congressional Budget Office, as reported in *Time*, October 10, 1988, p. 29.

8. *Poverty Remains High Despite Economic Recovery* (Washington, D. C.: Center on Budget and Policy Priorities, August 31, 1988).

9. James P. Grant, *The State of the World's Children 1987* (New York: Oxford University Press, 1987), pp. 13–15.

10. James P. Grant, *The State of the World's Children 1989* (New York: Oxford University Press, 1989), p. 1.

11. This and the following information on Sri Lanka, Bangladesh, and Costa Rica are drawn from Giovanni Andrea Cornia, "A Survey of Cross-Sectional and Time-Series Literature on Factors Affecting Child Welfare," *World Development*, 12, no. 3 (March 1984), 187–202.

12. Giovanni Andrea Cornia, "Economic Decline and Human Welfare in the First Half of the 1980s," in Giovanni Andrea Cornia, Richard Jolly, and Frances Stewart, eds., *Adjustment with a Human Face*, vol. 1, *Protecting the Vulnerable and Promoting Growth* (Oxford: Oxford University Press, 1987), pp. 11–47, see p. 398.

13. Grant, *The State of the World's Children 1989*, pp. 16–17.

14. Mahbub ul-Haq, "Employment in the 1970s: A New Perspective," in *Education and Development Reconsidered: The Bellagio Conference Papers* (New York: Praeger, 1974).

15. Grant, *The State of the World's Children 1989*, p. 20.

16. J. Larry Brown et al., *Hunger in America: The Growing Epidemic* (Boston: Physician Task Force on Hunger in America, Harvard University School of Public Health, 1985).

17. Lance Taylor, "Macro Effects of Myriad Shocks: Developing Countries in the World Economy," in David E. Bell and Michael R. Reich, eds., *Health, Nutrition, and Economic Crises: Approaches to Policy in the Third World* (Dover, Mass.: Auburn House, 1988), pp. 17–37.

18. David E. Bell and Michael R. Reich, "Introduction and Overview" in David E. Bell and Michael R. Reich, eds., *Health, Nutrition, and Economic Crises* (Dover, Mass.: Auburn House, 1988), pp. 1–13.

19. Grant, *The State of the World's Children 1989*, p. 30.

20. Ibid., pp. 30–31. The point is fully developed in Susan George, *A Fate Worse Than Debt: The World Financial Crisis and the Poor* (New York: Grove Press, 1988).

21. S.B.J.A. Halstead, A. Walsh, and K. S. Warren, eds., *Good Health at Low Cost* (New York: Rockefeller Foundation, 1985).

22. Marian Zeitlin, Hossein Ghassemi, and Mohammed Mansour, *Positive Deviance in Child Nutrition: With Emphasis on Psychosocial and Behavioural Aspects and Implications for Development* (Tokyo: United Nations University, 1989).

23. James P. Grant, *The State of the World's Children 1984* (New York: Oxford University Press, 1983), p. 150.

24. Leonard A. Sagan, *The Health of Nations: True Causes of Sickness and Well-Being* (New York: Basic Books, 1987), pp. 177–79.

25. Barbara L. Wolfe and Jere R. Behrman, "Is Income Overrated in Determining Adequate Nutrition," *Economic Development and Cultural Change*, 31, no. 3 (April 1983), 523–49.

Chapter Eight

WAR

Some of the 14 million children who die each year before reaching their fifth birthday are casualties of war. This chapter examines the ways in which military activities may produce benefits for children, and then reviews the ways in which they may harm children. Children are increasingly subjected to the trauma of warfare. Several national and international agencies do excellent work on behalf of children, but there is much more to be done. New institutional arrangements are needed to protect children, always the most vulnerable group in situations of armed conflict.

BENEFITS TO CHILDREN

There are several ways in which military establishments or warfare may benefit children.

Military establishments can provide the security needed for raising children properly. Armed forces often provide the security needed to maintain orderly commerce and orderly societies, allowing life to go on in a normal and productive way. Under some conditions the military can deter disruptive violence.

Under some conditions children benefit from warfare. There have been many instances in which children—with others—have been liberated by force from oppressive circumstances. World War II provides the major example in recent history.

Military establishments sometimes provide direct medical and other services for children during conflict situations. In some cases armed forces show special compassion for children. For example, according to one account of activities of the National Resistance Army and its opposition to the Uganda National Liberation Army in Uganda in the early 1980s:

the popularly supported NRA could not turn its back on the needs of the local people. Abandoned children were cared for in small numbers in the beginning, but by 1983 more and more school-aged children were absorbed into the NRA. As UNLA operations intensified and threatened remote NRA camps where these children were kept, a decision was taken to disperse the children and give them basic self-defense training to reduce risks. NRA officers "adopted" these children and looked after food, clothing and shelter.[1]

Benefits to children may be delivered out of compassion, to win recruits, or for public relations purposes in an effort to "win the hearts and minds" of the local population.

In some countries and for some individuals, military service may provide one of the few available means of assuring adequate nutrition and providing family income. In Ethiopia, for example, even during the worst famine periods in the hardest-hit areas, soldiers have not gone hungry, and their children probably have done better than others. At times food can be an important factor in the recruitment of child soldiers:

In Uganda... children in national and revolutionary armies are often better fed and protected than non-combatant youth. "I have a gun, food and a place to sleep," one nine-year-old Ugandan soldier recently told a relief worker. "That's more than I had in my village."[2]

HARM TO CHILDREN

Wars can hurt children in several different ways.

Wars sometimes kill and maim children through their direct violence. Children are killed in general attacks on civilian populations, as in Hiroshima. Some wars, such as that in Afghanistan in the 1980s, have been especially lethal to children. In Nicaragua, many children have been maimed or killed by mines.[3]

Children are being counted among the casualties of warfare at a steadily increasing rate:

In World War I about 5 percent of those who died were civilians; in World War II, it was about 48 percent; today in conflicts such as in Lebanon, the number is as high as 90 percent and many of these are children.[4]

Wars now kill more civilians than soldiers, and many of these civilians are children. This means that the proportion of children's deaths out of all deaths in warfare is rising steadily.

It has been estimated that "about nine million children have died in wars and 'police action' that have occurred since 1945 and about three times that have been injured and maimed."[5]

Of course, as outspoken anti-nuclear pediatricians such as Benjamin Spock and Helen Caldicott tell us, future wars are likely to be enormously deadly to all age groups.

Why have children become so much more vulnerable? Historically, conflicts involving set-piece battles in war zones away from major population centers killed very few children. However, wars are changing form, moving out of the classic theaters of combat and into residential areas where civilians are more exposed.

But it is not only a matter of exposure. Increasingly, children are being drawn into warfare as a matter of policy.

Children are being deliberately targeted. In the massacre at Lidice, Czechoslovakia, the Nazis systematically killed or dispersed all the children. It has been estimated that the holocaust of World War II killed a million children. Terrorists often make a point of going after children. Neil Boothby explains:

As paradoxical as it may be, this is occurring precisely because children are so precious to many of us. To destroy what is of highest value to someone is clearly among the most effective forms of terrorism imaginable; to kill and injure children is to rob a family or an entire group of its future. What better way to undermine whatever popular support may exist for any given cause than to attack the very beings we love and value most in life?[6]

The casualty rate for children is increasing not only because they are more exposed, and not only because they have become deliberate targets, but also because children are being used as soldiers.

Often children are pressed to participate in armed combat as soldiers, harming them both physically and psychologically. Children can be the agents as well as the victims of violence. Increasingly, older children (10 to 18 years old) are engaged not simply as innocent bystanders but as active participants in warfare:

thousands of children are currently bearing arms in at least 20 ongoing conflicts. Even children as young as nine years old are used as frontline combatants in unwinnable battles, as decoys to lure opposing forces into ambush and as human mine detectors to explode bombs in front of advancing adult troops.[7]

In many cases the treatment of child recruits has been far less benign than what has been suggested regarding Uganda. In some cases children "have been expected to commit violent murders against unarmed civilians as a kind of rite of passage into combat forces... boys were sometimes forced to kill other children of similar ages in order to save their own lives and enter into paramilitary groups, acts most undertook only after severe beatings."[8]

In Peru, "according to deputies of the Peruvian Parliament, the Sendero Luminoso ("Shining Path") guerrilla movement more and more frequently uses *minors to perform assassinations* because under Peruvian law they cannot be charged for crimes committed before the age of 18."[9]

The minister of education of Iran said that in 1987, 150,000 schoolchildren volunteered to fight in the Iranian army; they represented 60 percent of all volunteers in the army.[10]

There are many reports of forced recruitment of schoolchildren as combatants by the Mozambique National Resistance (or Renamo). They have been used as scouts and spies, and as part of their training as guerrillas, they have been forced to kill prisoners.[11]

The child soldiers of Uganda

will carry with them the scars of violence and war. They are mature beyond their years, but the respect shown them is frequently because of the weapon they proudly carry.... Child soldiers are increasingly deployed in guerrilla and conventional wars in developing countries, yet we have little or no information on how this affects them.[12]

Neil Boothby says, "In my clinical experience, psychological disturbance has been greater among children who perpetuated violence than among those who were victims of it."

With the increasing prevalence of irregular warfare, it is often difficult to distinguish between children who are combatants and those who are not. In the *intifadeh* uprising in the West Bank and Gaza, the Palestinians have made a point of not carrying arms. Many of the children involved have been killed or severely beaten by the Israeli Defense Forces:

the number of people under 18 years old killed between 8 December 1987 and 27 September 1988 is estimated... to be 104.... 67 of these 104 children were shot. The causes of death of the other 37 victims vary from beatings resulting in death to suffocation by tear-gas.[13]

Wars sometimes harm children indirectly, through their interference with normal patterns of food supply and health care. Famines are often due more to warfare than to drought: "More than half the civilian deaths in current hostilities resulted from war-related famine. Most of those were in Sub-Saharan Africa, where ruthless sabotage supported by South Africa against its neighbors targeted schools and health centers as well as food supplies."[14]

In 1980–86 in Angola and Mozambique, about half a million more children under 5 died than would have died in the absence of warfare. In 1986 alone 84,000 child deaths in Mozambique were attributed to the war and destabilization.[15] The high mortality rates in Angola and Mozambique are due not only to South Africa's destabilization efforts but also to their civil wars. The famines in Ethiopia in the mid-1980s and again in the late 1980s would not have been so devastating if it were not for the civil wars involving Tigre, Eritrea, and other provinces of Ethiopia. Civil war has also helped to create and sustain famine in the Sudan.[16]

Many children died of starvation during the wars under the Lon Nol and

Pol Pot regimes in Kampuchea in the 1970s. In February 1975 40 percent of the children admitted to the Catholic Relief Services Children's Centre died, most within 24 hours of admission.[17]

In Afghanistan, before the withdrawal of Soviet troops in February 1989:

More than 30,000 children run the risk of major illness or even death as a result of malnutrition among the deteriorating food and health conditions in the Kabul area. ... Already living on the edge, these children, along with nursing mothers and pregnant women in the poorest sections of Afghan society, are viewed by health experts as being least able to withstand the rigors of the Afghan winter and the food shortages that are affecting the city as the war moves into its final stages.[18]

The interference with food supplies and health services is often an unintended by-product of warfare, but in many cases it has been very deliberate. According to the distinguished nutritionist Jean Mayer:

Starvation has been used as an instrument of policy many times: against the South during the American Civil War, against France by the Prussians in 1870, against the Central Powers by the Allies during the First World War, against the city of Leningrad by the Germans during World War II, and against the Viet Cong by the United States during the Vietnamese conflict. In the situation in Nigeria, where I was present as an observer, starvation was being used as a weapon of terror by the Nigerians and as a weapon of propaganda by the Biafrans. At no time did I see any shortage of food in the Biafran army, which was nonetheless defeated. The persons who are most vulnerable in a fight like that, as the present situation in Ethiopia illustrates, are not combatants but children, pregnant and nursing women, and the elderly—those who die first in a famine. The weaponry of starvation is worse than indiscriminate, like bacteriological warfare; it discriminates against those who, by any standard, least deserve it.[19]

In the genocidal killing of the kulaks in the Ukraine and surrounding areas in the early 1930s, about 4 million children died as a result of the deliberately imposed famine and other "de-kulakization" programs.[20] According to one account, in the late 1960s in the Nigerian civil war, "a number of great and small nations, including Britain and the United States, worked to prevent supplies of food and medicine from reaching the starving children of rebel Biafra."[21]

In October 1987 in Ethiopia, 16 trucks of the World Food Programme carrying 530 tons of food were destroyed by the Eritrean People's Liberation Front, killing one driver and injuring several others. Seven Catholic Relief Services trucks in the same convoy also were destroyed. In April 1988 the government, pursuing its military objectives, excluded international agencies from the north, thus effectively stopping international relief efforts in the region.

Wars cause great psychological damage to children. The psychological trauma that war causes to children received a great deal of attention during World War II.[22] As Alison Acker observes:

The war in Central America has an emotional effect, too. Children who have watched their parents murdered, who have been raped or tortured themselves, children who have been orphaned, abandoned, imprisoned, and beaten, may well have been damaged for life. There is no one officially measuring the trauma, much less attempting to heal the traumatized, only a dedicated few who battle official indifference.

It is remarkable how few studies there have been of children from other wars. There is scant information on the children of the concentration camps in Germany and Poland, on the Vietnam boat people's kids, on the children of the disappeared people of Chile and Argentina.[23]

The book *Fire from the Sky: Salvadoran Children's Drawings* conveys a sense of the effect these wars can have on children.[24]

The impact of the Hiroshima bombing on children has been studied, and there have been several efforts to explore children's perceptions of the prospect of nuclear war.[25] The effects of the long-lasting civil violence in Northern Ireland on children has been documented,[26] as has the impact of the war in Lebanon.[27] The effects of militarization on children in the Philippines also has been documented.[28]

A 1987 analysis of the effect of continuing violence on the children of Uganda found that "the Ugandan youth are not indoctrinated with hatred or desire for revenge. They have no real enemies, but they are tired of war, violence, coups, and army men. They do not hate. They do not love. They hope."[29]

Studies of U.S. children's reactions to the Vietnam war seem not to have been therapeutic in purpose. They have been more "pure" research, and some have been concerned with themes such as "accepting the necessity for war."[30]

The psychological impacts of warfare on children have been investigated frequently. There have not been nearly as many studies of the direct physical impacts of warfare on children.

Even short of active warfare, the establishment of armed forces can be harmful to children in several ways.

High expenditures on armed forces can result in inadequate provision of resources for the care of children. Many have observed the contrast between the small budget allocations for health and the enormous allocations for defense in many countries of the world. President Dwight Eisenhower made the much-quoted observation that "Every gun that is made, every warship launched, every rocket fired, signifies, in the final sense, a theft from those who hunger and are not fed, those who are cold and not clothed." World Bank figures show that the 43 countries with the highest infant mortality rates (over 100 deaths per 1,000 live births) spend three times as much on defense as on health.[31]

In 1986 Pakistan's Finance Minister, Mahbub-ul-Haq, asked:

must we starve our children to raise our defence expenditures? For the sad fact is that from 1972 to 1982, the health and education expenditures of the low-income developing countries went down . . . while, at the same time, the defence spending of the developing world rose from $7 billion to over $100 billion. When our children cry in the middle of the night, shall we give them weapons instead of milk?[32]

UNICEF asks if we can really say it is too expensive to save children "when 3.5 million children a year are dying of diseases which can be prevented by immunization at an additional yearly cost which is less than the price of five advanced fighter planes?"[33]

Soldiers often father mixed-race children who are likely to be abandoned. Active warfare, occupations, and the establishment of overseas bases often lead to the births of large numbers of children of foreign soldiers and local women. Most of these children must be raised without fathers, and often they are abandoned altogether. The lucky ones are adopted or live in homes such as the Elizabeth Saunders Home for Mixed-blood Children established outside Tokyo after World War II,[34] but many end up scavenging in the streets.

Many children of U.S. servicemen are abandoned near the U.S. military bases in the Philippines:

The *Philippine Daily Inquirer* reported that there are about 3,000 abandoned and neglected children of American and Filipino parentage "who have mostly ended up on the streets as beggars, vendors, scavengers, baggage boys, shoe shine boys, and car and bus cleaners."[35]

There are "nearly 85,000 Amerasian children in varying states of need in nine Asian nations and many more elsewhere throughout the world," fathered by U.S. servicemen, businessmen, and civilian government workers.[36] These children are treated as social outcasts.

Largely as a result of the efforts of the Pearl S. Buck Foundation, Asian-American children fathered by U.S. soldiers and civilians during the Vietnam War and some of their relatives have been allowed to emigrate to the United States. A new Amerasian Act was signed into law in December 1987, with about $5 million budgeted to fly the children and their accompanying relatives to the United States by 1990. There are between 8,000 and 15,000 Amerasian children eligible for resettlement. Under the U.S. Orderly Departure Program the children and their relatives can emigrate at the rate of 1,900 a month.[37]

Warfare can result in large numbers of unaccompanied children. UNICEF was born out of the plight of the many thousands of children cast adrift in Europe after World War II.[38] Wars, natural disasters, and other kinds of problems have led to the repetition of similar situations all over the world.[39] Children who are orphaned or are separated from their parents are fortunate to be survivors, but they are especially vulnerable to direct physical violence, disease, malnutrition, and impaired social development.

PUBLICITY, EDUCATION, AND RESEARCH

Many different actions could be undertaken on behalf of children living under repressive conditions or subjected to armed conflict. Their conditions should be publicized as part of a politics of embarrassment. UNICEF's *Children on the Front Line* and Alison Acker's *Children of the Volcano* are outstanding examples of this sort of work. Defense for Children International-USA has prepared a very powerful analysis of the situation in South Africa.[40] Exposure may elicit anger and further repression, but it also may draw more constructive responses. The risks must be estimated in specific contexts.

Some of the many efforts in behalf of children by individuals, private organizations, and governments have been recognized in the Nongovernmental Organizations Committee on UNICEF's periodical, *Action for Children*, but they should be acknowledged and supported even more extensively and systematically.

Some publication might also serve as a sort of brokerage, helping to link resources and talent to places where they are needed. There are many people in developed countries who would devote their talents to helping serve children in developing countries if only suitable channels could be established.

Energetic educational programs are needed to make the general public more aware of the plight of children and the rights of children in conflict situations. Some programs should be designed for specific groups having special concerns with the welfare of children, including government leaders, military officers and soldiers, health workers, relief and welfare organizations, mothers, and children themselves. Suitable training programs could be devised to show how physical and psychological harm to children could be minimized in conditions of war and repression. Work along these lines has been initiated by the Project on Children and War at Columbia University's Center for the Study of Human Rights.

There is an immediate need for public education throughout the world to implement the new Convention on the Rights of the Child, described in Chapter 16.

CHILDREN'S RIGHTS IN CONFLICT SITUATIONS

International human rights law regarding children in warfare has focused on assuring that children will not be targeted and will not be used as soldiers. Despite past declarations and resolutions, "in reality, however, neither of these basic rights has been implemented."[41]

Article 38 of the new convention addresses the issue of armed conflict:

1. States Parties undertake to respect and to ensure respect for rules of international humanitarian law applicable to them in armed conflicts which are relevant to the child.

2. States Parties shall take all feasible measures to ensure that persons who have not attained the age of 15 years do not take a direct part in hostilities.

3. States Parties shall refrain from recruiting any person who has not attained the age of 15 years into their armed forces. In recruiting among those persons who have not attained the age of 18 years, States Parties shall endeavour to give priority to those who are oldest.

4. In accordance with their obligations under international humanitarian law to protect the civilian population in armed conflicts, States Parties shall take all feasible measures to ensure protection and care of children who are affected by an armed conflict.

The convention is legally binding on those nations which have signed and ratified it. As indicated in Chapter 16, however, there are questions as to how effectively it will be implemented.

UNICEF'S ROLE

In the context of its broader efforts in behalf of *Children in Especially Difficult Circumstances*, UNICEF has undertaken major initiatives for dealing with *Children in Situations of Armed Conflict*.[42] (*Children in Especially Difficult Circumstances* includes *Working Children and Street Children*, *Children Endangered by Abuse and Neglect*, and *Children Affected by Natural Disasters*.) A discussion paper, *What More Can be Done for Children in Wars?* was prepared and circulated within UNICEF in April 1984.

In April 1986 the UNICEF Executive Board adopted a resolution on *Children in Especially Difficult Circumstances* that called for collaboration with other agencies working on the issues but did not propose any new initiatives for UNICEF itself. In the words of the Canadian representative, "in dealing with the situation of children in especially difficult circumstances, UNICEF has chosen not to launch a new programming thrust, but rather to build gradually on the success of existing programmes."[43]

A policy paper sent from headquarters to UNICEF field offices on October 31, 1986, on children in especially difficult circumstances, provided guidelines and possible courses of action for dealing with children in situations of armed conflict. It also included a brief appendix on children as a zone of peace. Emphasis was placed on coordination with other international organizations, and with local nongovernmental organizations, provided they had the endorsement of their governments.

UNICEF sponsored the International Conference on Children in Situations of Armed Conflict in Africa: An Agenda for Action, held at Nairobi in July 1987. The conference passed a resolution saying that the safety and protection of children and women during armed clashes should be an overriding concern of both combatants and noncombatants. African governments and the Organization of African Unity were urged to promote the concept of children as a zone of peace.[44]

UNICEF has not initiated any substantial new programs in relation to children in armed conflict. UNICEF's action plan for 1986–90 and the 1987 report of the Executive Board did not mention *Children in Especially Difficult Circumstances*.[45] UNICEF's annual *State of the World's Children* reports give little attention to *Children in Especially Difficult Circumstances* as a programmatic category.

ICRC'S ROLE

The International Committee of the Red Cross (ICRC), together with the League of the Red Cross and Red Crescent Societies and the recognized national Red Cross and Red Crescent societies, is one of the three components of the International Red Cross. ICRC is the founding body of the Red Cross. Since its beginning in the Franco-Prussian War of 1870, its mission has centered on conflict situations: "As a neutral intermediary in case of armed conflicts or disturbances, it endeavors on its own initiative or on the basis of the Geneva Conventions to protect and assist the victims of international and civil wars and of internal troubles and tensions, thereby contributing to peace in the world."[46]

Although it is financed by voluntary contributions from governments, the ICRC is not an international organization. It is a private Swiss organization. The committee is limited to 25 members, all Swiss. It is supported by a large number of delegates—all of whom must be Swiss citizens.

The ICRC is the guardian of international humanitarian law. Its major concern is the implementation of the four Geneva Conventions of 1949 and the two protocols of 1977. In fact it was the ICRC's efforts that led to the adoption of the 1949 Geneva Convention Relative to the Protection of Civilian Persons in Time of War, and it prepared the initial negotiating text that led to the 1977 protocols. (Further details are provided in Chapter 16.) However, as a private organization, it is not constrained by the language of those agreements, and often goes beyond their specific mandates.

In its work on behalf of the victims of armed conflict the ICRC

has always been particularly sensitive to the plight of children during wartime. Since the Second World War especially, it has endeavoured to alleviate their sufferings by helping in the drafting of laws for their protection, and by undertaking operations in countries affected by conflicts.[47]

However, because of its belief that the problems of children are always closely intertwined with those of adults, "the ICRC does not have specific programmes for children; or, to put it more precisely, the ICRC's programmes for children are always situated within a broader general context of assistance to the victims of conflict."[48]

From time to time the ICRC's monthly *Bulletin* describes its activities relating to children in conflict situations. The June 1984 issue ran an item "Children Must Be Protected from the Horror of War," and the August 1988 issue had a hospital picture captioned "Twelve-year-old Said Rahman lost both his hands and one eye after picking up a mine while tending sheep in Afghanistan."

Usually the ICRC does not use publicity; it rarely takes public critical positions. It works as quietly as it can, understanding that "its low-profile diplomacy enables it to operate on both sides of a conflict."[49] However, the ICRC has been known to publicly denounce serious and repeated violations of international humanitarian law.

In contrast with the ICRC, the League of Red Cross and Red Crescent Societies does have activities focused on the health of children, as described in the League's *Child Alive Newsletter*. It addresses health problems of children in normal village circumstances, and not specifically in situations of armed conflict.

The ICRC worked actively to strengthen the Convention on the Rights of the Child as it was being drafted because it weakens the protection for children already established in international humanitarian law. It objected that the article on armed conflicts

asks States only to take "all feasible measures" in order that children affected by armed conflict receive care and protection.... Like Additional Protocol I, the present text prohibits the recruitment of children under 15, and calls on States to take all feasible measures to prevent children under 15 from taking a direct part in hostilities. However, there is no reference to children under 15 being indirectly involved in the acts of war. This can include reconnaissance work or transporting arms and food for the armed forces.[50]

At the twenty-fifth International Conference of the Red Cross, held at Geneva in 1986, 117 governments and the whole International Red Cross and Red Crescent movement adopted a resolution stressing that "protection accorded by the new Convention should be at least the same as that accorded by the Geneva Conventions and the two Additional Protocols." The ICRC failed to persuade the negotiators to strengthen the language of Article 38.

A NEW LIAISON GROUP?

A great deal has already been accomplished for children in situations of armed conflict. Building on those sound foundations, much more can be done.

UNICEF, ICRC, and several other organizations play major international roles in looking after the interests of children in conflict situations. They make enormous contributions, but they are constrained, sometimes by their own wise choices. There are gaps in coverage. UNICEF focuses on children but does not sponsor programs focused on situations of armed conflict. ICRC focuses on conflict but not particularly on children. There are situations that do not get the attention they require. As Neil Boothby points out:

there is still no viable structure for safeguarding and reporting on children's rights. In war and refugee situations, the International Committee for the Red Cross (ICRC) and the United Nations High Commissioner for Refugees (UNHCR) have mandates to do so. But normally both agencies undertake their tasks through quiet diplomacy with national governments. . . . Critics suggest that this tactic sometimes leads to situations in which protection issues can neither be aggressively pursued nor publicly disclosed.[51]

The implementation provisions of the Convention on the Rights of the Child also are limited. The proposed Committee on the Rights of the Child will be confined by the language of the convention, and will not be free to initiate new programs. Also, the committee's responsibilities will cover all of the many different concerns addressed in the convention, so situations of armed conflict will occupy only a part of its agenda.

There is now no well-endowed international agency publishing independent analyses of national policies and practices with respect to children in situations of armed conflict. There is no central agency systematically supporting and defending the many nongovernmental agencies around the world that work for children in conflict situations on a local, national, or regional basis. There is no agency identifying the gaps in coverage. There is no body to coordinate the established agencies' work in this area.

Many organizations are trying to fill in the gaps. Defense for Children International investigates and publicizes violations of the rights of children, giving particular attention to issues of international importance. In January 1988 Amnesty International launched a special action on behalf of children who are victims of the misuse of state power. But compared with the need, these actions are relatively small-scale and fragmented.

To strengthen work already under way and to develop new lines of action, it would be useful to bring together representatives of the major governmental and nongovernmental agencies concerned with the issue in a *Liaison Group on Children in Armed Conflict.* The group could include representatives of UNICEF, national committees for UNICEF, ICRC, Red Crescent organizations, the U.N. High Commissioner for Refugees, Defense for Children International, Save the Children, OXFAM, CARE, World Vision, the Pearl Buck Foundation, Amnesty International, Radda Barnen, and others. It could go beyond the formal rights and their associated instruments of implementation to consider legal, political, and other kinds of measures to protect the interests of children in situations of armed conflict. The group could meet at least once a year to exchange views and to consider new and better ways to address the problems of children in situations of armed conflict.

With the proportion of children being killed and injured in warfare increasing at an alarming rate, more should be done to recognize and implement the rights of those who are most needy and most powerless in situations of armed conflict. It is important to move beyond nonbinding resolutions and practically unenforceable assertions of rights to the formulation of concrete political strategies for the implementation of those rights. The new Convention on the Rights of the Child awaits implementation by the nations of the world. A liaison group that brings together representatives of concerned agencies could help to assure that there will be a broad variety of coordinated and sustained actions on behalf of children in situations of armed conflict.

NOTES

1. Cole P. Dodge, "Child Soldiers of Uganda: What Does the Future Hold," *Cultural Survival Quarterly*, 10, no. 4 (1986), 31–33.

2. Neil Boothby, "Children and War," *Cultural Survival Quarterly*, 10, no. 4 (1986), 28–30.

3. Ron Arias, "Agonies of the Innocents," *People Weekly*, February 29, 1988, pp. 46–53.

4. Sandra Singer, "The Protection of Children During Armed Conflict Situations," *International Review of the Red Cross*, May–June 1986, pp. 133–68.

5. Michael Jupp, "The Human Rights of Children," *International Health News*, 8, no. 1 (January 1987), 1.

6. Boothby, "Children and War," pp. 28–30.

7. Ibid.

8. Ibid.

9. *International Children's Rights Monitor*, 5, no. 1 (1988), 21.

10. Ibid., p. 23.

11. Dominique Leveille, "Children Used by the Guerrilla in Mozambique: Younger Than the War Itself," *International Children's Rights Monitor*, 5, no. 1 (1988), 24.

12. Dodge, "Child Soldiers of Uganda," pp. 31–33.

13. "Children of the Uprising," *International Children's Rights Monitor*, 5, nos. 2/3 (1988), 19. Also see articles on child warriors in *Time*, June 18, 1990, 30–52.

14. Ruth Leger Sivard, *World Military and Social Expenditures 1987–88*, (Washington, D. C.: World Priorities, 1987), p. 28.

15. *Children on the Front Line: The Impact of Apartheid, Destabilization and Warfare on Children in Southern and South Africa* (New York: UNICEF, 1987).

16. *Review of African Political Economy*, no. 33 (August 1985), special issue on war and famine.

17. Meng Try Ea, "War and Famine: The Example of Kampuchea," in Bruce Currey and Graeme Hugo, eds., *Famine as a Geographical Phenomenon* (Dordrecht, Netherlands: D. Reidel, 1984), pp. 33–47.

18. Richard M. Weintraub, "30,000 Afghan Children at Risk," *The Guardian* (Manchester) 140, no. 7 (February 12, 1989), 17.

19. Jean Mayer, "International Agreements in the Food and Health Fields," in Alan K. Henrikson, ed., *Negotiating World Order: The Artisanship and Architecture of Global Diplomacy* (Wilmington, Del.: Scholarly Resources, 1986), pp. 3–17.

20. Robert Conquest, *The Harvest of Sorrow: Soviet Collectivization and the Terror—Famine* (New York: Oxford University Press, 1986), p. 297.

21. Dan Jacobs, *The Brutality of Nations* (New York: Alfred A. Knopf, 1987).

22. See, for example, Anna Freud and Dorothy T. Burlingham, *War and Children* (New York: Medical War Books, 1943); Alice Cobb, *War's Unconquered Children Speak* (Boston: Beacon Press, 1953).

23. Alison Acker, *Children of the Volcano* (Westport, Conn.: Lawrence Hill, 1986), pp. 24–25.

24. William Vornberger, ed., *Fire From the Sky: Salvadoran Children's Drawings* (New York: Writers and Readers Publishing Cooperative, 1986).

25. Arata Osada, *Children of the A-Bomb: The Testament of the Boys and Girls of Hiroshima (Tokyo: Uchida Rokakuho, 1959);* Child Study Association of America, *Children and the Threat of Nuclear War* (New York: Duell, Sloan & Pearce, 1964); Florence Weiner, *Peace Is You and Me: Children's Writings and Paintings on Love and Peace* (New York: Avon, 1971); *Children of Hiroshima* (London: Taylor & Francis, 1981); Helen Caldicott, *Missile Envy: The Arms Race and Nuclear War* (Toronto: Bantam Books, 1986), pp. 251–56; Phyllis La Farge, *The Strangelove Legacy: Children, Parents, and Teachers in the Nuclear Age* (New York: Harper & Row, 1987).

26. Jeremy Harbison and Joan Harbison, *A Society Under Stress: Children and Young People in Northern Ireland* (Somerset, England: Open Books, 1980).

27. Jennifer W. Bryce, *Cries of Children in Lebanon: As Voiced by Their Mothers* (Amman, Jordan: UNICEF Regional Office for the Middle East and North Africa, 1986).

28. Gabriela Commission on Children and Family, *Children of War, Children of Hope* (Manilla: GCCF, 1989).

29. Cole P. Dodge and Magne Raundalen, eds., *War, Violence and Children in Uganda* (Oslo: Norwegian University Press, 1987). Also see Cole P. Dodge and Paul D. Wiebe, eds., *Crisis in Uganda: The Breakdown of Health Services* (New York: Pergamon Press, 1985).

30. Howard Tolley, Jr., *Children and War: Political Socialization to International Conflict* (New York: Teachers College Press, 1973).

31. James P. Grant, *The State of the World's Children 1986* (New York: Oxford University Press, 1986), p. 72.

32. Grant, *The State of the World's Children 1987* (New York: Oxford University Press, 1987), p. 17.

33. Ibid., p. 9.

34. John C. Caldwell, *Children of Calamity* (New York: John Day, 1957).

35. *International Children's Rights Monitor*, 5, no. 2/3 (1988), p. 10.

36. John A. Shade, *America's Forgotten Children: The Amerasians* (Perkasie, Pa.: Pearl S. Buck Foundation, 1981).

37. Beverly Creamer, "Children of the Dust: Hoping for New Lives in America," *Honolulu Advertiser*, May 9, 1988, p. B–1.

38. Maggie Black, *The Children and the Nations: The Story of UNICEF* (New York: UNICEF, 1986).

39. Everett M. Ressler, Neil Boothby, and Daniel J. Steinbock, *Unaccompanied Children: Care and Protection in Wars, Natural Disasters and Refugee Movements* (New York: Oxford University Press, 1988).

40. Michael Jupp, *Children Under Apartheid* (New York: Defense for Children International-USA, 1987).

41. Boothby, "Children and War," pp. 28–30.

42. *Children in Situations of Armed Conflict*, E/ICEF/1986/CRP.2 (New York: UNICEF, 1986); *Overview: Children in Especially Difficult Circumstances*, E/ICEF/1986/L.6 (New York: UNICEF, 1986).

43. *United Nations Children's Fund, Executive Board, Summary Record of the 3rd Meeting*, E/ICEF/1986/SR.3 (New York: United Nations Economic and Social Council, April 23, 1986), p. 12.

44. "Protection Urged for Children in Armed Conflict," *UNICEF Intercom*, no. 46 (October 1987), p. 17.

45. *Medium-Term Plan for the Period 1986–1990*, E/ICEF/1987/3 (New York: United Nations Economic and Social Council, March 5, 1987); *United Nations Children's Fund, Report of the Executive Board (20 April–1 May 1987)*. Economic and Social Council Official Records, 1987, supp. no. 11 (New York: United Nations, 1987).

46. This self-description is published regularly in the ICRC's *International Review of the Red Cross*.

47. Denise Plattner, "Protection of Children in International Humanitarian Law," *International Review of the Red Cross*, May–June 1984, p. 140.

48. *ICRC and Children in Situations of Armed Conflict* (Geneva: International Committee of the Red Cross, July 1987), p. 13.

49. Peter T. White, "A Little Humanity amid the Horrors of War," *National Geographic*, 170, no.5 (November 1986), 647–79.

50. "Protection of Children in Armed Conflicts," *International Committee of the Red Cross Bulletin*, no. 156 (January 1989), 4.

51. Boothby, "Children and War," pp. 28–30.

Chapter Nine

REPRESSION

There is direct governmental violence against children even in the absence of warfare. According to Amnesty International:

In the 1980s there is widespread imprisonment, torture, and killing of children by governments. In South Africa alone, according to official statistics, the government detained approximately 2,000 children under 18 between July 1985 and January 1986. . . . Immediately after arrest, children may be beaten for several hours while under interrogation. Children have been hit with fists, sjamboks (whips), rifle butts, and kicked. . . .

In Iraq, the authorities arrested approximately 300 children and teenagers in the northern town of Sulaimaniya in late 1985. At least 29 of the detainees were reported to have later been secretly executed. . . .

At about 3 p.m., August 1, 1986, government soldiers entered the small village of Morakondre in Suriname in search of armed opposition troops. When they left, Cakwa Kastiel, a three-year-old child, was dead. He had been shot in his mother's arms.[1]

Careful research on the many cases of violence against children in South Africa shows that these are not "isolated incidents where one policeman oversteps the mark but rather a consistent pattern that is occurring country-wide."[2]

In Chile, documented violence against children in 1987 took various forms:

204 minors under 18 were detained, 35 of whom were under 15 and 8 under 12 years old. 126 of them were arrested because of their participation in street demonstrations. 45 reported having been hit during arrest or detention, 7 reported having been tortured during detention, 16 of whom were under 3 years of age.[3]

The number of children who suffer direct violence at the hands of their governments is small, however, in comparison with the number who suffer more subtle repression.

Most of the 14 million children under 5 who die each year do not die from bullets or torture or from some mysterious cause beyond human control, but from the ravages of malnutrition and of very ordinary diseases. Arguably, since the earth's resources are more than sufficient to allow every individual to be well nourished and healthy, and thus these children's deaths are in principle avoidable and unnecessary, they can be viewed as resulting from a form of violence we can call repression or *structural violence*. Not all, but a very large share of these 14 million children would survive under a social order in which resources and benefits were distributed more equitably.

STRUCTURAL VIOLENCE

Structural violence is indirect, in contrast with the sort of direct violence suffered by those caught in the crossfire of revolutions and international wars. It is due not so much to specific actions of individual persons as to the social structure in which individuals are embedded. In Johan Galtung's formulation of structural violence

the basic idea is that there is such a concept as "premature death." This we know, because we know that with some changes in social structure in general, and health structure in particular, life expectancy can be improved considerably. More particularly, it may be possible to give to the whole population the life expectancy of the class enjoying appropriate health standards, that is, the "upper classes." The level enjoyed by them would be an indicator of the *potential* possibility to "stay alive" in that society; for all but the upper classes that would be above the *actual* possibility to stay alive. The difference, *when avoidable*, is structural violence.[4]

A guerrilla in El Salvador explained the concept to a U.S. volunteer physician this way:

You gringos are always worried about violence done with machine guns and machetes. But there is another kind of violence that you must be aware of, too.

I used to work on the hacienda. . . . My job was to take care of the *dueño's* dogs. I gave them meat and bowls of milk, food that I couldn't give my own family. When the dogs were sick, I took them to the veterinarian in Suchitot or San Salvador. When my children were sick, the *dueño* gave me his sympathy, but not medicine as they died.

To watch your children die of sickness and hunger while you can do nothing is a violence to the spirit. We have suffered that silently for too many years. Why aren't you gringos concerned about that kind of violence?[5]

With direct violence there is a specific event, an identifiable victim, and an identifiable perpetrator. In contrast, structural violence is not visible in specific events. Its effects are most clearly observable at the societal level, as systematic shortfalls in the quality of life of certain groups of people.

The distinction between direct and structural violence is comparable with that between child abuse and child neglect. Abuse is about doing something, while neglect is about *not* doing something. Both are wrong. And it is neglect rather than abuse that accounts for most children's deaths.

Most children's deaths cannot be described as murders. But that does not mean they are accidental or natural. There is such a thing as negligent homicide. There is a difference between deliberate and negligent homicide in regard to questions of criminality, but the victims end up just as dead. Negligent homicide is still homicide, in that the deaths are avoidable and unnecessary.

We draw too sharp a line between *deliberate* and *neglectful*. *Deliberate neglect* describes the pattern of many governments' responses to the needs of children. The term is not an oxymoron; it is not self-contradictory. If the failure to attend to children's needs persists over time, even in the face of repeated complaints and appeals, that neglect can be described as intentional or deliberate. Neglect can be described as the failure to do something that should be done—and that failure may or may not be intentional. If it persists and is obvious, it must be regarded as intentional.

In direct violence, *intentions* are a major factor in judging an individual's blame for injuring another. In structural violence, however, the key is *priorities*. Societies are guilty of structural violence when the interests of politically weak groups such as children are not taken adequately into account when allocating the society's resources. Stronger people's interests always seem to be more important.

Government officials say that of course they do not want children to go hungry or to die—and they don't. The problem is that they give so many other concerns a higher priority. Where there are serious problems of hunger or homelessness or children's mortality, decision makers claim they *cannot* deal with the problem because they don't have the resources. Often the truth is that they *will not* respond to the problem. Children's welfare could be sharply improved if it were of high priority to the governments. *Cannot* is an attempt to evade responsibility. The *cannot* defense should not be accepted as an excuse where low priority—*will not*—is the truthful explanation.

The priorities of societies are made very visible in their budget allocations. Some sectors, such as the military, are treated very generously, while children's interests are given very little support.

Armed forces absorb an extraordinarily large share of the available resources in many societies. But they have their most negative effects on children as a result of their use in maintaining repressive regimes. Under such regimes children are not so much victims of direct violence from the armed forces as they are victims of indirect violence in the form of poverty, malnutrition, and disease.

Ruth Leger Sivard has categorized third world countries for their repressiveness in terms of whether there is *no*, *some*, or *frequent* official violence against citizens. If we check these data against the infant mortality rates, we find that those countries which impose *no* official violence against citizens have an average infant mortality rate of 54, while those which impose *some* or *frequent* violence have average infant mortality rates of about 90.[6]

Whether direct or indirect, violence means depriving people of what they value with no justification or legitimation other than the fact that some are more powerful than others. If I do not have a decent chance of feeding my children, staying healthy, and otherwise fulfilling my basic needs simply because I am politically weak while others around me are politically strong, then that political system is doing violence to me.

If we accept the estimate that about 9 million children have died in wars between 1945 and 1987, we get an average of less than 215,000 children's deaths due to warfare each year. These deaths account for only about 1.5 percent of the 14 million children under 5 who die each year. (The 9 million estimate includes children over 5 years old, which means that the proportion of children under 5 dying from warfare is far smaller). Most of the total 14 million deaths can be attributed to structural violence. Thus, *far more children's deaths result from the indirect, structural violence of repression than from the direct violence of warfare.*

The situation in Chile or in South Africa may not be formally one of war, but it is certainly not one of peace. We should be concerned not only with negative peace, understood as the absence of warfare, but also with positive peace, understood as the presence of justice. The opposite of peace is warfare *or* repression.

Grossly undemocratic societies are characterized by gross inequalities. They are inherently unstable unless they are held together by force and intimidation. Thus repression requires militarization. It would be a mistake to think that ending active warfare would in itself lead to great gains in child survival. Structural violence must be ended as well.

It may be objected that some countries are so absolutely poor that people would go hungry no matter how benign the leadership. But even the poorest countries find adequate food and health care for their government leaders and their armed forces. In a major study of 28 developing countries, the most striking find regarding the patterns of children's mortality was "the gross inequalities which exist within so many of the countries considered":

There are truly enormous differences.... It is by no means unusual for the ratio between the group with the highest neonatal mortality and that with the lowest in the same country to be between two and four; for post-neonatal mortality to be between two and five; and for child mortality to be between 4 and 30.[7]

Extensive premature deaths are a direct sign of repressive social systems.

In epidemiological studies the relative seriousness of different diseases is sometimes gauged by the degree to which they shorten people's lives. The aggregate number of lost years of life is measured as Years of Potential Life Lost.[8] Assessed in these terms, it is recognized that each child's death must be regarded as more serious than deaths from causes such as warfare, heart disease, or cancer, which tend to strike older people. The idea of structural violence goes further in that it recognizes that premature death does not strike people randomly, but very systematically affects certain groups of people much more than others. Children, the poor, and certain ethnic groups regularly suffer especially high losses of potential years of life.

RACISM

Patterns of repression against particular groups become clear when we distinguish infant mortality rates by race. In 1983, in South Africa the infant mortality rate for "colored" people was 50.7 while that for whites was 12.6. The rate for blacks in 34 urban magisterial districts in 1980 was 85.9. For rural Transkei it was 130. In Soweto the rate for blacks was estimated at 25.5 in 1983.[9] According to one report, in South Africa the infant mortality rate for whites is 12, while for rural blacks it is 282.[10] It has been estimated that in South Africa:

half (50 per cent) of all deaths in the African and "coloured" populations occur in the under-five age group... while among whites only seven percent of all deaths involve children under five. ... Both "coloured" and African children are between 14 and 15 times more likely than their white compatriots to die before their fifth birthdays.[11]

In the United States the infant mortality rate for blacks is almost twice that for whites: 18.4 versus 9.4 in 1984.[12]

The mortality rates for some ethnic groups are regularly higher than would be expected for their income levels, indicating that there is something more than poverty at work. In Fiji the infant mortality rate for ethnic Fijians is about 30, while that for Indians is about 40. The Indians are economically stronger but politically weaker than the indigenous Fijians. Apparently the Indians' political powerlessness is more important than their wealth levels in determining their infant mortality rates.

Differences in mortality rates by race cannot be explained in biomedical terms. The descendants of immigrants tend to acquire patterns of infant mortality more like the ones in the country of residence than the ones in the country of origin, which means that the differences are not simply genetic.[13]

Differences in infant mortality rates by race constitute rather pure indicators of structural violence, since in each case the different races live in the same country, with identical contexts of aggregate natural resources, climate, total wealth, and so on. That the differences are the result of social and political forces is suggested by the fact that in virtually every case it is the politically weaker minorities which have the higher infant mortality rates.

A measure comparable with the Years of Potential Life Lost is the number of "excess deaths": "Excess deaths" expresses the difference between the number of deaths actually observed in a minority group and the number of deaths that would have occurred in that group if it experienced the same death rates for each age and sex as the White population."[14]

Thus the number of excess deaths suffered by particular groups is a measure of the structural violence they suffer. During 1979–81 blacks and other minorities in the United States averaged 58,942 deaths each year in excess of what would be expected based on rates for whites. This is more than the total number of U.S. casualties in the Vietnam war. Minorities in the United States suffer more casualties from structural violence every year than the country suffered in the entire Vietnam war! Of these 58,942 excess deaths, 6,178 (about 10.5 percent) were deaths of infants.[15]

In 1983, 11,060 black babies died before their first birthday.[16] If around 6,000 of these can be designated as "excess deaths," it can be argued that more than half of the 11,060 black babies died *because* they were black.

GENDER DISCRIMINATION

The fact of discrimination against females has been well documented elsewhere and does not need to be demonstrated here.[17] Our special concern is with the ways in which gender discrimination affects children's mortality.

The effect is felt in several ways. One is that often there is discrimination against female infants. The result is direct infanticide,[18] or more frequently an indirect and subtle form of infanticide that is accomplished by giving females less care.[19] Whether or not it is intended to result in premature death, it has that effect:

Among 45 developing countries for which recent data are available, there are only 2 where mortality rates for girls age 1–4 years are not higher than mortality rates for boys in the same age range, suggesting that less food, health care, and other social benefits which enhance survival chance are going to girls in those countries.[20]

A study in the Punjab area of India showed that the mortality rate for girls was almost double that for boys:

it seems that women take better care of their sons than their daughters. During the newborn's crucial first year of life, women spend 2.3 times more money on their sons than on their daughters. This means that boys are better nourished (more fat and protein), better dressed (warm clothing when nights are cool), and better cared for when they are ill.[21]

Other studies in the Punjab found that 20.3 percent of girls were severely malnourished, compared with 0.1 percent of boys. Families invest less food and medical care in girls than in boys. Boys are breast-fed longer, and are given more food after weaning. Boys are more likely to be taken for preventive and curative health care.[22]

There may be comparable patterns of discrimination in richer areas, but with greater amounts of food, health, and other resources to cushion its effects, the discrimination does not have significant mortality impacts.

GOBI programs may be applied by mothers in a discriminatory way. Systematic efforts should be made in child survival programs to persuade mothers not to discriminate against their girls. Discrimination against female children even by women is largely due to the fact that females are commonly viewed as being of less economic value to the family.

A second way in which gender discrimination affects children's mortality is that females who reach maturity and bear children may be considerably weakened by the discrimination they suffer. The higher levels of malnutrition and disease they have as a consequence of discrimination results in higher mortality rates for their children. Children's mortality rates are higher in countries with higher levels of gender discrimination.

A third, less obvious way in which gender discrimination affects children's mortality is the fact that child survival programs tend to emphasize interventions that must be undertaken at significant cost in time and effort to the mother. Carol MacCormack observes:

The four primary strategies put forward by UNICEF for child survival—growth monitoring, oral rehydration therapy, breastfeeding and immunization—all have financial implications for women. For example, a sick child with a common rota virus infection, who has diarrhoea, vomiting and is peevish with fever, will require an enormous amount of mothering time if oral rehydration fluid in sufficient quantity is coaxed into its mouth, spoonful by spoonful.[23]

Instead of pursuing the child survival objective by piling new burdens onto already overburdened women, it would be possible to use means that are advantageous to women, such as increasing their education, providing child care services, and increasing their earnings. But liberating women with such programs might threaten men's prerogatives.

The systematic bias of national governments in favor of economic growth and militarization, and against health and welfare programs, itself reflects gender discrimination, emphasizing typically masculine values of power and individuality, and de-emphasizing concerns with nurturance and community associated more with feminine values.[24]

AGEISM

There is repression against weaker countries, and there is repression against weaker people in all kinds of countries. This is apparent not only in racism and sexism but also in ageism. In many countries, the interests of the very young and the very old are not well served. According to the Children's Defense Fund, in the United States "the percentage of children living in poverty has increased from one in seven 20 years ago to one in five today." The fund's president, Marian Wright Edelman, observes, "Our children are growing poorer while our nation is growing richer."[25]

In the United States the elderly do quite well. A study by the Bureau of the Census showed that in 1988 more than 15 million elderly Americans were lifted out of poverty as a result of Social Security payments:

But if the near-elimination of poverty among the elderly is a national achievement, then the creation of a poverty culture among the young is every bit as much a national scandal. Sen. Daniel Patrick Moynihan, a leading authority on income distribution, reminds us that a child under 18 is seven times more likely to live in poverty today than a person over 65.

The reasons for this disparity are not hard to discern: Old people vote, and children don't. Moreover, there is an element of semantic trickery: Social Security is defined as an "entitlement," while aid that would lift children out of poverty is defined as "welfare."[26]

Despite the fact that most of the elderly are not poor, the U. S. government spends 11 times as much on each senior citizen as it does on each child:

Today, the cost of caring for the elderly rivals defense as the largest share of federal spending. . . . The royal treatment is rooted in politics. The 30 million elderly carry so much weight at the polls that they have been able to perpetuate an elaborate mythology concerning their status and the budget.[27]

TRADE GUNS FOR BUTTER?

Many observers say that too much money is spent for defense in both the rich and the poor countries, and that some of that money might instead be used to relieve hunger and promote children's survival and development. One of the most renowned proponents of this view is Ruth Leger Sivard, the various editions of whose *World Military and Social Expenditures* provide the basic data. The idea is prominent in the work of the Children's Defense Fund, especially in its *A Children's Defense Budget.*[28]

Offering no explanation for the skewed priorities, the arguments imply that the misallocations are simple mistakes. The critics almost seem to expect that once they show how many children could be saved if one less battleship were purchased, the political leaders will thank them for pointing out the error and correct it in the next budget cycle.

But the budgets stay sharply skewed in favor of defense year after year. And the same criticism goes on and on. Sivard publishes a new edition of her book every year or two. The fact that military expenditures often exceed social expenditures is already well established, and does not need to be endlessly reconfirmed.

If security means the protection of our most precious assets, child survival should be high on the agenda of all defense departments. It is not. Why not? Whose interests are served by military establishments and warfare?[29]

Many essays suggest that national security should be redefined to take fuller account of human welfare, but the essays don't have much effect. Perhaps they all make the same mistake—believing that the purpose of defense systems is what it is claimed to be by defense establishments. Perhaps the real, operational function of defense establishments is not so much to maintain the security of the people as a whole as it is to maintain the power of the powerful. This proposition seems to explain observed patterns better than the conventional accounts, and it certainly helps to explain why proposals for alternative understandings of security are not welcomed.

Why would leaders in developed or developing countries agree to spend less on maintaining their armed forces if those armed forces keep them in power? The director of the Institute for the Study of Rural Resources in Bangladesh asked:

Whose security is being defended, that of an economic or political class, or that of the entire population of the country? Wages are kept down and cheap labour enclaves maintained, strikes are prevented and supplies of raw material are obtained from the Third World at low prices, all in the name of national security. . . .

Militarization of the police and of paramilitary organizations is going ahead at a tremendous pace in the Third World today. And this militarization is required to support the internal power structure and to maintain the *status quo* within various developing countries.[30]

The linkage between hunger and military expenditures is not simply in the budgetary allocations; it is also in the ways in which armed forces are used to sustain repressive regimes. More hunger and more children's deaths result from the structural violence of repression than from the direct violence of warfare.

Defense budgets protect the interest of the powerful through the ways in which the arms are used, and also by the ways in which the money spent rewards political allies of the powerful. To some extent defense budgets constitute a form of welfare for the rich.

Governments suggest that defense establishments serve all of their people's interests, but defense serves mainly the rich, not the poor. Poor people are still trying to get, while the rich want to protect what they already have. Poor people don't buy burglar alarms or hire guards to stand outside their doors. They don't have a stake in the status quo in the way the rich and powerful do. No wonder poor people are far more concerned with development than with defense. If the poor were the ones who allocated the world's resources, we could be sure that far less would be spent on defense and far more on child survival.

Governments suggest that military threats, whether internal or external, affect virtually all the people's interests, and large "defense" establishments serve all the nation's citizenry more or less equally. But we must consider that the interests of governing elites are different from those of the population as a whole, and especially that they are different from the interests of the poor. Analysis on the basis of class makes the issue clear. Security is a rich people's issue, while child survival is a poor people's issue. The decisions are made by the rich because the rich are also the powerful. As a result there is an enormous bias in the system in favor of defense and against child survival.

It appears that always and everywhere, the highest priority of the powerful is to assure that they will remain in power. This proposition explains their behavior much better than their rhetoric.

Weapons are symptoms of the insecurity of the powerful. While government leaders may be preoccupied with hardware and its role in ensuring their power, for most people in the world security is about having enough to eat, and something to wear, and a place to live, and some way to keep their children alive and well. Conventional governmental security policy diverts resources away from these fundamentals of real human security.

PRIORITIES, NOT POVERTY

Some health and welfare programs can be understood as little more than pacification programs, means for quieting the demands of restless populations. They have the function of protecting the larger social system from being disturbed.[31]

Usually those who decide about such programs choose first on the basis of securing their own interest, which is mainly the maintenance of the current equilibrium situation, and only secondarily on the basis of humanitarian instincts. Where populations are not mobilized to make strong demands regarding health and welfare services, the decision makers' interests are likely to be fulfilled well before the needs of the people. This accounts for the persistently short budgets for health and welfare services.

A simple hypothesis can be proposed. *Worldwide, health systems—like food systems, educational systems, defense systems, or legal systems—serve power more than they serve need.* How else can we understand the fact that in international trade in food, on balance it is the poor who feed the rich? How else can we understand why government subsidies to agriculture exceed government grants to the needy? How else can we understand why most doctors are found where people are rich and healthy rather than where they are poor and sick?

Costa Rica, Sri Lanka, China, and the state of Kerala in India all have shown that if health is given high priority, it can be achieved even with low per capita incomes.[32] Few other governments have sought to emulate their achievements. Public health is not nearly so important to governments as its advocates would like to believe.

Widespread malnutrition and disease are due to poverty, but even more fundamentally to powerlessness. In some few cases people may be poor because there is an absolute shortage of resources where they live. More often the difficulty is that the disposition of resources around the poor is determined by other people who have other priorities. Most people are not lazy or unproductive. Their problems arise from the fact that, having very little bargaining power, much of the benefit of their labors is siphoned off by purchasers, suppliers, landlords, and others with whom they interact, others who have greater bargaining power. The poor, being powerless, are endlessly marginalized.

The child survival problem is, at its core, a matter of conflict—differences of interest among different groups regarding the allocation of resources. There is violence in that conflict, in that some parties regularly use their power to enforce their own claims while excluding others, with no basis for those claims other than power itself. That violence may be indirect and structural, rather than the direct and visible violence we associate with crime and warfare, but it is violence nonetheless.

Most children die from ordinary forms of malnutrition and disease, not from mysterious and unmanageable causes such as AIDS. If enough resources and attention are given to small children, most will thrive. At the societal level, a reasonable rough measure of that attention is the size of the budget devoted to serving children's interests.

Contrary to common assumptions, poor countries, like poor people, do have money. Poor countries are not uniformly poor; most have a middle class and a wealthy elite. They all manage to muster sufficient food and medical services for the wealthy. Soldiers don't go hungry. But most countries spend very little on children. Poverty is their explanation. But even very poor countries seem to find money for monuments and armaments. The limited allocation of national resources to serving the interests of children is due more to the ways in which available funds are allocated than to the absolute shortage of funds.

Thailand, for example, is regarded as a third world country, but it has substantial resources at its disposal. It is a matter of considerable pride that its infant mortality rate dropped from 103 in 1960 to 40 in 1987. But why should it still be as high as 40 in the late 1980s? The answer is suggested in a study from the 1970s, whose results

reveal substantial socioeconomic differentials in infant and child mortality and suggest that the overall level would be considerably reduced if the same health care were provided for the rural and socioeconomically disadvantaged populations as is apparently enjoyed by the numerically small, advantaged groups in urban areas.[33]

The Northeast region of Thailand has the lowest gross regional product per capita in Thailand, and the worst health status. The number of mal-nourished children in Thailand has been going down, but it is still the worst in the Northeast. Why should there be any malnutrition in one of the leading rice-exporting countries in the world?

Instead of getting more health services to respond to the need, the Northeast gets less. "In Bangkok one physician serves an average of 1,230 people, while in the Northeast the corresponding figure is 29,348."[34]

In China, provinces with high infant mortality rates, such as Guizhou, Sichuan, and Yunnan, are among those with the lowest per capita government expenditures on health.[35]

In many countries better care is taken of farm crops than of the current crop of children. Often livestock have higher immunization rates than children.

That the issue is national priorities rather than national poverty is nowhere more clear than in the richest country in the world. The infant mortality rate in the United States is now about 10 per 1,000, which is quite good. But how do we come to terms with the fact that about 20 other developed countries have even lower rates, rates that are declining even faster than in the United States?

Children, especially poor children, are not attended to because they do not have the power to demand attention from public and private agencies. For children who are abused for their labor or for their bodies, the situation is worse than being ignored. The powerful often find ways to use children to serve their own interests, whether those interests are economic or sexual or military. Whether it is a matter of neglect or of direct abuse, it is the interests of others that are served; the interests of children are ignored.

NOTES

1. "Children Under Attack by Governments," *Amnesty Action*, January/February 1988, p. 2.

2. Michael Jupp, "Apartheid: Violence Against Children," *Cultural Survival Quarterly*, 10, no. 4 (1986), 34–37.

3. *International Children's Rights Monitor*, 5, no. 1 (1988), 23.

4. Johan Galtung, *The True Worlds: A Transnational Perspective* (New York: Free Press, 1980), pp. 438–39.

5. Charles Clements, *Witness to War* (New York: Bantam, 1984), pp. 259–60.

6. Ruth Leger Sivard, *World Military and Social Expenditures 1986*, (Washington, D. C.: World Priorities, 1986), pp. 24, 36–41.

7. J. N. Hobcraft, J. W. McDonald, and S. O. Rutstein, "Socio-Economic Factors in Infant and Child Mortality: A Cross-national Comparison," *Population Studies*, 36 (1984), 193–223.

8. Centers for Disease Control, *"Premature Mortality in the United States: Public Health Issues in the Use of Years of Potential Life Lost,"* Morbidity and Morality Weekly Report, supp. 35, no. 2S (December 19, 1986).

9. A.A.B. Herman and C. H. Wyndham, "Changes in Infant Mortality Rates Among Whites, Coloureds and Urban Blacks in the RSA over the Period 1970–1983," *South Africa Medical Journal*, 68 (August 17, 1985), 215–18.

10. *World Development Forum*, 2, no. 14 (August 15, 1984), 1, as quoted from the *Rand Daily Mail*.

11. Francis Wilson and Mamphela Ramphele, "Children in South Africa," in *Children on the Front Line: The Impact of Apartheid, Destabilization and Warfare on Children in Southern and South Africa* (New York: UNICEF, 1987), pp. 39–67.

12. Dana Hughes, Kay Johnson, Sara Rosenbaum, Janet Simons, and Elizabeth Butler, *The Health of America's Children: Maternal and Child Health Data Book* (Washington, D. C.: Children's Defense Fund, 1987).

13. C. Arden Miller, "Infant Mortality in the U.S.," *Scientific American*, 253, no. 1 (July 1985), 31–37.

14. Margaret M. Heckler, *Report of the Secretary's Task Force on Black and Minority Health*, vol. 1, *Executive Summary* (Washington, D. C.: U.S. Department of Health and Human Services, 1985), p. 63.

15. Ibid., p. 5. Also see "Black/White Comparisons of Premature Mortality for Public Health Program Planning—District of Columbia," *Morbidity and Mortality Weekly Report*, 38, no. 3 (January 27, 1989), 1–5.

16. Heckler, *Report of the Secretary's Task Force . . .*, p. 177.

17. Ruth Leger Sivard, *Women: A World Survey* (New York: Pantheon, 1977); *Country Rankings of the Status of Women: Poor, Powerless and Pregnant* (Washington, D. C.: Population Crisis Committee, 1988).

18. Kanti B. Pakrasi, *Female Infanticide in India* (Calcutta: Editions Indian, 1970); Barbara D. Miller, *The Endangered Sex: Neglect of Female Children in Rural North India* (Ithaca, N. Y.: Cornell University Press, 1981).

19. Minja Kim Choe, "Sex Differentials in Infant and Child Mortality in Korea," *Social Biology*, 34, no. 1–2 (1988), 12–23; Stephen W. Mosher, *Broken Earth: The Rural Chinese* (New York: Free Press, 1983); Stephen W, Mosher, *Journey to the Forbidden China* (New York: Free Press, 1985).

20. Carol P. MacCormack, "Health and the Social Power of Women," *Social Science & Medicine*, 26, no. 7 (1988), 677–83.

21. Robert Charbonneau, " 'The Trouble with Girls . . . ': Sexual Discrimination in the Punjab," *IDRC Reports*, 17, no. 4 (October 1988), 6.

22. MacCormack, "Health and the Social Power of Women," p. 679. Boys are breast-fed longer partly because of gender bias, but also partly because boys tend to be larger.

23. Ibid., p. 677.

24. Cecelia Kirkman, "Militarism and Violence Against Women: The War at Home," *The Nonviolent Activist*, 3, no. 7 (October/November 1986), 3–6; Carol Cohn, "Sex and Death in the Rational World of Defense Intellectuals," *Signs: Journal of Women in Culture and Society*, 12, no. 4 (1987), 687–718.

25. David Broder, "Magic of Childhood Is Too Often a Myth," *Sunday Star-Bulletin and Advertiser* (Honolulu), December 25, 1988, B-1.

26. "Making a Dent in Poverty," *Honolulu Advertiser*, December 29, 1988, p. A-10. This editorial originally appeared in the *Baltimore Evening Sun*.

27. *U.S. News & World Report*, October 31, 1988, p. 55.

28. Children's Defense Fund, *A Children's Defense Budget, FY 1988: An Analysis*

of Our Nation's Investment in Children (Washington, D. C.: CDF, 1987). Also see Stephen Coats, *Military Spending and World Hunger: Let Them Eat Missiles*, Bread for the World Background Paper no. 62 (Washington, D. C.: Bread for the World 1982); Marian Wright Edelman, "How the Military Budget Hurts America's Children," *Food Monitor*, no. 41 (Summer 1987), 3–5, 23; Lester Brown, "Redefining National Security," in Lester Brown et al., *State of the World 1986* (Washington, D. C.: World-watch Institute, 1986), pp. 195–211. It is sometimes charged that large defense budgets *cause* widespread hunger and child mortality. While money not spent on arms might conceivably be used to alleviate the symptoms of hunger, that does not mean that large defense budgets in themselves cause hunger. Enormous amounts of money are spent on things such as, say, cars or space exploration, but no one says that those expenditures cause hunger.

29. In the United States, national defense is the exclusive responsibility of the federal government, while other human concerns are addressed primarily at the state and local levels. Thus there is really no reason to expect parity between federal defense expenditures and federal expenditures on health, welfare, and education. The appropriate comparisons are not about federal allocations alone, but about the allocations to these sectors overall, from all sources.

30. Muzammel Huq, "The Structure of Hunger," *UNESCO Courier*, September 1980, p. 16.

31. Fred Block, Richard A. Cloward, Barbara Ehrenreich, and Frances Fox Piven, *The Mean Season: The Attack on the Welfare State* (Washington, D. C.: Institute for Policy Studies, 1987).

32. John C. Caldwell, "Routes to Low Mortality in Poor Countries," *Population and Development Review*, 12, no. 2 (June 1986), 171–220.

33. John Knodel and Apichat Chamratrithirong, *Infant and Child Mortality in Thailand: Levels, Trends, and Differentials as Derived Through Indirect Estimation Techniques* (Honolulu: East-West Population Institute, 1978), p. 1.

34. Sirilaksana Chutikul, *Malnourished Children: An Economic Approach to the Causes and Consequences in Rural Thailand* (Honolulu: East-West Population Institute, 1986), p. 5.

35. United Nations Children's Fund, *Children and Women of China: A UNICEF Situation Analysis* (Beijing: UNICEF, 1989), pp. 22, 93.

Chapter Ten

POPULATION

Many people worry that saving children on a large scale would aggravate the problem of worldwide population growth. They believe that hunger and poverty persist mainly because of excessive population growth rates in third world countries. Apparently premature deaths, while tragic, are nature's way of keeping population growth in check.

THE DEMOGRAPHIC TRANSITION

Won't saving babies lead to runaway population growth? Won't the result be that we simply have millions more living at the edge of starvation? The key is the demographic transition. Poor, less developed countries have high birth rates and high death rates, and low life expectancies. Richer, more highly developed countries have low birth rates and low death rates, with high life expectancies. Developed countries have fewer people, and they live longer and better.

During the industrial revolution in Europe in the eighteenth century, living conditions improved and death rates went down. The immediate effect was that population growth rates increased sharply.

The remarkable thing was that as development progressed, birth rates came down as well, without any systematic population policies or family planning programs. This demographic transition, occurring over a number of decades, was experienced by all modern, developed countries.

During the industrial revolution, economies grew, living conditions improved, mortality rates fell, and fertility rates fell, with the net result that real incomes rose continuously. But it was really not all so simple:

In Europe, and later in Japan, the pattern of declining mortality and fertility was not so orderly—nor is it today in the developing countries. In a few places fertility decline preceded mortality decline; in others, fertility did not start falling soon after mortality did. And economic growth—if narrowly perceived as industrialization, urbanization, and the shift from family to factory production—was neither necessary nor sufficient for the demographic transition.

In England fertility within marriage did not begin to fall until the 1870s, almost 100 years after the start of the Industrial Revolution and at least as long after a sustained decline in mortality had begun.[1]

One reason for the delay in England was that while there was considerable economic growth, "at least after 1820, it was the upper- and middle-income groups that captured most of the income gains."

The demographic transition occurs at different rates in different ways at different times for different reasons. One major demographic change was the decline in death rates in countries undergoing industrialization, resulting in relatively rapid population growth rates in Western countries. A second major change was the decline in birth rates following industrialization, which decreased these countries' growth rates below the world average.

A third major demographic trend began around the time of World War II. A dramatic decline in death rates occurred in the underdeveloped countries. . . . This decline was caused primarily by the rapid export of modern drugs and public health measures from the developed countries to the underdeveloped countries. The consequent "death control" produced the most rapid, widespread change known in the history of human population dynamics.[2]

Thus there has been a transition of the transition. During the industrial revolution rapid population growth was associated with increasing wealth, but after World War I rapid population growth has become associated with poverty.

DEMOGRAPHICS AND DEVELOPMENT

Some writers say the demographic transition occurs "with time," but of course the passage of time in itself does not cause changes. There is broad agreement that the explanation lies in improved health care and in socio-economic development. Within this consensus, however, there is disagreement regarding the relative contributions and the exact nature of the health care and development that are required:

The accepted argument is that imported, low-cost mass medical and public health projects have accelerated the mortality declines in developing countries since the 1930s. . . . during the last four to six decades these developing-country mortality declines have been dissociated with social and economic phenomena because of the nearly absolute reliance on the transfer of health and medical technology.[3]

The economic-growth-driven demographic transition in the wake of the industrial revolution may have been a unique historical event. In many poor countries today, death rates are declining not because of genuine development and improvement of overall living conditions, but because of the importation of specific health care techniques such as immunization programs. Some countries may now be stuck in their underdevelopment. And with the conditions of poverty and the institutional structures that prevail in many poor countries, technical innovations in health care can accomplish just so much.

Economic growth, too, can accomplish just so much. There is now a growing school of thought that says growth does matter, but its effects can be negative. Environmental degradation accompanies uncontrolled commercial exploitation of resources, and pollution often runs out of control. There can be more direct negative connections between economic growth and health. Wealth can become excessive. For example, in a study of the Pacific island of Nauru:

The considerable adult male mortality appears to be related to the rapidly acquired affluence and the ready availability of motorcycles, cars, imported foods, tobacco, and alcohol. The data suggest that modernization of the economy in Pacific Island nations can lead to new and serious public health problems.[4]

Sudden new wealth often leads to social decay, as evidenced by increasing gambling, alcoholism, obesity, and other kinds of excesses.

THE EPIDEMIOLOGICAL TRANSITION

The workings of the demographic transition can be studied through examination of the causes of death in different phases of the development of nations. Epidemiological transition theory recognizes three major stages.

The first is the era of pestilence and famine. Infectious diseases such as typhoid, tuberculosis, cholera, diphtheria, and plague are dominant, as was the case in the Middle Ages and in Europe through most of the eighteenth century. Mortality rates were high and life expectancies were low.

In the second stage, infectious diseases are gradually controlled, mortality rates decline, and life expectancies begin to increase. The consensus is that in this stage the major causal factors are improved hygiene, sanitation, housing, and nutrition. Medical care does not contribute very much.

In the third stage of the epidemiological transition, degenerative diseases such as cancer, heart disease, and stroke become dominant. Mental illness becomes more common. Stress and environmental factors become major causes of illness and death. Mortality declines, and life expectancies become high. The elderly account for a large portion of the population.[5]

A new fourth stage has been suggested. In this "hubristic" stage, deaths are increasingly attributable to individual behaviors and life-styles. Smoking, alcoholism, drug use, and suicide become major factors:

Hubris is an excessive self-confidence, a belief that you cannot suffer, that you are invincible. Morbidity and mortality in the hubristic stage are affected by man-made diseases and increasing modernization as well as individual behaviors and potentially destructive life-styles. Increases in physical inactivity, pernicious dietary practices, and excessive drinking and cigarette smoking can contribute to heart disease, diabetes, chronic nephritis, lung cancer, and cirrhosis of the liver and such social pathologies as accidents, suicides, and homicides.[6]

With this formulation, the pattern observed in Nauru is not anomalous. Rather, it reflects a recognizable pattern that can be linked to findings such as the extraordinarily low life expectancy of native Hawaiians and the high alcoholism and suicide rates among Micronesian youth.

Some may describe this pattern as reflecting a kind of arrogance, but I think this self-destructive behavior is better understood as indicating a deep and pervasive sense of powerlessness. Alcoholism, drug use, and obesity are most prominent among groups with little control over their own life circumstances.

COMMON PROPERTY

The prevailing explanations for changes in population growth rates centered on economic growth and health care services miss the essentially political character of demographic change. Frances Moore Lappé and Rachel Schurman have shown how important it is to understand the role of social power:

the powerlessness of the poor often leaves them little option but large families. Indeed, high birth rates among the poor can best be understood . . . as a defensive response against structures of power that fail to provide, or actively block, sources of security beyond the family.[7]

A well-off fisherman who has plenty of options, such as the possibility of moving to other fishing spots, will simply move on when the catches are not good. But a poor and desperate fisherman who has no good alternatives can do only one thing when the resource dwindles: he puts out more lines. Economically, a poor family's producing more and more children is comparable with a desperate fisherman's putting out more and more lines. The fisherman's and the family's behaviors are shaped by the nature of the alternatives they face.

A rich fisherman puts out more lines because he can. A poor fisherman puts out more lines because he has no good alternatives. Similarly, it appears that, up to a point, richer people have more children because they can, while poorer people have more children because they must. The pattern is suggested by a study in southern Egypt. The number of children was higher for whose who worked larger farms. But for any given farm size, the number of children was lower among those who owned their land than among tenants.[8]

Of course people will continue to have babies even when the opportunities these children will face are meager. When people are desperate and have few alternatives, the "lottery mentality" takes hold, convincing people they have some possibility of doing well even if their concrete experience tells them their chances are slim. Fishermen keep fishing long after the fish are gone.[9] Of course they do give up when there is no longer any doubt that the resource has dried up. In extreme situations such as famines, when it becomes evident that there are no prospects at all, fertility rates decline sharply.

The metaphor here is that described by Garrett Hardin as the "tragedy of the commons."[10] Prior to the enclosure movement in England, when pastures were open, the incentives faced by each individual led him to place more and more cattle to feed on the common pastures. Of course that ultimately led to destruction of the commons' environment. The strategy of adding more and more cattle made sense for individuals because while each benefited from feeding his own cattle, the negative effects were distributed through the community as a whole. As the economists say, there were "negative externalities" that had little immediate and direct impact on the individuals.

When the threat of destruction became apparent, those who were more powerful and could make strong claims on the resources fenced in large sections for their private use. The benefits drawn from the area still were large, but the distribution of those benefits was radically changed.

Large private landholdings, often tied closely to antidemocratic regimes, have quite direct effects on fertility:

So, we must ask what are the consequences for fertility when at least 1 billion rural people in the third world have been deprived of farmland? In many countries, including Brazil, Mexico, the Philippines, India, and most of the Central American countries, landholdings have become increasingly concentrated in the hands of a minority during a period of rapid population growth. . . .

In this context, without adequate land or secure tenure, and with no old-age support from the government or any other source outside the family, many poor people understandably view children as perhaps the only source of power open to them. For those in extreme poverty, children can be critical to one's very survival.[11]

In general, under antidemocratic institutional arrangements, where people have little say about how the resources around them are to be managed, most people have little effective access to resources and few opportunities. Under such conditions of apparent scarcity, birth rates and children's mortality rates will remain high.

In the logic of the situation, a more equitable remedy to the tragedy of the commons would be for the participants to join together, analyze the problem, and realize that they would all be better off if they created some means to manage the commons. If they agreed on fair rules by which they could jointly limit the access of individuals to the commons, in the long term they would all be better off.

Population growth and poverty are related to the nature of the physical environment, but not so directly as is suggested by concepts such as carrying capacity. The connection is always mediated by a social structure that governs the ways in which resources are used and, more to the point, governs the ways in which the benefits of resource use are allocated. The critical issue is not the size of the population itself or the size of the population in relation to overall resource endowments. It is the nature of the social arrangements that mediate access to resources. Arrangements that are open to full and equal participation by all affected parties are likely to lead to more even distribution of the benefits from the resources, and thus to adequacy for all.

The major environmental problem worldwide is the fact that many people lack adequate opportunities to make good use of the physical resources around them. Landlessness, lack of capital, inadequate markets, and other constraints prevent their undertaking the productive work they would gladly do if they had decent opportunities. When people have decent opportunities, they are producers and not just consumers.

In some places this lack of opportunity may be due to an absolute insufficiency of resources. A small island may have so many people living on it that it must either import food or export people. But that sort of situation is rare. In most cases the problem is that the available resources are not well managed for the purpose of supporting the local population. Bad management may be in the form of anarchy—the absence of management—but more frequently it is an inequitable, undemocratic form of management, one that concentrates the benefits from the use of the resources in the hands of a few. Plantation agriculture, for example, is often wrongly praised as being highly efficient. Its real appeal is the fact that plantations concentrate the benefits of the work of many laborers into the hands of a few owners.

POLICY IMPLICATIONS

Many people see population growth alone as the source of poverty, hunger, destruction of the environment, and many other major problems of our times. Their remedies are simple and direct: "policy makers tend to see high fertility as the intractable villain, creating acute population pressures and oppressive socioeconomic conditions in developing societies; consequently, programs to treat these onerous problems have been geared almost exclusively to birth control."[12]

These programs usually are not based on any explicit analysis of the roots of the social problems or of population growth in the concrete local circumstances; they are based on prevailing myths and metaphors.

People from developed countries, through their governments and through many well-funded private agencies, are keen to promote family planning in third world countries. Their work is generally well intended, and based on the belief that it will help the third world. But it is based on very shallow analyses of the problems.

If the main concern is to protect the earth's resources and to control the rate of pollution and depletion, it is important to expose:

the myth that the impact of the population explosion stems primarily from poor people in poor countries who do not know enough to limit their reproduction. Numbers per se are not the measure of overpopulation; instead it is the impact of people on ecosystems and nonrenewable resources. While developing countries severely tax their environments, clearly the populations of rich countries leave a vastly dispro-portionate mark on the planet.

The birth of a baby in the United States imposes more than a hundred times the stress on the world's resources and environment as a birth in, say, Bangladesh. Babies from Bangladesh do not grow up to own automobiles and air conditioners or to eat grain-fed beef. Their life-styles do not require huge quantities of minerals and energy, nor do their activities seriously undermine the life-support capability of the entire planet.[13]

In this light, since each baby born in a rich country will consume far more resources and generate far more polluting wastes than each baby born in a poor country, population control is more urgent in the rich countries than in the poor countries.

Conventional population control programs imply blaming the victim. They press poor countries to make substantial adjustments and assume that people in richer countries need not make any adjustments. Indeed, the pressure on the third world appears to be designed to protect the first world from having to make any changes. Certainly none of the proposed strategies involve any significant costs to the first world. If there is such a terrible imbalance between population and resources, why not promote programs of consumption control in the first world?

Pressing people in the third world to have fewer children can mean asking them to forgo one of the very few assets to which they have access. Even if their children's economic prospects are not promising, they are asked to take fewer lottery tickets, and cut back on the hope that comes with taking the chance that at least one of their children will do well.

Popular magazines headline the population story as one of "Too Many Mouths."[14] They view third world babies simply as gaping mouths needing to be fed. Why don't they acknowledge that babies come with hands, too? They surely would become net producers if given a decent opportunity to do so. This was clearly demonstrated when China's new policy of allowing families to earn private income "unexpectedly created an incentive to have more children to help earn the income."[15]

Lappé and Schurman cite a leading demographer who acknowledges that "98 percent of the resources and effort should be devoted to social and economic development," but he and his organization focus their work narrowly on population control.[16] Demographers recognize that socioeconomic development is important in limiting population growth, but their recommendations usually propose only conventional family planning programs. Socioeconomic development programs should have high priority among the options they advocate.

If farmers in the third world were paid at the same rate as first world farmers for each bushel of grain they produced, they would become much more productive and would be much more secure regarding their own futures. Birth rates and infant mortality rates in their communities would decline rapidly. Why don't those concerned with reducing population growth rates ever recommend a policy of equal pay? The appropriate remedy for poverty, hunger, and children's mortality is to improve people's opportunities. People need to be secure in knowing that they will be able to live out their lives with dignity.

Reducing population growth rates may not reduce the extent of hunger and poverty at all. In Thailand, for example, fertility rates have been cut in half since the 1960s, but many the children still suffer from malnutrition.[17] Thailand suffers not from overpopulation but from a very skewed distribution of control over its abundant resources. India, too, has reduced its fertility levels sharply, but this has not resulted in significant improvements for the poor.

With any given gross national product (GNP), lowering population growth rates automatically means higher levels of GNP per capita. That is arithmetic, not social progress. Lowering population growth rates could result in the poorer section of the population's capturing even smaller shares of the GNP.

The White House Task Force on Combating Terrorism, chaired by then-Vice President George Bush, concluded that "population pressures create a volatile mixture of youthful aspirations that when coupled with economic and political frustrations help form a large pool of potential terrorists."[18] The response is not to analyze and correct the injustices faced by the poor, but simply to reduce their number. Many people view population control in the third world as essential to first world security. Their perspective is narrowly self-interested. It amounts to using population control as a form of cultural genocide against the poor, the ultimate remedy of those who blame the victims.

Family planning programs are useful, but they are not enough. They become dangerous when they are advocated as alternatives to social change. Population growth itself is not the cause of hunger, poverty, and children's mortality. Focusing too narrowly on population issues means blinding oneself to fundamentally important social, economic, and political factors underlying these problems. As argued in Chapter 14, if the problem at its root is one of powerlessness, the remedies must be based on strategies of empowerment.

Improved child survival rates and overall development help to limit the rate of population growth, but under any plausible scenario the transition process will not be fast enough. Population growth is a problem requiring carefully planned programs. While rapid population growth is a problem that needs attention, it should not be assumed that population growth is the source of the child survival problem. An overly narrow focus on population growth as the root of social and environmental problems can distract attention away from the basic political forces at work.

NOTES

1. World Bank, *World Development Report 1984* (New York: Oxford University Press, 1984), p. 60.

2. Paul R. Ehrlich and Anne H. Ehrlich, *Population, Resources, Environment: Issues in Human Ecology* (San Francisco: W. H. Freeman, 1972), pp. 20–22.

3. Brian F. Pendleton and Shu-O. W. Wang, "Socioeconomic and Health Effects on Mortality Declines in Developing Countries," *Social Science & Medicine*, 20, no. 5 (1985), 453–60, see 453.

4. Richard Taylor and Kiki Thoma, "Mortality Patterns in the Modernized Pacific Island Nation of Nauru," *American Journal of Public Health,* 75, no. 2 (1985), 149–55, see 149.

5. Abdel R. Omran, "The Epidemiologic Transition: A Theory of the Epidemiology of Population Change," *Milbank Memorial Fund Quarterly*, 49, no. 4 (October 1971), 1, 509–38.

6. Richard G. Rogers and Robert Hackenberg, "Extending Epidemiologic Transition Theory: A New Stage," *Social Biology*, 34, no. 3–4 (1988), 234–43, see 240.

7. Frances Moore Lappé and Rachel Schurman, *The Missing Piece in the Population Puzzle*, Food First Development Report no. 4 (San Francisco: Institute for Food and Development Policy, 1988), p. 2.

8. World Bank, *World Development Report 1984* (New York: Oxford University Press, 1984), p. 109.

9. Having children is a way of creating options when the opportunities are bleak psychologically as well as economically. See Leon Dash, *When Children Want Children: The Urban Crisis of Teenage Childbearing* (New York: William Morrow, 1989).

10. Garrett Hardin, "The Tragedy of the Commons," *Science*, 163 (December 13, 1968), 1234–48. Current perspectives are described in Panel on Common Property Resource Management, *Proceedings of the Conference on Common Property Resource Management* (Washington, D. C.: National Academy Press, 1986).

11. Lappé and Schurman, *The Missing Piece*, pp. 20–21.

12. Omran, "The Epidemiologic Transition . . . ," p. 511.

13. Paul R. Ehrlich and Anne H. Ehrlich, "Population, Plenty, and Poverty," *National Geographic*, 174, no. 6 (December 1988), 914–45, see 917.

14. Anastasia Toufexis, "Overpopulation: Too Many Mouths," *Time*, January 2, 1989, pp. 48–50.

15. Ehrlich and Ehrlich, "Population, Plenty, and Poverty," p. 922.

16. Lappé and Schurman, *The Missing Piece*, p. 36.

17. Ibid., p. 52.

18. Quoted in Werner Fornos, *Regional Powder Kegs: Charting U.S. Security in an Exploding World* (Washington, D. C.: Population Institute, 1988), p. 4.

Chapter Eleven

ALTERNATIVE SOCIAL SYSTEMS

Different political-economic-cultural-social structures can lead to different levels of children's mortality. The most obvious comparison to be made is that between socialist and capitalist countries.

In 1987, 58 countries categorized as capitalist had an average infant mortality rate of 55.8, while 24 countries categorized as socialist had an average infant mortality rate of 79.3.[1] Thus capitalist (market-oriented) economies have lower children's mortality rates than socialist (or Communist, or centrally planned) economies.

Why does this difference exist? The intervening variable of wealth explains it at least in part. Capitalist countries are richer than socialist countries.

Some would say this demonstrates that capitalism is inherently superior. Others would say that capitalist nations are richer partly because they exploit other nations. Poorer countries tend to turn socialist as a matter of self-defense, to avoid exploitation by other countries. They are not poor because they are socialist; they are socialist because they are poor.

Is there a difference in child mortality rates between capitalist and socialist countries apart from that associated with the differences in their wealth levels? If we compare socialist and capitalist countries of approximately equal wealth levels, which will show higher children's mortality levels? Analysis of data from the World Bank's 1983 *World Development Report* indicates that "Within each level of economic development, the socialist countries had infant mortality and child death rates approximately two to three times lower than the capitalist countries."[2]

The study cited here emphasizes that *the socialist countries have achieved more favorable quality-of-life outcomes at equivalent levels of economic development.* But that should be counterpoised against the equally strong observation that *capitalist countries have achieved more favorable quality-of-life outcomes.* Socialist countries tend to have lower children's mortality rates at any given level of economic development, but children's mortality rates are lower with high levels of economic development, which is associated with capitalist countries.

Thus policymakers concerned with reducing children's mortality rates could pursue either the socialist or the capitalist path—either finding ways to do better with what they have, or increasing what they have. This is the fundamental dilemma of choosing between distributing a modest level of resources more equitably and working to increase the overall pool of resources, even if that means accepting continuing inequalities. Is it better to cut a small pie into parts that are more equal in size or to accept inequalities while making the pie larger?

In Chapter 1 we saw that the United States has a low and decreasing infant mortality rate, but infant mortality is decreasing even faster in a number of other countries. In contrast with all other industrialized countries, which have had steadily declining infant mortality rates, the Soviet Union has seen some increases in the rate in the 1970s and 1980s. We must acknowledge that even before the reforms of the late 1980s, the socialism-capitalism distinction was a weak basis for analyzing the status or the behavior of nations:

It might be thought that the major factor explaining why some governments are committed to the relief of malnutrition while others are not has to do with ideology. Perhaps the most common hypothesis is that explicit policy attention to public health, nutrition, mass education, and the like (and significant resource allocations for these purposes) is a product of communism.... There are several problems with such a comprehensive explanation, however. It is strong on intent but, in many instances, weak on capability. Also, one does not have to be a socialist to desire an end to injustice and human misery. Furthermore, many political leaders who claim to be socialist, usually with some diluting ethnic or regional prefix, have little tangible to show for their rhetoric. The actualities are more complex than the imagery.[3]

One cannot assume any correspondence between the structure of health services and the ideological posture of the nation as a whole. Countries have not been so sharply divided in practice as their ideological rhetoric might suggest. Most capitalist countries have a public sector that is centrally planned, and socialist countries have had some market-oriented activity, and this mixing is increasing with the reforms of the 1980s and 1990s. This sort of crossing can be found in the health sector in particular. Although India is nominally a free-market economy, its government does not charge for any public social service, and for many people public health services are the only services they get. In the United States, the health care system is mixed, and increasingly shifting away from private fee-for-service operations to broad-coverage health insurance programs and health maintenance organizations, which in effect establish pockets of socialized medicine. In many socialist and Communist countries there is a widespread invisible market in health services, with physicians who are underpaid by the government supplementing their incomes with direct fees for service. In China the system of barefoot doctors has collapsed and private medical practice has returned.

Those countries in western Europe and Scandinavia which describe themselves as mixed economies, with substantial elements of both central planning and free markets, are all high-income countries with low infant mortality rates. Ideological purity may itself be a serious impediment to national development.

As acknowledged in Chapter 7, income levels alone do not determine levels of children's mortality. A major reason for this is that countries which have better-than-expected infant mortality rates tend to devote an unusually large proportion of their resources to health, particularly to the health of the poor. Why do they do that?

A study of this question in relation to Costa Rica, Sri Lanka, and the state of Kerala in India found that:

Unusually low mortality will be achieved if the following conditions hold: (1) sufficient female autonomy; (2) considerable inputs into both health services and education, both essentially of the modern or Western model, and with female schooling levels equaling or being close to male levels; (3) health services accessible to all no matter how remote, poor, or socially inferior to those providing them; (4) ensuring that the health services work efficiently, usually because of popular pressure (and, in addition, disciplining rural health workers by having a physician in charge); (5) providing either a nutritional floor or distributing food in some kind of egalitarian fashion; (6) achieving universal immunization; and (7) concentrating on the period before and after birth, usually by providing antenatal and postnatal health services and having deliveries performed by persons fully trained for this purpose.[4]

The question of how to make such things happen cannot be addressed at the household level alone; societal decision makers must become fully engaged. Grass-roots political activism appears to be an important factor. The following chapters suggest some directions for that activism.

CAPITALISM WITH A HUMAN FACE

As argued in Chapter 7, in addition to its being highly efficient at creating wealth, capitalism has a very negative characteristic: it tends to pump wealth from the poor toward the rich.

One response to the criticism has been to seek alternatives to capitalism, usually described as some form of socialism. Socialism is commonly characterized in terms of state ownership of the means of production. Others characterize socialism as emphasizing the social objective of minimizing poverty rather than maximizing individual and national income.

Another approach is to try to fix capitalism. Is there any way to assure that poverty is systematically alleviated while capitalism's effectiveness in producing wealth is retained? The practice of nations makes it clear that the most practical solutions lie somewhere toward the middle.

Perhaps the best approach would be to have countries organize their economies on the basis of capitalism but at the same time, through a system of progressive taxation, transfer a significant share of the wealth toward the bottom.

Hong Kong and the Nordic countries—Denmark, Finland, Iceland, Norway, and Sweden—are capitalist with firm social welfare floors. The Nordic countries describe themselves a social democracies:

Economically, the Nordic countries are highly industrialized and affluent. They have a high standard of living, reasonably well distributed among different socio-economic groups. A high proportion of women are gainfully employed, and the unemployment rate is low.

They are pronounced welfare states where the drawbacks of a market economy system are balanced by a large public sector and a guaranteed minimum income for individuals irrespective of the market value of their labour or assets ("mixed economy"), and modified by a dense social security net, designed especially to look after people in illness, incapacity and old age.

Moreover, there is

the solidaristic and universalist nature of social legislation. The welfare state is meant to integrate and include the entire population, rather than target its resources towards particular problem groups. Social policy is actively employed in the pursuit of a more egalitarian society.[5]

They all have very extensive maternal and child health services. Many of the infectious diseases that used to affect children have been practically eradicated, and children's mortality rates are extraordinarily low in the Nordic countries.

These countries are decidedly capitalist, but still provide generous income supports for those at the bottom. They extend this philosophy worldwide by contributing an extraordinarily large share of their national incomes to development programs in third world countries.

In the sort of mixed model proposed here, private enterprise would be free to pursue its own private interests, primarily profit. Where wholly free enterprises would not serve the public interest, as democratically determined, the major function of government would be to alter the structure of incentives faced by private enterprise to assure that the public interest was in fact served. Government would influence the incentives faced by private individuals and corporations partly by regulation and partly by its powers of taxation. To the extent feasible, public services would be privatized, carried out by private agencies under contract with the government.[6]

The public interest in some issues (the merits of tobacco and alcohol, for example) might be subject to debate, and would be resolved by democratic procedures. However, in the social design suggested here, the public interest in the alleviation of poverty would be firmly established in the basic constitution of the government. It would be mandated that every poor family was unconditionally entitled to receive, on application, an income grant assuring that it had at least an established minimum quality of life. The minimum acceptable income could be set at, say, twice the amount of money required to purchase a minimally adequate diet and minimally adequate housing. A guaranteed minimum income would be more efficient for providing welfare support than an administratively top-heavy patchwork welfare system like that now in place in the United States. A guaranteed minimum income would establish a form of modified capitalism that takes advantage of its positive features and acknowledges, and compensates for, its negative features.[7]

An income floor of this sort would radically change the shape of developed capitalist economies. With fewer poor people at the bottom end of the labor pool anxious to work, menial jobs would be compensated more generously, and wages in general would go up. The number of employment opportunities would diminish because, in the face of higher labor costs, owners would increasingly substitute capital for labor. There would be fewer people working, but also less unemployment in the sense that fewer people would be seeking jobs.

The negative aspects of capitalism could be further contained by promoting protectionism with respect to the production of food staples, especially in poor countries. Foreign investment would be controlled to assure that the benefits retained were sufficiently large and well distributed. Such measures could help to assure that the productive resources of nations would be responsive to the demands of their own people rather than to those of outsiders.

This approach may be politically infeasible, but it is at least conceivable. If we explore why it is infeasible, we discover that it is because those who are now in power do not see it as being in their interests to make the transition. If programs of this sort were to be implemented, they could be undermined by the powerful.

The interests of poor people would be served if society were to be restructured to provide an income floor—but they don't have the power to bring about that restructuring. Seeing that a plausible alternative can be designed, we now can make a clearer analysis of why things remain as they are. The current system fails to serve the interests of most people in the world. It is not that there are no alternatives. The problem is that the people who have an interest in change do not have the power to bring it about, while those who have the power do not have the interest.

In capitalist economies, democracy, defined in terms of everyone's having an equal say in the determination of outcomes, is an illusion. Our most important votes are those we make with our dollars in the marketplace. Political power is strongly correlated with wealth. If political systems worldwide were in fact shaped on the basis of equality, we can be sure that the billions of poor people in the world would vote for systems different from what they now have.

Capitalism is a very impressive system for producing wealth. It could be even better if those who defend it would allow themselves to see that it has important defects. It has a dark side. Shining a light on the problems does not necessarily amount to an attack on capitalism. Acknowledging the defects creates the opportunity for correcting and compensating for problems, and thus defending the essence of capitalism. Humanizing capitalism through devices such as the guaranteed minimum income could in the long run prove to be an important means of defending the institution.

Let us reframe this conceptual exercise and put the proposal in more moderate terms. In the United States the fundamental objective of government is economic growth. In managing the economy for maximum growth, various economic instruments are used to control such things as inflation levels and unemployment levels. It is not government policy to seek zero unemployment. Rather, the unemployment level is tuned to a level that appears to be optimum for the working of the overall economy.

Thus the unemployed are to some extent forced to pay a price for the effective functioning of an economy that benefits many others. Viewed in these terms, the unemployed should be entitled to some compensation for being forced to live in poverty so that others can live comfortably. In this perspective, unemployment compensation or welfare in general would not be grudgingly given, and the unemployed would not be accused of indolence. Instead it would be recognized that the condition of the poor results in part from the nature and structure of the social system.

The system of unemployment compensation in the United States is now designed for limited-term assistance to workers in transition. Those who are more permanently unemployed do not receive unemployment compensation. They may receive some form of welfare, such as food stamps, but these grants are viewed as charity, not as entitlements.

If the condition of the poor results from the nature of the capitalist system, it may be judged that the system should be abandoned altogether. An alternative view is that the system should be retained because, although it unfortunately results in some negative effects on some people, overall it does a large number of people a great deal of good, and thus should be retained.

If it is retained, honesty and decency require some compensation for those who are hurt by the system. Unfortunately, since the poor are also weak, there is no compelling political demand that the rich compensate the poor. Strategies of empowering the poor, helping them to articulate and press their demands, can help to correct this imbalance of power.

CONVERGENCE

On July 2, 1988, on the occasion of the Communist Party Congress at which he formally presented his proposals for reform, Soviet leader Mikhail

Gorbachev spoke of attempting to create "socialism with a human face." He echoed the words of Czechoslovak leader Alexander Dubcek two decades earlier. The radical changes in eastern Europe suggest intriguing possibilities for socialism's meeting with capitalism on some middle ground.

Capitalist systems take on aspects of socialism, particularly through their welfare programs and other public works. Socialist systems throughout the world have been modifying their ideologically extreme positions and are taking on important aspects of capitalist systems. Incremental, evolutionary reforms can result in radical structural change. The Soviet Union is going through what Gorbachev has described as a revolution without guns. As both capitalist and socialist systems move away from the ideological extremes and toward the center, we begin to feel that either kind of system could work. It does not make much difference if one's country is socialist tinged with capitalism or capitalist with streaks of socialism. Most countries could manage reasonably well no matter which flag they flew.

Perhaps the most important lesson the West has to learn from the European reform movements is that even those with the greatest pride in their national systems must not be blinded by the virtues of their systems. They are well advised to look for, acknowledge, and correct the dark side. Critical analysis should not reflexively be treated as an attack on the system, but as a realistic approach to adapting and saving it. Capitalist institutions such as the World Bank have begun to acknowledge that economic growth alone is not enough, and other kinds of measures are needed to assure human welfare. It would be magnificent if the World Bank and the leading capitalist countries dropped their defensiveness, and began plainly to acknowledge that there are disadvantages to capitalism. The capitalists, too, might then undertake bold reforms with the vision and courage that have been shown in eastern Europe.

DESIGN PROCESS, NOT OUTCOME

People can be poor and miserable in capitalist or in socialist systems. The critical issue is not the form of the social structure as described in terms of abstract ideological blueprints, but more fundamentally the fact that some people are powerless and cannot make much of a claim on the society's resources.

The intellectual exercise of designing new social orders may not have much real impact. Perhaps we need to give more attention to social processes within the social order—whatever that order may be—to assure that those at the bottom have an increased voice in shaping that social order. In the following chapters we set aside the search for the optimum social design and instead look into the possibilities for alleviating powerlessness directly at the local level.

NOTES

1. In Raymond D. Gastil, "The Comparative Survey of Freedom 1987," *Freedom at Issue*, no. 94 (January–February 1987), 19–34, the countries of the world are

categorized as capitalist, capitalist statist, mixed capitalist, mixed socialist, or socialist. For this calculation only the first and the last of these categories were examined. Infant mortality rates for these countries for 1987 were those listed in James P. Grant, *The State of the World's Children 1989* (New York: Oxford University Press, 1989), pp. 94–95, 108.

2. Shirley Cereseto and Howard Waitzkin, "Economic Development, Political-Economic System, and the Physical Quality of Life," *American Journal of Public Health*, 76, no. 6 (June 1986), 661–65.

3. John Osgood Field and F. James Levinson, "Nutrition and Development: Dynamics of Political Commitment," *Food Policy*, 1, no. 1 (November 1975), 53–61.

4. John C. Caldwell, "Routes to Low Mortality in Poor Countries," *Population and Development Review*, 12, no. 2 (June 1986), 171–220.

5. Lennart Kohler and Gunborg Jakobsson, *Children's Health and Well-Being in the Nordic Countries* (London: Mac Keith Press, 1987), pp.1–2.

6. Calvin A. Kent, ed., *Entrepreneurship and the Privatizing of Government* (Westport, Conn.: Greenwood/Quorum, 1987); Raymond Vernon, ed., *The Promise of Privatization: A Challenge for American Foreign Policy* (Cambridge, Mass.: Harvard University Press, 1988).

7. Robert Theobald, ed., *The Guaranteed Income: Next Step in Socioeconomic Evolution?* (New York: Doubleday/Anchor, 1967).

Chapter Twelve

SHOULD CHILDREN BE TREATED AS HUMAN CAPITAL?

Why should any society allocate limited national resources to alleviating malnutrition or to child survival and development? One major line of argument is that it is a sound investment for national economic growth. Ruth Leger Sivard, for example, argues:

Health protection, like education, is both the instrument and product of economic development. The preservation of health makes a difference in the quality of life people can have. As a social investment, it also has a positive multiplier effect on the world economy, reducing absenteeism and increasing the productive years of men and women. Inadequate health protection wastes human resources and adds to the burden on the whole of society, through the cost of treating illness and the loss of working capacity.[1]

James Grant, the director of UNICEF, has suggested that some of the newly industrialized countries achieved their extraordinarily rapid growth partly because they invested substantial resources into looking after the poor, particularly their children. According to UNICEF's Richard Jolly:

Much evidence already exists of the economic returns to investment in human resources. To fail to protect young children at the critical stages of their growth and development is to wreak lasting damage on a whole generation, the results of which may well have effects on economic development and welfare for decades ahead.[2]

In the U.S. context Marian Wright Edelman, the president of the Children's Defense Fund, argues: "Our future prosperity now depends in large part on our ability to enhance the prospects and productivity of a new generation of

This article first appeared under the title "Children as Human Capital?" in the *Food and Nutrition Bulletin,* vol. 10, no. 4, 1988.

employees that is disproportionately poor, minority, undereducated, and un-
trained."[3]

If it could be demonstrated that public investment in nutrition and child
survival accelerates national economic growth, that would attract the support
of growth-oriented leaders for such programs.

AN EMPIRICALLY QUESTIONABLE ARGUMENT

Whether for poor countries or for rich countries, these arguments are ultimately unconvincing. Governments that already face high levels of unemployment and spend little on treating illness would have difficulty in taking
them seriously. The argument that investments to improve nutritional standards or child survival rates are justifiable as stimulants to economic growth

is based on the faulty presumption that increasing a person's capacity or potential will
necessarily result in growth in both his and his country's productivity. The translation
of improved individual capacities into greater individual and national productivity is
by no means automatic. It is largely dependent on the ability of the society to make
effective use of such capacities.[4]

The human capital rhetoric may have tactical value. When the president
of the Children's Defense Fund argues that our prosperity depends on looking
after our children, we know that she is using this argument more as a way
of winning support for children than as a way of promoting national prosperity.
If someone made a convincing argument that we would achieve greater
prosperity by investing our money in machines rather than in children, surely
she would forgo prosperity and continue to defend children. She knows that
there is intrinsic value in children; they need to be saved for their own sakes,
and not merely as an investment toward achieving something else. Her rationale for advancing the human capital argument would be that emphasizing
material benefits can help to persuade policymakers to support child survival
programs.

The point has merit. The risk is that it could be factually wrong. It may not
be generally true that healthier, better-nourished people are more productive.
One study concedes that "the most persuasive criticisms of the contention
that nutrition interventions lead to economic growth is the weakness of the
empirical evidence to date."[5] An empirical study of the question found that
"no positive and consistent effect on the productivity in market production
activities of the supplemented workers can be demonstrated."[6] Investments
in the promotion of children's growth "have been estimated to improve Gross
National Product (GNP) by 0.6–2.2 per cent due to the improved productivity,"[7] a very unattractive rate of return.

There is abundant evidence that over broad ranges, improved nutrition and larger body size increase work *capacity*.[8] But that should not be confused with increased *productivity*. Productivity requires motivation as well as capacity. There are many circumstances in which work performance improves with improved nutrition, but globally the dominant pattern seems to be just the opposite. People who are well fed or overfed often are reluctant to do any hard physical work. With better diets people are likely to have more capacity but be less motivated to work. It is obvious that many people who are poor and badly nourished work very hard. Even more important, they work cheap.

One can look at poor workers in fields and factories anywhere in the world and see that people can be badly nourished and still be highly productive. These people may sleep a great deal, fall ill very often, and live shortened lives, but they definitely are workers. They are efficient "machines," generating a great deal of output with little input. Indeed, there is evidence that, within broad limits, people who eat less are more efficient, in that they produce more work output for each unit of energy input.[9]

One study showed that cane cutters in Jamaica cut only 3.1 tons per day, while West Indian cutters in Florida cut 8.6 tons per day.[10] If Jamaican cutters received food supplements and increased their productivity, who would benefit? The distribution of benefits between the cutters and the enterprises would depend in part on whether the cutters were paid on an hourly or a piecework basis, but given their low wages, it is likely that either way most of the benefits would go to the enterprises. One major effect of increasing productivity could be that fewer cutters would be employed, a significant disadvantage from the societal perspective. Total production might not be increased, in which case wages to individuals might go up while the overall wage bill went down.

If I were a profit-maximizing plantation owner, it probably wouldn't be worthwhile for me to spend money on improving the workers' diets in the hope of improving their productivity. If I could draw from a large pool of unemployed people ready to work at cheap rates, I wouldn't be much concerned about the marginal productivity of any particular individuals I hired.[11] In fact, "in labour-surplus economies, planners often conceptualise increased productivity not as an asset but as an additional problem which exacerbates unemployment problems."[12]

Even if there is no large labor surplus, the increment in productivity may not be sufficient to justify the plantation owner's paying the increased food cost. It may be cheaper to hire additional labor. The plantation owner's concern is overall production, not productivity per laborer.

In the Jamaican study weight-for-height was chosen as the primary measure of nutritional status, with individuals who were low in weight compared with the standard for their height categorized as malnourished. Instead of providing nutrition supplements to bring up the workers' weight levels, an alternative strategy for the enterprise owners would be to hire only those whose weight was at or close to the standard for their height. A hiring policy that was discriminatory according to nutrition status would be a serious disadvantage to those who were undernourished.

As pointed out in Chapter 6, it is conceivable that "increased nutrient intakes partly go to increase productivity rather than to improve indicators of health." Thus increased productivity sometimes might be at the expense of health, rather than a result of health. Whether or not this is true at the level of the individual, it certainly can be true at the level of the family unit. In Brazil, "Energy costs of sisal laborers are so great in relation to wages that systematic deprivation of adequate calories to the non-productive dependents of sisal workers is necessary."[13]

If the central concern is productivity or wage earning in the short term, it is economically sensible to distribute food supplies in favor of wage earners, even if that means depriving women, children, and the elderly. The result is the commonplace skewed distribution of food within the household, discussed in Chapter 6.

Nutrition supplementation might improve nutrition status and thus improve the productivity of individuals in some cases. Even so, it might not be economically efficient to provide supplements. The benefits might be small. Another problem is that the benefits of nutrition supplementation might not go to the enterprise. One empirical study of the effects of nutrition supplementation found that "After work the unsupplemented group spent most of their time resting or sleeping while the supplemented subjects remained active doing other tasks of their own or participating in recreational activities."[14] The researchers pointed out that dietary supplementation would permit the worker to participate in his own development and that of his family—and, therefore, his community—by providing extra energy for leisure time work and recreation. They could have looked at it another way. An employer who is narrowly concerned with profit maximization might feel it would be wasteful to pay for nutrition supplementation when much of the benefit goes to the workers and the community, after work hours, and not to the enterprise.

In asking whether the benefits of nutrition supplementation or child survival programs would be worth the cost, it is important to ask not only what are the benefits and what are the costs but also who benefits and who bears the costs.

Distinctions should be made not only between employer and employee but also between public interests and private interests. In the United States it is frequently claimed that the Special Supplemental Food Program for Women, Infants, and Children, known as WIC, saves three dollars for each dollar invested in the program. Benefits were estimated in terms of the hospital costs that were averted by reducing the number of low-birth-weight babies with WIC food supplements.[15] Since the intention is to justify public expenditures on the WIC program, the argument is clear if those hospital costs would have been borne by the public.

But what if hospital costs for the low-birth-weight babies would be paid privately? Under a narrow economic analysis, it is not obvious that public expenses which yield only private benefits are warranted, no matter how positive the economic cost/benefit ratio appears to be.

Also, according to this argument for WIC, if low-birth-weight children were not hospitalized, there would be no cost to be averted and thus no possible benefit from WIC supplementation. Where public health care expenditures are low, so that little in the way of expenditures can be averted, the argument does not work.

The linkage between nutritional status and work output depends on the social context in which the work is embedded. After the Sandinista victory over Somoza in Nicaragua, people were well fed for the first time in decades, so they were "much less anxious to earn wages by harvesting cash crops."[16] They reduced their effort on the plantations, but at the same time many tended their own garden plots.

If a worker's incremental efforts benefit others more than himself, the better-nourished worker may be inclined to work less. However, if workers enjoy the full benefits of their own labor, as they do in their own vegetable gardens, better-nourished individuals are likely to work harder. This is why labor productivity on smallholdings is regularly much higher than it is on large holdings.

Studies of productivity in relation to nutrition status have been about wage labor such as cane cutting, coal mining, and ditch digging. The benefits have been measured primarily in terms of production output (such as amounts of cane cut) and not in terms of laborers' earnings where they are paid on a piecework basis. Apparently the objective has been to increase productivity per laborer without increasing wages, thus benefiting employers, rather than to find ways to increase incomes to laborers.

The effect of improved nutrition on productivity in forms of self-employment such as home vegetable gardening or on women's ability to work more effectively around the home have not been assessed. It seems the linkage between nutrition and productivity has been of interest only where someone other than the worker stands to benefit from increased productivity. The focus has been on the benefits to the employer, not to the laborer.

If the payoff from nutritional supplementation for laborers is uncertain, it is even more uncertain for nutrition and other health programs for children. As suggested in relation to WIC, there can be a benefit in terms of health care costs that are averted. It is clear that "children are the poor man's capital,"[17] and that under many circumstances it is economically wise for the poor to invest in their children.[18] But the question posed here is whether investment in children is a feasible strategy for national leaders whose primary concern is the acceleration of national economic growth. Economic benefits from investments in child survival and development must be discounted because of the long delays and considerable uncertainties. While investment in children may sometimes be associated with national economic growth, that is not the same as showing that an investment in children will regularly lead to *greater* returns in economic growth than investment elsewhere in the economy. Governments have many other opportunities for investing the limited resources they have available, and they regularly view investment in options such as industry as yielding a larger, more certain, and quicker economic benefit.

A MORALLY QUESTIONABLE ARGUMENT

There is real danger in the human capital approach to justifying national nutrition and child survival programs. Where would this line of analysis lead in regard to nutrition programs for the elderly? What would be done to save handicapped children? In this narrowly economic mode of dealing with welfare needs, there is little room for human dignity. The function of human life is economic production. The alleviation of malnutrition and the saving of children are seen as means toward, and not the objective of, development. The argument has got it backward, assuming that the function of people is to serve the economy, rather than the reverse.

The stories of abuse in the employment of young children are so numerous and so grotesque that child labor is prohibited in many developed countries. Yet the human capital approach implies that young children should be sent out to earn money as quickly as possible. If we would not want to take the human capital approach to the treatment of children in developed countries, why should it be acceptable in less developed countries?

There is something distasteful about designing programs to make people into more efficient cane cutters and ditch diggers. Health and development programs should be designed to liberate them from that sort of labor.

If UNICEF relied on the argument that investing in children leads to economic growth, and then found that investing in something else leads to a bit more economic growth, what rationale would remain for saving children?

The argument that nutrition or child survival programs can be justified in terms of improved productivity seems to be a bit of liberal wishful thinking, an instrumentalist rationalization for something that should be viewed as intrinsically desirable. If it does not stand the empirical test in most of the third world, those who rely on the human capital approach would be left with no argument with which to defend their programs.

Narrowly economic cost/benefit analysis fails to recognize that minimizing suffering is itself a social value, one for which there is a real public interest. Alan Berg agrees that "Improved nutrition as a means of reducing deaths, lessening the severity of infections, and preventing various forms of retardation, blindness, anemia, and other malnutrition-related problems is, in itself, sufficient justification for investment in better nutrition."[19] But he is overoptimistic when he adds that "adequate nutrition is now widely accepted as part of the purpose of development and need not be justified as a means to development." A survey of national development plans and budgets would show that only small shares of national resources are devoted to the alleviation of malnutrition.

The human capital argument is morally defective because it shows no consideration for the hungry or for the children themselves. The best reason for ending hunger or saving children is that it is not right for people to remain hungry or for young children to die unnecessarily. No other reason should be necessary. Any other reason is inadequate.

The appropriate reason for ending hunger and saving children is not calculation of instrumental values but compassion or, more precisely, love. The linkage is not so much physical and mechanical; it is essentially spiritual. We should be concerned with the fact that some are harmed by existing social systems for its own sake. People should be able to live in dignity. No other reason should be necessary.

Arguments such as "a dollar spent on the Childhood Immunization Program saves $10 in later medical expenses," or "for every low-birthweight birth averted . . . the United States health-care system saves between $14,000 and $30,000," or "for every $1 invested in quality preschool education, we can expect a substantial return of $6 in the reduced costs of remedial education, welfare, crime, and other social services"[20] fail to acknowledge that "we" are composed of different groups with different interests and different capacities to pursue those interests. Speaking of an undifferentiated "we" means being blind to politics. How do you convince the powerful that money spent on poor children is a sound investment that will yield significant benefits not only to the recipients but also to the powerful themselves? The data are not persuasive.

Moral considerations *ought* to be sufficient to motivate nutrition and child survival work, but we know that usually they are not. The instrumentalist argument that investments in improving the welfare of children can lead to national economic growth is shaky on both empirical and moral grounds. But where a truthful and convincing instrumentalist argument can be made, it certainly should be used along with the moral argument.

NOTES

1. Ruth Leger Sivard, *World Military and Social Expenditures 1986* (Washington, D.C.: World Priorities, 1986), p. 22.

2. James P. Grant, *The State of the World's Children 1987* (New York: Oxford University Press, 1987), p. 16.

3. Children's Defense Fund, *A Children's Defense Budget FY 1988: An Analysis of our Nation's Investment in Children* (Washington, D.C.: CDF, 1987), p. xii.

4. Peter Hakim and Giorgio Solimano, "Nutrition and National Development: Establishing the Connection," *Food Policy*, 1, no. 3 (May 1976), 249–59.

5. David E. Sahn and Nevin S. Scrimshaw, "Nutrition Interventions and the

Process of Economic Development," *Food and Nutrition Bulletin,* 5, no. 1 (February 1983), 2–15.

6. Maarten D. C. Immink, Rafael Flores, Fernando E. Viteri, Benjamin Torun, and Erick Diaz, "Economics and Human Capital Formation," *Food and Nutrition Bulletin,* 6, no. 1 (March 1984), 12–17.

7. Judith S. McGuire and James E. Austin, *Beyond Survival: Children's Growth for National Development,* spec. iss. of *Assignment Children,* 1987, p. viii.

8. G. B. Spurr, "Nutritional Status and Physical Work Capacity," *Yearbook of Physical Anthropology,* 26 (1983), 1–35.

9. R. Martorell, A. Lechtig, C. Yarborough, H. Delgado, and R. E. Klein, "Small Stature in Developing Nations: Its Causes and Implications," in S. Margen and R. A. Ogar, eds., *Progress in Human Nutrition,* vol. 2 (Westport, Conn.: Avi, 1978); P. V. Sukhatme, "Poverty and Malnutrition," in P. V. Sukhatme, ed., *Newer Concepts in Nutrition and Their Implications for Policy* (Pune, India: Maharashtra Association for the Cultivation of Science, 1982), pp. 11–63.

10. Michael C. Latham, "Nutritional Problems in the Labor Force and Their Relation to Economic Development," in N. S. Scrimshaw and M. Behar, eds., *Nutrition and Agricultural Development: Significance and Potential for the Tropics* (New York: Plenum, 1976).

11. Alan Berg, *The Nutrition Factor: Its Role in National Development* (Washington, D.C.: Brookings Institution, 1973), pp. 20–23.

12. J. O. Field and F. J. Levinson, "Nutrition and Development: Dynamics of Political Commitment," *Food Policy,* 1, no. 1 (1975), 53–61.

13. Daniel R. Gross and Barbara A. Underwood, "Technological Change and Caloric Costs: Sisal Agriculture in Northeastern Brazil," *American Anthropologist,* 73 (1971), 725–40.

14. Spurr, "Nutritional Status and Physical Work Capacity," pp. 1–35.

15. Eileen T. Kennedy, "Evaluation of the Effects of the WIC Supplementary Food Program on Prenatal Patients in Massachusetts" (Ph.D. diss., School of Public Health, Harvard University, 1979).

16. Susan George, *Ill Fares the Land: Essays on Food, Hunger, and Power* (Washington, D.C.: Institute for Policy Studies, 1984), p. 15; Joseph Collins, *Nicaragua: What Difference Could a Revolution Make?,* 2nd ed. (San Francisco: Institute for Food and Development Policy, 1985), pp. 75–76.

17. Theodore W. Schultz, ed., *Economics of the Family: Marriage, Children, and Human Capital* (Chicago: National Bureau of Economic Research, 1974).

18. Marc Nerlove, Assaf Razin, and Efraim Sadka, *Household and Economy: Welfare Economics of Endogenous Fertility* (New York: Academic Press, 1987).

19. Alan Berg, *Malnourished People: A Policy View* (Washington, D.C.: World Bank, 1981).

20. Sheila M. Smythe, "Safeguarding Our Children's Health," Rae Grad, "The Fight Against Infant Mortality," and Owen B. Butler, "Investing in the Very Young," all in *The GAO Journal,* no. 3 (Fall 1988).

Chapter Thirteen

MOTIVATING THE POWERFUL

The abundant literature on empowerment very properly focuses on the task of empowering the weak. It is important also to ask how the powerful might be induced to become more fully engaged with issues of hunger and children's mortality.

Low-cost techniques for addressing child survival problems are now readily available; the key is finding the will to use them:

Perhaps the most important aspect of efforts to improve childhood survival is what might be called "political and social will": the resolve to commit resources at national and international levels and to develop broad-based health and child-spacing programs that will both initiate and sustain the dramatic increases in infant and child survival now within reach.[1]

UNICEF says:

there is no automatic process which translates technical advances into widespread improvements in the lives of the majority. Only conscious policies, backed by political commitment and the mobilization of the necessary social and economic resources, can translate this new potential into a new reality for the world's children.

The real challenge is therefore no longer scientific or technical. It is political and social. It is the challenge of generating the political will and the social organization to put today's knowledge to use on the necessary scale and at an affordable cost.[2]

Whose political will are we talking about? What are its sources? Which comes first, the will of the people or the will of their governments? There is a problem of will both at the level of central decision makers and among the people in general.

Many studies show in great technical detail how specific nutrition or public health interventions could promote child survival, but do not address the question of whether national leadership is motivated to pursue such programs. Naiveté has been common: "Rather uncritically, nutrition planners tended to believe the advocacy arguments for governments to invest in nutrition and then to assume that, once suitably enlightened, political leaders and economic planners would accept these arguments with equal ardor."[3]

Means for enhancing child survival such as immunization programs can be proposed, but if national leaders are not much concerned with child survival, the programs will not be carried out. Governments have many other priorities. In the budgets of individual nations and of the world as a whole, very limited resources are devoted to saving children. Given the variety of interests that national policymakers pursue and the politically powerful constituencies to which they are responsive, it cannot be assumed that governments are highly motivated to promote child survival.

Governments are much more responsive to the stronger than to the weaker segments of their populations, and child survival is not nearly as large a problem for the strong as it is for the weak. Governments are unresponsive to the problem of children's mortality partly because their more influential constituents don't treat it as a problem of great importance.

Moreover, many political leaders are embarrassed by such problems and tend to minimize or deny them. In 1974 Emperor Haile Selassie denied that famine was sweeping Ethiopia. The same impulse is reflected in President Reagan's November 1988 veto of legislation calling for a study of the nutritional status of the U.S. population. Leaders who deny problems cannot act on them.

MOBILIZATION FROM BELOW

Child survival usually does not loom as a major concern even in the minds of the politically weak. This is partly because of their so-called fatalism, their resignation to oppressive conditions because of the sense that nothing can be done about them. When the poor are mobilized, it tends to be around issues other than health. They tend to focus on issues such as poverty and land ownership. Revolutionary movements are likely where large segments of the population are landless,[4] but there is no such high likelihood of revolution because of high infant mortality rates.

One reason is that access to land is very visible and tangible, and it is often clearly associated with policies and interests of local and national elites. Mortality rates, however, are abstract and invisible. When a particular child dies, that may be seen as due to fate or chance, not as due to the policies of the elite. After all, it is hard to see how the elite would have any direct interest in having children die. How can they be blamed? What good would it do to protest?

Sufficiently motivated people can do many things to persuade their leaders to be attentive to child survival and other basic social issues.

Leaders who are not sufficiently responsive can be replaced with those who are. This change may occur on a revolutionary basis, as it has in China, Cuba, and Nicaragua, or it may occur on a more evolutionary basis, with social structures and political leaders being changed through a slower, more systematic process. This has been the pattern in Kerala and in Sri Lanka. In Sri Lanka in 1928 the Donoughmore Commission recommended that the British government give the vote to women specifically as a way of making children's health a major item in election agendas. In Kerala the people's own clear desire for strong social programs, together with a highly participatory and responsive political system, have shaped the progressive leadership that has emerged. It is in the leadership's political interest to pursue social programs.[5]

MOBILIZATION FROM ABOVE

The following chapters address the question of empowering people to take initiatives regarding their children's survival. The question here is, If the initiative does not originate with the local people, how might outsiders stimulate governments to undertake action for children's survival?

UNICEF's programs of social mobilization for children's survival are based on the premise that governments can be induced to launch children's survival campaigns. How can leaders be helped to internalize the child survival problem as their own? How can child survival be shifted to higher priority? Apart from pressure from below of the sort just discussed, there appear to be two ways to get leaders to support action for child survival.

First, there is the moral or altruistic motivation, according to which child survival is viewed as an end in itself. As argued in Chapter 12, moral considerations *ought* to be sufficient to motivate child survival work, but we know that usually they are not. Moral concern can be stimulated in various ways so that the presumably latent intrinsic interest in the welfare of children can be brought to the surface.

Second, it is possible to work with the prevailing values of political leaders as they are, not as we might wish them to be. Where the leadership's moral concern for child survival appears weak and the leaders cannot be replaced, other inducements may be used. Incentives can be devised so that child survival work is seen as instrumental to the achievement of other objectives that are valued by the leaders, such as rapid economic growth, generous foreign aid grants, and enthusiastic popular political support.

Of course there are great differences among leaders regarding what will move them. Some are interested in popular endorsement, while others are concerned only with the support of a narrow oligarchy. Some are preoccupied with the idea of economic growth, and others are not. Some care what the leaders of other nations think of them; others do not. In undertaking a campaign to win national support for child survival programs, one needs to analyze and address the specific interests and views of the key decision makers.

In Chapter 12 we examined the proposition that investments in improving the welfare of children can lead to economic growth, and thus might provide good instrumental reasons for promoting child survival. We concluded that the argument is shaky on both empirical and moral grounds. But where a convincing argument can be made, it should be used.

In Chapter 11 it was suggested that humanizing capitalism could be a way of defending the institution of capitalism. This defense-of-the-system argument might appeal to leaders in capitalist societies.

Leaders may ignore high mortality rates among children partly because they don't see that anything practical can be done about them. They may become responsive if they can be shown concrete means and strategies for enhancing child survival, such as immunization and the promotion of breast-feeding. Just as the weak can be empowered by providing them with new tools, so the powerful can be empowered by showing them that there are practical ways to save children. In general, one ought to operate on the assumption that there is latent concern in these leaders, and that concern can be called forth when it becomes clear that something reasonable can be done. Their interest in children might not be intense enough to induce them to act when they believed the cost would be high, but they might be sufficiently motivated to act when they are shown that the cost would be low.

Some leaders may be so unconcerned with the plight of children that even low-cost child survival programs are uninteresting to them. In such cases it may be necessary to resort to other inducements, such as properly packaged foreign aid programs.

It is important to go beyond consideration of money costs and show that supporting programs for children's survival can yield considerable political benefits. Leaders are likely to be responsive if they can be given credit for the achievement of improved child survival rates. Rather than going in with programs under the UNICEF banner, UNICEF's child survival work is based on providing technical and material support for national programs. There are active public relations efforts, such as television programs and posters, showing the nation's leaders administering the first inoculation in the immunization program. To the extent possible, it is the government that gets the glory. Thus the child survival problem that previously had appeared as a burden and an embarrassment for national leaders can be transformed into an opportunity for them.

In a variation on the idea of publicly praising leaders for their activity in child survival, they can be complimented for doing things that they are close to doing but actually aren't quite doing. A tennis instructor will praise her student for doing a backhand in a way that the instructor describes in detail, and soon afterward the student matches behavior to description. Similarly, Pope John Paul II, addressing the World Conference on Fisheries Management and Development in 1984, said, "It is natural that the main concern of the present Conference is the rapidly increasing need for food resources to satisfy the hunger of millions of people suffering malnutrition in the poorest countries of the world." Malnutrition actually was not the main concern, but the pope's words may have helped bring about the unanimous approval of a new program on the use of fisheries resources in alleviating malnutrition. It can be helpful to praise individuals and nations for behaving in ways they are only approaching.

Pressure from the outside can be helpful. Other nations, international development agencies, and private organizations can threaten economic sanctions or exposure, or, more positively, they can offer material incentives, advice, praise, and positive publicity both within and outside the country. Good examples are provided by *War on Want's* successful campaign against infant formula, by the way threats of quarantine and economic sanctions helped reticent nations decide to commit themselves to smallpox eradication, by USAID's direct support for a broad variety of child survival programs, and by UNICEF's active support of national child survival and development programs.

Criticizing leaders publicly for not attending to the issue of child survival is likely to be a diplomatic and strategic error. Harsh criticism closes off dialogue. Treating national leaders as if they were allies in the child survival effort and showing them the possibilities for action is much more likely to turn them into allies in fact.

EMPOWERING OURSELVES

Many private voluntary organizations in developed countries focus on programs such as devising means of subsistence agriculture for people in less developed countries. But often they don't have good access to their purported "clients," the needy in less developed countries. They may not have a realistic grasp of the problems of the poor and the many constraints they face. Well-meaning people in developed countries want to help empower the weak, but they are frustrated because they are not in a good position to do so.

Perhaps these organizations could work more effectively if they took their clients to be the many people around them in the developed countries who are eager to find meaningful ways to respond to the worldwide hunger problem. There are many people who would be very responsive if they could find ways to use their specific talents, resources, and interests. They have much to contribute, and should not be asked only for their money.

An organization could focus on particular kinds of "clients," such as business people or fraternal organizations. Years ago someone got the attention of the Rotary Club, and now the club makes a major contribution to the control of polio worldwide. As suggested in the following section, universities could become more fully engaged with the child survival issue. Businesses, especially multinational corporations, have much to offer. They have not only material resources but also a great deal of organizational and analytic talent. Multinational businesses with operations in less developed countries have good access to the needy. They can help to channel not only their own resources but also the resources of others in developed countries to the places they are needed. They can help to organize child survival programs where they have overseas operations.

It is not only the poor, and it is not only national leaders, who need to be empowered. We, too, can be strengthened in our commitment and our skills for addressing child survival and other major issues that concern us.

MOBILIZING UNIVERSITIES

At an international conference on Health Leadership Development and Child Survival held at Honolulu in February 1987, UNICEF's Executive Director, James Grant, said, "We look to universities for development of effective solutions and, secondly, to inform and lead society toward enacting those solutions." Universities constitute an underutilized resource in the child survival effort. Universities in both developed and developing countries already play a role in promoting child survival and development, but they could do more.

Universities can contribute not by providing services directly to families but by providing support services for other agencies. In general, universities can contribute to child survival work in areas of *teaching, research,* and *service.*

Teaching about child survival issues could be strengthened in several ways. Established courses on maternal and child health could add reviews of the child survival movement to show how specific activity fits into the larger picture. More attention could be given to the favored instruments of the child survival movement, with close study of both their advantages and shortcomings. Universities could develop courses on the social dimensions of the child survival movement. Many questions need to be explored regarding social marketing, the quality of national and international policies, and the structural character of social systems.

Programs in child survival could be prepared that would draw on the health sciences, social sciences, anthropology, and other fields. Universities could offer mixtures of degree programs, certificate programs, short courses, extension work, and in-service training, depending on local needs. They could also help to prepare materials for social mobilization programs for the wider community.

Each national child survival and development program could be tied to one designated university. That university could serve as its major training and research arm and provide support service as needed, in coordination with the appropriate government ministries.

University-based research already supports the work of international agencies, national governments, and private voluntary organizations in their work on child survival, but that research could be broadened and intensified. At the Honolulu conference James Grant suggested research on social mobilization practices and strategies, the analysis of specific situations within countries, monitoring and evaluation of programs, and advancing medical technology. Universities should retain their independence and be prepared to adopt a critical stance, but to some extent their research agendas should be shaped according to the needs of local child survival and development agencies. This would require close working relationships between the universities and the agencies, and the allocation of some resources to support research.

Enhancement of the role of universities could be undertaken in conjunction with UNICEF's project, Institutional Strengthening and National Capacity Building for Child Survival and Development, launched in 1987. The program, focused initially on five countries in Africa, is designed to help build national capacities for child survival work at three levels:

(1) *at the university or institution of higher learning level,* [to] establish and develop centers or "chairs" for interdisciplinary training and research for child survival and development, through interdepartmental and interfaculty cooperation;
(2) *at the community or district level,* [to] enable representatives from service rendering ministries, such as those of health, agriculture, community development, along with staff and students from the university, and concerned non-governmental organizations, ... to develop operational methods and models suitable for replication, and to get practical training in activities related to child survival and development, in the context of urban and rural development through community participation;
(3) *at the regional and international level,* to link the above-mentioned individual country projects with each other, as well as with other appropriate knowledge sources in different parts of the world (knowledge-networking), in the spirit of north–south and south–south cooperation, through exchange of information, "twinning" of universities, and collaboration on specific activities at community-based demonstration areas.[6]

There are many constraints to improved child survival work, such as the lack of programs at specific sites, insufficient national budgetary resources, insufficient field experience and training. "The removal of these constraints requires priority emphasis in universities and professional schools, through their pre-service training and in-service refresher training."

Telecommunications can play an important role. In Uganda:

Teleconference facilities have been established between the Departments of Paediatrics of Makerere University, the College of Health Sciences of the University of Nairobi and the Memorial University of Newfoundland, Canada. This facility provides a teaching mechanism through which lectures and discussions delivered to students in the University of Nairobi are transmitted by satellite and can be listened to simultaneously by students at the University of Makerere and in Newfoundland and vice versa.

Working in collaboration with other agencies, universities could do a great deal to accelerate the worldwide movement for child survival and development.

NOTES

1. Kristina Galway, Brent Wolff, and Richard Sturgis, *Child Survival: Risks and the Road to Health* (Columbia, Md.: Institute for Resource Development/Westinghouse/ USAID, 1987), p. 7.

2. James P. Grant, *The State of the World's Children 1987* (New York: Oxford University Press, 1987), pp. 11–12.

3. John Osgood Field, "Multisectoral Nutrition Planning: A Post-Mortem," *Food Policy,* 12, no. 1 (February 1987), 15–28.

4. Roy L. Prosterman and Jeffrey M. Riedinger, *Land Reform and Democratic Development* (Baltimore: Johns Hopkins University Press, 1987).

5. John C. Caldwell, "Routes to Low Mortality in Poor Countries," *Population and Development Review,* 12, no. 2 (June 1986), 189.

6. *Project: Institutional Strengthening and National Capacity Building for Child Survival and Development,* E/ICEF/1987/P/L.32 (New York: UNICEF, March 1987). Also see Eira Gorre-Dale, "Institutions to Link up for CSDR," *UNICEF Intercom,* no. 48 (April 1988), 13, 23.

Chapter Fourteen

CHILDREN'S SURVIVAL AND COMMUNITY DEVELOPMENT

Chapter 12 asked whether promoting the welfare of children contributes to economic growth. No systematic linkage was found, and the conclusion was that children should be saved for reasons other than the promotion of national-development-understood-as-economic-growth. We could instead change our understanding of national development.

As shown in Chapter 7, economic growth certainly helps to improve child survival rates. But in Africa and elsewhere, the prospects for rapid economic growth are not promising. Moreover, it was also shown that there is not a one-to-one association between child survival and economic growth. Economic growth in itself is not enough to address the problem of child survival. Indeed, it may not be enough to serve as a basis for overall national development. The persistence of the child survival problem in rich countries in itself indicates there is a need for fundamental rethinking of the meaning of national development.

Child survival can be viewed as a clinical problem, an effort to keep children alive to their fifth birthdays by all available technical means. Heroic measures can be undertaken in special rehabilitation centers to save children on the verge of death. In this way, child survival rates could be improved without changing anything in the society that sends children to the rehabilitation centers.

This approach can be quite futile. According to the chief of the social work office of Bloom's Children's Hospital in San Salvador:

It is a vicious cycle. We don't cure children, we simply revive them so that they can go out and starve once more. Sometimes they get sick from simple infections that become serious for children without any resistance, children who don't get enough to eat. Three-quarters of Salvadorean children under five suffer from some grade of malnutrition.

There is food in the country but the poor cannot afford it. We have a twelve-year-old girl now, dying of malnutrition. Her father has a cow and chickens and grows beans and corn. He owes all of it to the man who owns his land, so his daughter and the rest of the family are starving. If he didn't hand over the milk, the eggs, and his crops, someone would come and take them, so what could the man do? It is a social and economic problem, not a medical one. We just bandage the wound; we don't cure anybody here.[1]

Another approach, advocated here, is to view the challenge of child survival as a way of concretizing the overall problem of development. Improved children survival rates are not very meaningful if children reach their fifth birthdays but are doomed to lives of misery. Child survival is an integral part of development and should not be separated from it. Successful child survival programs improve the survival rate not as an isolated phenomenon but as part of overall improvement in the quality of life.

Moreover, improvements in child survival rates should not be something done to a passive community; the community itself should be fully engaged in initiating and sustaining the required changes.

MEANINGS OF DEVELOPMENT

What, then, is development?

Historically, the idea of development that flourished after World War II focused on the idea of economic growth for the rapid industrialization of nations. Industrialization was understood less as a means for reducing the numbers of poor people than as a means for strengthening the nation as a whole, particularly in its relationships with other nations. More attention was given to the question of how people could be used to help achieve industrialization than to the question of how industrialization might help people. Gross national product was used to measure levels of industrialization, not levels of human welfare. Development often meant the accelerated exploitation of natural resources.

The idea that economic growth ought to be pursued chiefly for the purpose of reducing poverty did not arise until later. The idea was pressed in the 1960s, and it was not until the 1970s that the objective of reducing poverty came to prevail, at least in the rhetoric of development.

By the mid-1970s the mainstream argument—that economic growth is the chief instrument, if not the very embodiment, of development—was discredited in the eyes of many observers. The challenge was based not on the failure of economic growth to achieve the original objective of industrialization, but on its failure to achieve the newly invoked objective of alleviating poverty.

In the 1970s the response was that poverty should be alleviated through programs of growth with equity. Attention to the issue of distribution of wealth took many forms: meeting basic needs, redirecting investments, strengthening agriculture, increasing local self-reliance, establishing the New International Economic Order. The means varied, but the meaning of development remained centered on production and distribution of goods, measured in economic terms.

Some analysts, dissatisfied with the emphasis on economic measures, formulated indicators of progress more closely linked with the well-being of individuals. The most prominent of these was the Physical Quality of Life Index (PQLI), a composite measure based on life expectancy, infant mortality, and literacy.[2] As Jon Rohde suggested:

Donor participation in framing development goals has too long been based on the sole principle of economic growth. Rather than justifying social programmes in health, nutrition, or family planning in terms of their economic rates of return, we should be justifying financial investments in terms of their impact on health, nutrition, and population, for these are the *true* measures of development. All too long we have been measuring the success of our development efforts on the basis of changes in GNP. We should insist on the use of real measures of quality of life, such as the PQLI—physical quality of life index—an index calculated on infant mortality, life expectancy, and literacy.[3]

The emphasis remained on the material aspects of development, on life-support systems rather than on life itself. However, a few analysts began to focus on nonmaterial aspects of development, emphasizing ideas of liberation, finding ways to overcome domination and oppression. Too often people are limited to being the objects of other people's action. They do not see themselves as having the power or even the right to act on and affect the world around them. The task of development therefore is, in Paulo Freire's terms, to raise the consciousness of people so that they come to respect themselves and their capacity and their right to act on the world.[4]

Development, then, should be understood as involving a transformation of consciousness, with individuals who had seen themselves as victims beginning to see themselves as somehow in control of their own worlds. In this perspective, development can be defined as *the increasing capacity of define, analyze, and act on one's own problems.*

Thus development in its essence should be understood not so much in terms of economic or physical life-support systems as in terms of life itself. Good nutrition, good housing, low child mortality, and long life expectancies are supporting bases for a good quality of life, and they may be correlated with it, but they do not constitute it. The central aspect of life that is of concern in development work is individuals' and communities' condition of consciousness, how they view themselves and the world, and how they understand their relationship to that world. The core issue is whether one views oneself as a helpless victim, subject to forces beyond one's control, and even beyond understanding and beyond criticism, or whether, in contrast, one views oneself as a force in the world—among others—with some effectiveness, and deserving of respect from both self and others.

Human development refers to increasing consciousness of oneself and of one's own capacities in relation to the surrounding world. Development does not refer only to increase, whether of size or of any other measure. Rather, one develops when one can do something one could not do before. The essence of development is transcending limits, moving from cannot to can. To develop means to gain power, not over others but over oneself, and with others.

The purpose of development should be understood not simply in terms of achieving economic growth or even in terms of alleviating poverty. More fundamentally, we should see that true development means the alleviation of powerlessness.

It is not meaningful in any human sense to define development simply in terms of national economic growth. What family, when asked about its concerns, would say that its greatest aspiration is to help increase the gross national product? Economic growth is useful, but as a means toward, not as the end objective of, development.

If development is the increasing capacity of a community to define, analyze, and act on its own problems, then development projects should be centered on the community's objectives. If child survival is recognized as a major problem by the community, then that should be a major objective of its development programs and projects.

The objectives should be determined by the community, and the planning and action should be the community's as well. Planning and acting to improve child survival rates can be a means toward achieving the development of individuals and communities, but only if that is done by them and with them, and not for them. Work on child survival can be an effective means through which people define, analyze, and act on their own problems.

POWERLESSNESS

Malnutrition, disease, and high levels of children's mortality are largely due to poverty. The correlation is imperfect, however. Other factors, such as medicine and public health measures, are important; and beyond these there are other, less readily measured, less tangible factors. Underdevelopment is due in part to poverty, but even more fundamentally to powerlessness. This can be seen in the pattern of "women and children last" at the dinner table. Poverty may put the family unit at risk of malnutrition, but it does not explain the discrepancies in nutritional status within the family. Women and children are relatively powerless within the household. Small children in particular cannot fend for themselves, and are thoroughly at the mercy of others.

As pointed out in Chapter 7, China, Costa Rica, Sri Lanka, and the state of Kerala in India have had much lower children's mortality rates than would be expected on the basis of their average gross national products. Some individuals and some nations do well even though they are poor, and others manage to be miserable even with a great deal of money. Several of the oil-exporting countries of the Middle East have extraordinarily high levels of infant mortality despite their high levels of gross national product per capita.

The importance of powerlessness becomes evident when we look at middle- and upper-class malnutrition, which, by definition, does not arise from poverty. Analysts of eating disorders such as anorexia and bulimia recognize that the problems are not only psychological but also social. Speaking of women's sometimes excessive preoccupation with thinness, one doctor said, "Caught between demands of those around them and their own needs, they feel powerless."[5]

Obesity also illustrates the pattern. In developed countries we are all subjected to persistent pressure to eat, but some of us succumb more readily than others. According to data from the U.S. National Center for Health Statistics:

1. Women are more likely to be obese than men, regardless of age...;

2. Obesity is more prevalent in lower socioeconomic groups, particularly among females;

3. Rural populations tend to be more overweight than urban populations; and

4. Blacks, as a group, are more likely to be obese than whites.[6]

This suggests a strong association with powerlessness, and not simply with poverty.

Common forms of middle-class malnutrition reflect lack of control over one's circumstances and high vulnerability to pressures from outside. Thus their roots are similar to those which lead to the undernutrition of the poor. Both undernutrition and overnutrition result from powerlessness. Almost always, people who are malnourished suffer the effects of decisions made by others who have more power and different priorities. Malnutrition should not be treated as if it were a problem of individuals in isolation; it is a problem of the social order. A strong case can be made that not only malnutrition but also ill health in general is largely due to powerlessness.[7]

Poverty is not misery. Money is important, but there is something more than that determining the quality of people's lives. The key issue is, Do people have control over their own lives?

If poverty, disease, malnutrition, and excessive children's mortality have their roots in powerlessness, their remedies must lie in programs of empowerment.

EMPOWERMENT

The conventional response of citizens and public health workers to poverty and recession is one of submission:

Government health services in the developing world typically reach no more than 15 to 20 percent of the population. In the United States, federal support for health and nutrition programs is being reduced, with responsibility turned over to the States in the form of block grants. In both the U.S. and the developing world, therefore, increased emphasis must be given to the promotion of preventive self-care and to experimentation with low-cost outreach techniques that provide basic knowledge about health, nutrition, and child care to poor households.[8]

This is not the only possible response. Even while adapting to an economic squeeze by developing low-cost health care techniques, it is possible to resist and fight that squeeze. Instead of asking only how citizens and public health workers can adapt, one can also ask how they might become vigorous advocates of their cause, cultivating a power base of their own and making their demands felt.

Whether as individuals or in groups, people may persist in looking inward, without asking what might be done about a world that leaves them and their children chronically undernourished and ill. People will tend to blame themselves, saying they are too ignorant or too poor or too lazy to manage their own circumstances. There may be something to that, but we also know that to some extent this is learned, based on a persistent pattern of blaming the victim. People internalize their problems most strongly when they see little prospect of affecting the outside forces. The poor peasant may be slow to accuse the landowners. But continuing, focused reflection on these issues with the support of peers can help to enlarge analyses and thus enlarge the possibilities for action.

We should be wary of governments' promotion of local self-reliance when that may be little more than an excuse for evading the proper obligations of government. We should be wary of governmental claims of lack of money in the face of demands for child survival programs when even the poorest countries can find the means for purchasing monuments and armaments. People need to be empowered not only so that they can take care of themselves with their own meager resources, but also so that they can make effective claims to fair shares of the resources of their communities and nations.

There have been many calls for increasing participation by local people in child survival and other kinds of primary health care. For example, David Werner of the Hesperian Foundation points out that oral rehydration therapy is sometimes used ineffectively:

Often not enough attention is paid to the experience, traditions and ideas of the people. . . . If diarrhea control were approached more as a participatory process, I feel that a great deal could be learned from the people. In my brief visit I saw evidence that in some areas of the country people have traditional methods of diarrhea control that are reducing mortality from diarrhea more effectively than the WHO strategies.[9]

Werner describes a meeting with a women's organization in a poor barrio in which investigators from outside asked questions about traditional means of diarrhea control. The meeting "shows the potential for greater involvement of community people in what might be called 'participatory research.' Studies can be conducted *with* the people and not just *of* them." This represents a great advance over conventional forms of intervention that treat people as objects.

But it is possible to go further in designing strategies of empowerment. Real empowerment means something more than local people's following instructions or answering questions. It means their full participation in the analysis of the roots of their own problems, and it means their choosing action on the basis of their own analyses rather than someone else's. Empowerment is development: *To be empowered is to increase your capacity to define, analyze, and act on your own problems.*

Immunization, oral rehydration, and other child survival programs often treat local people as faceless, nameless units, there to be manipulated. They are targets. They are subjected to particular medicines, trained to undertake particular behaviors, and taught particular bits of information. Counted up, the number trained or informed constitutes an aggregate success rate. These programs tend to be weakening, not empowering.

One representative of an international agency working on a preschool education program in Latin America, came to view the conventional approaches to designing and carrying out programs "as a form of genocide."

When we planned and programmed *for* the poor instead of *with* the poor, setting objectives in our language instead of in theirs, we deprived them of the one thing they need in order to survive in a world of conflict—power, *kratos*. We described our work as "efficient" (a word notoriously associated with keeping costs down by keeping wages low), but we were not at all efficient in helping poor people attain what they need the most—the capacity to solve their own problems. We even talked about "educational services delivery systems" and "target populations", as if the aim were to keep the poor as passive as possible while we took care of them. It makes me sick to think about it. The United Nations, in its own way . . . through an elaborate ideology composed of welfare economics and management science, kept the poor powerless as effectively as the *huasos* [landowners] who have no ideology at all, but simply a common fear that the socialists will take their land again, and a common interest in cheap, submissive labor. We said we did not believe in class struggle, but we participated in the struggle—on the side of the dominant class.[10]

Empowerment is not merely behavioral in the sense that people begin to do "good" behaviors (such as breast-feeding) instead of "bad" behaviors (such as bottle-feeding). It is cognitive and value laden in that if you do something differently, you do it not because you were told to, but because you arrived at an understanding of the situation in which you decided for yourself that changing your behavior would be in your own best interests. The object of empowerment is not simply to convey new bits of information or to induce specific behaviors. It is to support people in making their own analyses so that they themselves can decide what is good for them.

While *mobilization* commonly refers to recruiting people to act on someone else's agenda, *empowerment* means increasing people's capacities to pursue their own agendas.

Child survival programs, like other public health programs, have been essentially adaptive, focusing on ways to cope with one's situation as if it were immutable. For example, conventional nutrition education advises the consumer on how to make the best possible choices with respect to the available options, which are described in terms of the locally available foods. With empowering nutrition education, however, there would be an examination of social and political possibilities, what they are and what they could be. There would be active analysis of concrete circumstances. In that analysis local people would not accept that the range of choices—whether of foods or of social conditions—is fixed and given. Instead, they would raise questions: Why are the options so narrow? How did it come to be that way? How and why did we come to be in this situation? Political analysis, in its essence, means asking: Who gets what benefits, and how is that decided? The analysis provides the basis for finding ways to expand and improve the range of possibilities.

In Yap, local merchants promoted soft drinks rather than coconut milk because selling soft drinks was more profitable. While working as a nutritionist there, Nancy Rody reversed the pattern of increasing consumption of Coca-Cola by launching a campaign based on the slogan "Things go better with coconuts." Empowerment arose through a form of education that went beyond comparison of the nutrients in the two products. It helped people to understand why Coca-Cola was promoted so vigorously and whose interests it served. Thus people gained increasing control over their own diets, serving their individual and their community interests.[11]

Empowerment work means helping people come to an understanding of their own problematic situations in their own terms. Child survival programs should be based on an understanding of the problem that goes beyond immediate biomedical factors. People whose children are dying are unable to manage their life situations adequately. Thus child survival programs should serve to empower, helping people to understand their situations, and helping them to make their own analyses of what to do about it. The principal tool of this work would be inquiry through mutually empowering dialogue. An approach is suggested in Chapter 15.

Children's survival rates can be viewed not simply as an indicator of health

status but also as an alternative measure of the overall level of development
of societies. Certainly it is a biased measure, one that is particularly sensitive
to the conditions of the poor. The more conventional measure of development, gross national product per capita, is also a biased indicator, one that
favors the interests of the rich.

It can be very useful to contrast the policies of nations that center on
accelerating economic growth with the policies of nations whose highest priority is the advancement of the people's health and welfare, as gauged by
indicators such as the children's survival rate. There is no doubt that material
wealth is needed if children's mortality rates are to be kept down. The key
question is whether wealth is to be seen as a means to other good things, or
to become elevated so much that it becomes an end in itself.

NOTES

1. Alison Acker, *Children of the Volcano* (Westport, Conn.: Lawrence Hill, 1986),
p. 81.

2. Morris David Morris, *Measuring the Condition of the World's Poor: The Physical
Quality of Life Index* (Elmsford, N.Y.: Pergamon/Overseas Development Council,
1979).

3. Jon E. Rohde, "Why the Other Half Dies: The Science and Politics of Child
Mortality in the Third World," *Assignment Children,* 61/62, no. 1 (1983), 64.

4. Paulo Freire, *Pedagogy of the Oppressed* (New York: Seabury Press, 1970).

5. "Disorders in Eating Start at an Early Age," *Sunday Star-Bulletin and Advertiser*
(Honolulu), May 3, 1987), p. J–7.

6. S. R. Weiss, "Obesity: Pathogenesis, Consequences, and Approaches to Treatment," in Felix E. F. Larocca, ed., *The Psychiatric Clinics of North America,* vol. 7,
no. 2 (Philadelphia: W. B. Saunders, 1984), pp. 307–19. However, one study on a
U.S. community showed that fatness was inversely related to income levels in females
but directly related to income levels in males. See Stanley M. Garn, Stephen M.
Bailey, Patricia E. Cole, and Ian T. T. Higgins, "Level of Education, Level of Income,
and Level of Fatness in Adults," *American Journal of Clinical Nutrition,* 30 (May
1977), 721–25.

7. Leonard A. Sagan, *The Health of Nations: True Causes of Sickness and Well-
Being* (New York: Basic Books, 1987).

8. Ford Foundation, *Child Survival/Fair Start* (New York: Ford Foundation, 1983),
p. 3.

9. David Werner, "ORT: The Need for Education and Participation," *Cultural
Survival Quarterly,* 10, no. 4 (1986), 24–27.

10. Howard Richards, *The Evaluation of Cultural Action: An Evaluative Study of
the Parents and Children's Program (PPH)* (London: Macmillan, 1985), pp. 209–10.

11. Nancy Rody, "Things Go Better with Coconuts: Program Strategies in Micro-
nesia," *Journal of Nutrition Education,* 10, no. 1 (January–March 1978), 19–22.

Chapter Fifteen

LOCALIZED MULTIPARTY PLANNING

Centralized planning in less developed countries has not been very effective.[1] Localized planning has advantages, but it also has disadvantages. Local people may lack material resources, technical expertise, and experience with comparable problems in other contexts. Local initiatives are likely to be viewed as threatening by the central government. These problems can be avoided if the central government and the local people can find ways to plan together, through a process described here as *localized multiparty planning*.

LOCALIZED ...

Child survival and, more broadly, development are commonly taken to be the responsibilities of national governments. It is usually the ministries of health in the national capitals that prepare child survival programs. Why should local people be the beneficiaries, but not the producers, of plans for their children's survival?

Participation is often interpreted in terms of involvement in decision making, implementation, supplying material and labor resources, or evaluation of programs. Here the focus is on participation in the *planning* of child survival programs. This means involvement in the formulation of the questions, the conceptual framework, the perspective, and the options, and not just having the opportunity to choose among options formulated by others. Full engagement in the planning of programs for child survival can be a potent means of empowerment for local people.

Full engagement of local people in the planning process can lead to better outcomes for four major reasons. First, planning is always contextual, and local people know the local context better than any outsiders. Second, broad participation in planning expedites the implementation of plans; people generally do not like to carry out schemes devised by others, regardless of their merits. Third, when people plan for themselves, they may make mistakes and they may harm themselves, but they normally will not be unjust to themselves. Fourth, the fundamental reason for localizing planning is that it expands people's capacity for defining, analyzing, and acting on their own problems. Participation in the planning process in itself constitutes a means of development.

It may seem foolish to advocate localized planning where communities do not have the power to carry out their plans. The formulation of ends without control over the necessary means can only lead to frustration. But power is not a tangible commodity available only in specific fixed amounts that must be divided up. People become weak by acting weak. People can gain power by acting as if they had power. A village may not have direct control over its nation's budget allocations, for example, but if it begins to formulate clear analyses and demands in the light of its interests, it will in the process manifest power, and it will gain influence over those allocations. It will awaken power that has lain dormant. This empowerment is the basis of development in its deepest sense.

Real political power arises not out of the barrel of a gun but out of social organization, out of groups of people working together in a coherent and systematic way to achieve common goals. Effective social organization derives from the sharing of goals. Members of a community, or of specific organizations within the community, who internalize the common purpose of child survival and share responsibility for its achievement can be extremely powerful.

It is not only goals but also the appreciation of obstacles and other considerations that must be shared. These common understandings arise out of continuing dialogue among the concerned individuals and organizations. That dialogue helps to build increasingly effective task orientation, and it also helps to build the sense of community.

Sophisticated, technical planning methods used by central governments often become instruments of mystification, expanding the influence of the outside planner or "expert" while shrinking the influence of the purported beneficiaries. Technique can thus serve as an instrument of dominance. The objective of child survival plans should not be simply to save children, but also to help local people work out ways in which they can act to save their own children. Thus there should be strong local involvement in the planning effort.

Dialogue should play a very central role in planning. Some argue that dialogue should take place among the professionals involved in the issues. Others speak of the importance of dialogue between the professionals and the local people, the dialogue of consultation. But dialogue should also take place among local people themselves. Local people need to work together to analyze their situations and discover their capacity to act on those situations.

Intervention agents tend to dominate planning activities because they are viewed as professionals. Power relationships in the dialogue can be evened out if the local people undertake discussion of the issues in small groups. A facilitator could help to guide the discussion toward definition and analysis of the problem, but otherwise recede into the background as the process goes on. The important discussions are not those between local individuals and the facilitator, but those among the local people.

There is special potential in working with groups, as Alcoholics Anonymous and Weight Watchers know so well. Local people need to reflect together on issues such as the deaths of their children. In that dialogue process they can learn from one another, and indeed they can produce knowledge that none of them previously had as individuals. They can come to new understandings about what they do, and also about what government officials or plantation owners or village chiefs do, to cause or to prevent children's deaths. They will get clearer about how and why they relate to one another in the ways they do. And as a result of that process they can come to clearer answers about what should be done in their specific circumstances.

Therese Drummond's description of how the methods of Paulo Freire can be used in nutrition education is applicable to many different kinds of child survival programs. She recognized that "poor health and poor nutrition of most of the world's population is caused more by a lack of access to the resources of land, credit, income, legal services, sanitation, etc. than by a lack of knowledge."

I believe that in the ideal situation nutrition education should be a part of a global effort for liberation from hunger, disease, and inhuman conditions; a joint effort of people and technical staff for achieving first and foremost a *humanizing* situation where dependence is destroyed. This implies conditions in which people are acting as subjects and not passively receiving information or being acted upon as objects. It is more than just "participation" of the people because it involves a whole basic philosophy and motivation on the side of both teacher-students and student-teachers. Nutrition education then is part of "conscientization" and the awakening of critical awareness among people who have many deprivations, including food and nutrient deprivations.

Since the global effort that we are discussing is much more than imparting facts, the "nutrition message" cannot be merely persuading people to eat what we think they should. Rather, the central problem is the creation of a humanizing set of conditions (basic to which is personal decision-making) through a problem-posing education. Therefore, the nutrition problems must be posed and the long, slow process of working out solutions must be gone through by the people, with the specialists supplying information when it is requested.[2]

The possibilities are illustrated by Alexandra Praun's work in Central America. Facilitators or *promotores* were trained to work with local groups, leading discussions on questions such as

1. The nutrition situation in our locality.
2. Why do children die?
3. Why don't we have enough food?
4. Foods in the community.
5. Local food preparation.
6. Local food taboos and traditions.
7. The agricultural services in the region.
8. The health services in the region.
9. Food aid programmes.
10. Communal/home gardens.
11. Chicken, rabbit, and pig farms.[3]

The theme "nutrition situation in our locality," for example, "was developed through a set of questions concerning: local food prices, food availability, local production, family diet, common child sicknesses, budget used for food and so on." Of course the appropriate questions would be different in different circumstances. They would not be addressed mechanically, as in some sort of examination, but would be used to stimulate an open-ended joint analysis of the local food situation.

In another case, in the Dominican Republic a women's nutrition training course was established:

Some 62 women started attending the course—structured along Paulo Freire's lines—which examined nutrition not only in technical terms but also in the social, political, and economic context of the women's lives. . . . They studied the nutritional situation of their own region, and of the entire country. They also made surveys in their own neighbourhoods to assess the nutritional problems of their families, friends, and neighbours, and to work out ways of dealing with them.[4]

As a result the women, calling themselves Women of the South, developed detailed critiques of the export orientation of the country's agriculture and of their own excessive dependence on food aid, launched a number of projects for food production and distribution, and undertook a systematic program of self-evaluation of their efforts.

Their realization of the limits of [conventional] nutritional education has led them to analyse the socioeconomic and political structure of their own society and their own role within it. They have become truly *conciente*, aware of themselves and their role, and their first question when faced with any problem is: "What can we, as women of the South, do?" They believe in their own power to instigate a social change, and to work with other organizations to create conditions in which children will be well fed, clothed, housed, and educated.

The natural method of development planning among ordinary people is dialogue. Planning at the community level thus entails a group of people arriving at their own analysis of their situation, including a confrontation with the conflicts they have among themselves and with others. It is a process of joint reflection providing a basis for action that will transform their situation.

National plans should provide for citizen participation in planning for the action that is to take place locally. The national plan should set the parameters but not work out all the details. Adaptations to local circumstances should be worked out with local people and local agencies.

MULTIPARTY . . .

Planning, for development in general or for child survival in particular, should not be viewed as the exclusive domain of either those at the top or those at the grass-roots level of society. *Multiparty planning* emphasizes full engagement by people at the bottom, middle, and top levels in the formulation of the major plans which affect their lives. Each party has distinct and complementary contributions to make, and all can develop—be empowered— by the process. There should be clarity about how the parties' roles differ, and how their efforts in the field can fit together.

It is important to include not only top and bottom but also middle-level agencies. Many nations have provincial, district, regional, or village health agencies as well as national departments of health. These middle-level workers are frequently bypassed, and thus become very frustrated. In many countries different private voluntary organizations undertake similar development work but barely know about one another's existence. Often there is little coordination between ministries of agriculture and ministries of health regarding problems of food and nutrition. There should be engagement and coordination not only across different levels (vertical) but also among agencies at the same level (horizontal). That is why we speak here of *multiparty,* and not simply *multilevel,* planning.

PLANNING

The basic elements of the planning process can be listed as

1. Describe the problem
2. Explain it
3. Formulate alternative responses to it
4. Evaluate the alternatives
5. Choose and implement the action.

Multiparty development planning focuses on decisive, clear identification of the different parties and their distinct roles in dealing with the issues of concern. Its main objective is to enhance the quality of the dialogue among all those involved in development work at a particular location.

The methods for multiparty planning can be quite simple. Some lead agency takes the initiative to arrange meetings of representatives of all agencies or organizations concerned with the issue. After a brief round of introductions, they are asked to describe their understanding of the issue, what they think should be done about it in general, and how their agency in particular relates to it.

For child survival, the local department of health could describe current mortality patterns, mothers could describe prenatal care and child care practices, and local health workers could talk about the problem and the remedies as they see them. A UNICEF representative could talk about the common causes of the problem, and report on child survival programs that have been attempted elsewhere.

After that background is established, discussion opens on what should be done about the local problem, and who will take what concrete actions. Doing all this in a thoughtful way will require a long series of meetings.

The major objective is *to prepare, in written form, an agreed statement on who is to do what to deal with the issue.* This is not a simple matter of enumeration; rather, it is likely to emerge only after long discussion and even negotiation among the different parties. The discussion may help some of them to discover and articulate what they can do.

In addition to the final written statement of roles and functions, some mechanism should be established to maintain communication among the different parties over time. Perhaps some combination of frequent small meetings of special interest groups, occasional large meetings of all concerned, and periodic newsletters would do the job.

Often it will not be useful to try to work out a detailed program of action. The articulation of roles and functions, and the establishment of means for communication, allow the action to evolve in a natural way. This in itself constitutes the core of multiparty planning. Planning is a systematic process of reflection that precedes and guides action, something that can be accomplished in many different ways in the context of multiparty planning meetings. The process can be embellished with specific technical exercises regarding the explicit formulation of objectives, strategies, and so on, but it also can function in a more evolutionary and intuitive way.

GUIDELINES

One good way to think out guidelines is to formulate—and reformulate—a letter to a friend working on a child survival program in a distant country. The first draft might go something like this:

Dear Fran—

The child survival program you are working with sounds very exciting. You and the others concerned might want to consider *localized multiparty planning* for the program, so that all involved will be clear about what they can to do contribute to the child survival effort.

You might begin by discussing the idea informally with the people you work with. If they are interested, you and they could begin by making a list of all the agencies that have a role, or should have a role, in local child survival activity. Of course you will want to review and expand this list of possible participants as time goes on.

You could then ask one of the parties involved to take the lead in arranging the multiparty planning meetings. That individual or agency would have to find a suitable place for the meetings, reserve it, and arrange for such things as refreshments and occasional social diversions. Physical arrangements should include chalkboards or large papers for writing things visible to everyone at the meetings. The arranger should consult with the others on an informal basis as these things are being worked out.

It will be important to find a suitable *facilitator* for the meetings. It might be best if the facilitator was not associated with the party arranging the meetings, to minimize any suggestion that the arranger wanted to dominate the proceedings.

At the first meeting the facilitator should begin by saying very briefly that the purpose of getting together is to address the child survival problem locally, and to see how the different agencies could work together in the effort. The facilitator ought to propose right at the beginning that the group as a whole should work toward preparing a written statement of who is to do what.

This might be a good time to post a list of all the agencies, organizations, and unaffiliated individuals who are participating in the meeting. Later this list could be used to enumerate who will be doing what.

The facilitator could then suggest a stepwise procedure. The first task would be to have the local child survival problem described in as much detail as possible, from as many different points of view as possible. How many of which children die? This would be the *description* phrase. The basic information could be sketched out on the chalkboard for all to see. At first it would be reported in bits and pieces, but then an attempt should be made to make a comprehensive statement describing the nature of the local child survival problem.

There may be some differences among observers about the nature of the problem. Differences in views should be discussed, but they do not have to be resolved.

The second major task would be to discuss *explanations* for the existence of the problem. What are the reasons for these early deaths? Different people will offer different kinds of explanations. Some may be different, but still compatible, perhaps because some focus on more immediate clinical causes, while others focus on societal causes, such as poverty or the lack of certain kinds of services.

There may be serious disagreements or incompatibilities in the explanations that are offered. These differences should be acknowledged, but it may not be necessary to resolve them.

The third major task would be to discuss the possible *remedies* for the problem. At the beginning the different possible courses of action could be discussed in rather abstract form, identifying different types of action. Then, as the major options become clear, it will be time to say who will do what. Of course some actions may already be under way. These ongoing actions and actors should be noted, but then the main question would be: Who else could do what else? This may mean giving further support to actions that have already been initiated, and also starting new lines of action.

After outlining the basis objective and the suggested procedure at the beginning of the first meeting, the facilitator should give everyone the opportunity to discuss that agenda. If they don't agree with it, it is not going to work. The participants in the meeting should have an opportunity to help shape the procedure.

It should be explained that the purpose is not to formulate a single course of action or a single project to which everyone would have to agree. Different individuals and agencies would be expected to do different things, according to what is right for them in terms of their own views, talents, interests, and resources. Instead of trying to find a single, common project on which all could collaborate, it might be better to ask each participant: In regard to child survival, (1) what actions are you taking? (2) what actions would you like to take? (3) how can you be helped? (4) how can you help others?

At the beginning the facilitator could write large headings on three different sections of the chalkboard: DESCRIPTIONS, EXPLANATIONS, REMEDIES. The facilitator would then summarize the main points under each heading as the information and ideas are formulated. If participants begin to talk about explanations or remedies while the agenda is still focused on descriptions, the facilitator could make a note under the appropriate heading, and say that the group will return to the thought later, when DESCRIPTIONS are completed.

In addition to the facilitator, there should be a skilled *recorder* who will take notes and summarize the group's discussions and positions. These minutes should be prepared in written form after each meeting and distributed for review at the beginning of the subsequent meeting.

The facilitator should draw the accounts of descriptions, explanations, and remedies regarding child survival from the participants in the meetings, and not press his or her own views. Of course occasional pointed questions from the facilitator would be acceptable, but the facilitator should not steer the proceedings too much.

One of the facilitator's main jobs would be to keep the meeting from getting bogged down in acrimonious debates over what is the right way to understand the problem and what is the right thing to do about it. Discussion of differences in views certainly can be useful, but as soon as the discussion becomes heated—an argument rather than a dialogue—the facilitator should acknowledge the differences and try to move on to the next steps.

Some differences are minor and can be ignored. However, some deep differences will be worth exploring and managing. Important conflicts should be acknowledged. They might be addressed in a systematic way by representatives of the different views in smaller, focused meetings outside the main meetings. In some cases skilled mediators could participate. The results should then be reported back to the main meetings.

Overall, the idea is to work toward preparation of a written statement of who is to do what. This written statement would then constitute the local program for child survival. Of course, as in most sound planning efforts, the important thing is the process and the dynamics that go into the preparation of the document, and not the document itself. The final paper is only a very fragmentary record of the shared understanding that emerges from the sustained dialogue of the planning meetings.

The facilitator should make it clear that all this will not be accomplished quickly, in a single meeting, but will involve a lot of hard work by all concerned over very many meetings. The process should not be rushed.

The group could appoint a small standing committee to monitor progress and to organize occasional follow-up meetings. These meetings could be used for sharing information about the different ongoing activities, and for evaluating progress. The group could consider amending the overall plan. These continuing meetings would help to assure that planning for child survival remains a dynamic process, with reviews and revisions as necessary.

This may seem like a long and arduous process, but the payoffs could be very great, not only in terms of improved child survival rates but also in terms of empowerment of the entire community.

Good luck, Fran. Please be sure to let me know how it works out.

Best regards,

PROBLEMS

Often there is not only a lack of communication among different agencies but also some hostility, condescension, and jealousy. Agencies normally like to have their areas of responsibility—their "turf"—clearly demarcated, and they do what they can to prevent intrusion by others. They don't want their credit for successes diluted by having to share it with others. They don't want critical examination by outsiders. The lack of communication among agencies, both horizontally and vertically, is no accident. There are distinct forces working against it. Thus communication cannot be left to chance, but must be deliberately arranged.

These sorts of problems, normally encountered in development work, will be reflected in the multiparty planning process. Even if they cannot be fully resolved, it may be useful to make the difficulties plainly visible. In the absence of a hierarchical command structure, it is only through this sort of interaction that full participation and coordination of all concerned parties can be obtained. It is important to appreciate that multiparty planning does not create these difficulties. It makes them more plainly visible and thus, with skillful handling, can make them more readily manageable.

Some problems will be unique to the meeting situation. There will be difficulties in getting some parties to attend. In some cases local people may not know that child mortality levels are high in their communities, or they may not view it as a problem. They may see it as something no one can do anything about. They may see it as something no one *should* do anything about.

There may be problems in working out orderly discussion procedures and in formulating the distinct tasks that need to be done. Perhaps initially no one will want to do some specific thing that needs to be done. Perhaps too many will want to do it. One persistent problem will be to find ways to keep a few powerful, articulate individuals from dominating the proceedings. Several different devices can be helpful. For example, arrangements might be made for a rotating chair, so that different people take turns managing the meetings. Also, the practice of discussing issues in small ad hoc groups which report back to the larger meeting can help to assure that everyone has good opportunities to speak.

Local people who are not used to participating actively in meetings may need special encouragement and support. In some cases it may be useful to ask them to talk among themselves and select representatives to speak at the meetings. For very poor people it may be sensible to provide some sort of subsidy for taking the time to attend the meetings. In the short term some people may have limited capacity for participation, but given its intrinsic value for empowerment, methods should be found to gradually stretch that capacity.[5]

The idealized form of localized multiparty planning sketched here cannot be achieved instantly. Compromises will be necessary. Sometimes it will be more practical to work with middle-range local leaders rather than with local people directly. One could work with—or help create—a local health committee. It may be more effective to begin with other prominent health and development concerns, and gradually work into the child survival issue. Often it will be necessary to put off political analysis and instead address more concrete and immediate issues.

The important thing is to pursue small successes and build on them. Empowerment is learned. One becomes empowered through practice, by repeatedly defining, analyzing and acting on one's own problems. The learning should be incremental, in small doses, with modest attempts and modest successes paving the way for bolder attempts and grander successes. As UNICEF's Karl-Eric Knuttson put it:

When goals exist and are accepted, the possibilities of introducing new skills, and building effective organizations to achieve them, are greatly facilitated. Addressing important goals of ordinary people in great numbers can also release their social energy and increase their control over other aspects of their situation and make it possible to pursue other important goals of development. In this way, one set of actions lays the foundation for the next in a pragmatic and durable way. It is only through such a phased integration over time, in which demonstrable results are achieved at each step, that energy and competence can be released in a cumulative way towards the next set of goals.[6]

One of the most serious problems in multiparty planning is identifying the incentives for participation. For agencies with adequate material resources and full legitimacy for doing child survival work, the option of working with others may not be very attractive. One hopes that the prospect of increased effectiveness will itself help to motivate collaboration. In some situations multiparty planning might be required by funding agencies. Localized multiparty planning could be formally mandated in national child survival programs.

Problems in planning are inevitable. The meetings that constitute multiparty planning provide a means for uncovering and addressing some of the difficulties that always plague development work. The identification of the problems provides the opportunity for addressing them in creative ways. As experience accumulates and the problems of the meetings are analyzed, it may become possible to train specialized facilitators for multiparty planning meetings.

Empowerment work is not easy to do. It is advocated here because it goes to the root of the problems of child survival in particular and of underdevelopment in general, addressing the fundamental issue of powerlessness. Empowerment strategies may be less effective than others in the short run, but they are likely to be much more effective in the long run.

Local people need to gain increasing understanding of and control over their own circumstances. If development is understood in terms of the empowerment of ordinary people, then the highest priority should be given to facilitating the planning dialogue among the people themselves, and between the people and the professionals. People cannot become fully developed unless they become involved in the planning for their own development.

The child survival issue is often addressed by agencies acting in isolation: "That's not our responsibility. It's the job of the mother, or the village health worker, or the doctor, or the department of health, or UNICEF." No matter how skilled and devoted, they are all very limited in what they can do alone. When the agencies do coordinate their efforts, it is often without the participation of the local people. The purported beneficiaries are not fully engaged in the process.

UNICEF's *The State of the World's Children 1988* speaks of the need to build "a grand alliance for children" involving teachers and religious leaders, mass media and government agencies, voluntary organizations and people's movements, business and labor unions, professional associations and conventional health services. Multiparty planning is a concrete means of building alliances for children, beginning with the essential linkages among local people themselves, and between local people and government and nongovernmental agencies.

NOTES

1. Naomi Caiden and Aaron Wildavsky, *Planning and Budgeting in Poor Countries* (New York: John Wiley, 1974).

2. Therese Drummond, "Rethinking Nutrition Education," in Kathryn W. Shack, ed., *Teaching Nutrition Education in Developing Countries or the Joys of Eating Dark Green Leaves* (Santa Barbara, Cal.: Meals for Millions Foundation, 1977), pp. 2–11.

3. Alexandra Praun, "Nutrition Education: Development or Alienation?" *Human Nutrition: Applied Nutrition,* 36A (1982), 28–34.

4. Lindsey Hilsum, "Nutrition Education and Social Change: A Women's Movement in the Dominican Republic," in David Morley, Jon E. Rohde, and Glen Williams,

eds., *Practising Health for All* (New York: Oxford University Press, 1983), pp. 114–32.

5. Practical ideas and a powerful conceptual framework for empowerment are in Guy Gran, *Development by People: Citizen Construction of a Just World* (New York: Praeger, 1983). More good ideas are in Michael Doyle and David Straus, *How to Make Meetings Work* (New York: Jove, 1982); and Jerry Silverman, Merlyn Kettering, and Terry Schmidt, *Action Planning Workshops for Development Management: Guidelines* (Washington, D.C.: World Bank, 1986).

6. James P. Grant, *The State of the World's Children 1987* (New York: Oxford University Press, 1987), p. 23.

Chapter Sixteen

LAWS AND INSTITUTIONS

The high rates of children's mortality, morbidity, abuse, and neglect are largely due to the powerlessness with which they and their families face the world around them. Strategies of empowerment can help to overcome that condition. But that bottom-up approach must be complemented with work from the top down, through the development of more responsive laws and institutions at both the national and the international levels.

Powerful countries resist the urgings of weaker countries, and within countries, powerful people resist the urgings of weaker people. The powerful respond to those with power. In many countries, ethnic minorities, women, the handicapped, and homosexuals have gained increasing recognition of their rights not because of the sudden awakening of compassion among the powerful, but because they themselves have worked vigorously to win that recognition.

But small children cannot make their own claims for recognition of their rights. Children require surrogates to speak in their behalf. A number of organizations, private and public, national and international, have emerged as advocates for children. International agencies such as UNICEF, Defense for Children International, and Save the Children do a great deal, and within countries there are organizations, such as the Children's Defense Fund in the United States, that are very effective. But despite the magnificence of their work, much remains to be done. Millions upon millions of children still die and still starve and still are exploited throughout the world. The explanation for the persistence of these problems is one that is very common in politics: those who have the problems are not the ones who have the power.

No matter what the intentions of political leaders may be, the massive horrors that befall children amount to a form of holocaust. Why are we deeply concerned with the abuse and neglect of children by their families, yet give so little attention to the abuse and neglect of children by their societies and their governments? The crime of silence is a crime no less for a negligent holocaust than it is for a deliberate holocaust.[1] Historians ask us to remember the holocaust of World War II, but sometimes we forget why we are to remember.

RINGS OF RESPONSIBILITY

What is our responsibility toward children? The principal obligation is to promote their development, understood as empowerment or increasing self-reliance. The task is to help increase children's capacity to define, analyze, and act on their own problems.

Who is responsible for children? The question here is not whose fault it is that children suffer so much (who caused their problems?), but who should take action to remedy the problems? Many different social agencies may have some role in looking after children, but what should be the interrelationships among them?

Most children have two vigorous advocates from the moment they are born, and even before they are born. Their parents devote enormous resources to serving their interests. These are not sacrifices. The best parents do not support their children out of a sense of obligation, or as investments. They support their children as extensions of themselves, as part of their wholeness.

In many cases, however, that bond is broken or is never created. Fathers disappear. Many mothers disappear as well. In New York City, each month hundreds of children are abandoned in the hospitals where they are born. In many cities of the world, bands of children live in the streets by their wits, preyed upon by others. Often children end up alone as a result of warfare or other political crises. Many children are abandoned because they are physically or mentally handicapped. Often parents become so disabled by drugs or alcohol that they cannot care for their children.

Often children who cannot be cared for by their biological parents are looked after by others in their communities. In many cultures children belong not only to their biological parents but to the community as a whole. The responsibility and the joy of raising children are shared in the wider community.

In many places, especially in "developed" countries, that option is no longer available because of the collapse of the idea of community. Many of us live in nice neighborhoods in well-ordered societies, but the sense of community—of love and responsibility and commitment to one another—has vanished. In such cases the remaining hope of the abandoned child is the government, the modern substitute for community. We look to government to provide human services that the social community no longer provides.

As children mature, the first priority is to help them become responsible for themselves. So long as they are not mature, however, children ought to get their nurturance from their parents. Failing that, they ought to get it from their local communities. Failing that, they ought to get it from the local governments. Failing that, they ought to get it from their state or provincial governments. Failing that, it should come from their national governments. Failing that, they ought to get it from the international community. The responsibility hierarchy looks like this:

self

family

community

local government

state government

national government

international community

This is straightforward. The point that needs to be added is that in cases of failure, agents lower on the list should not simply substitute for those higher on the list; they should try to *work through and strengthen those higher on the list* in fulfilling their responsibilities toward children. To the extent possible, local communities should not take children away from inadequate parents, but should help parents in their parenting role. State governments should not replace local governments, but should support local governments in their work with children. The international community should help national governments in their work with children. The same reasoning should apply to care for the physically handicapped and the mentally ill.

In this view, promoting the adoption of children—especially international adoption—should be undertaken only as a last resort, because it means giving up on the primary support systems closest to the child. UNICEF's policy of working with national governments in the formulation of programs identified as national (not UNICEF) programs for children's welfare and development is very good. UNICEF does not substitute itself for national governments; instead it supports them in their work in behalf of children.

The Reagan administration's idea that the states, rather than the federal government, ought to look after welfare programs within the states was sound, at least in the abstract. But states cannot automatically step in to meet needs when the federal government cuts off support, just as children do not immediately mature on being abandoned by their parents. The states should have received fuller support from the federal government to assure that, in the localization process, needy children and others became better, not worse, off.

The international community is the last resort, the outer ring of responsibility in looking after the welfare of children. Obviously it has not been very successful.

THE INTERNATIONAL RESPONSE

The rights of children have been formalized only recently in history. Their rights seem to be recognized even more reluctantly than the rights of animals, nature, or artifacts:

We know something of the early rights-status of children from the widespread practice of infanticide. . . . as late as the Patria Potestas of the Romans, the father had *jus vitae necisque*—the power of life and death—over his children. . . . he had the power of "uncontrolled corporal chastisement; he can modify their personal condition at pleasure . . . he can transfer them to another family by adoption; and he can sell them." The child was less than a person: an object, a thing.[2]

There has been real progress, but the legal rights of children are still weak, in developed as well as in developing countries. International law regarding the rights of the child is in its infancy largely because the international law of human rights of which it is a part is itself still very young.

The Geneva Declaration on the Rights of the Child adopted by the League of Nations in 1924 was revised and became the basis of the Declaration of the Rights of the Child adopted unanimously by the United Nations General Assembly in 1959. The declaration enumerates ten principles regarding the rights of the child, but it does not provide any basis for enforcement of those principles.[3]

The Universal Declaration of Human Rights was approved unanimously by the U.N. General Assembly in 1948. It was given effect in two separate instruments, the International Covenant on Civil and Political Rights and the International Covenant on Economic, Social, and Cultural Rights. The covenants describe children's rights in detail.[4]

The four Geneva Conventions of 1949, the major sources of the law of armed conflict, were discussed in Chapter 8. The Convention Relative to the Protection of Civilian Persons in Time of War is of particular importance for the protection of children. (The others are the Convention for the Amelioration of the Condition of the Wounded and Sick in Armed Forces in the Field; the Convention for the Amelioration of the Condition of Wounded, Sick and Shipwrecked Members of Armed Forces at Sea, and the Convention Relative to the Treatment of Prisoners of War.) The Geneva Conventions have been ratified by 165 states, making them the most widely ratified conventions in history.

After negotiations at the Geneva Conference on the Reaffirmation and Development of International Humanitarian Law beginning in 1974, two supplements, Protocols Additional to the Geneva Conventions of 12 August 1949, were adopted in June 1977. Protocol I applies to international armed conflicts, while Protocol II applies to noninternational armed conflicts. By June 1990, 96 states had become parties to Protocol I and 86 had become parties to Protocol II. The United States is among the countries that have not yet ratified them.[5]

In 1974 the U.N. General Assembly adopted the Declaration on the Protection of Women and Children in Emergencies and Armed Conflicts.[6] It made six points, including the proclamation that "attacks and bombings on the civilian population, inflicting incalculable suffering, especially on women and children . . . shall be prohibited"; but, as a nonbinding resolution, no means for enforcement were included.

There are now more than 80 international laws, covenants, and declarations setting out human rights for children.[7]

Major progress has been made. After ten years of negotiation and drafting by a working group of the Commission on Human Rights, on November 20, 1989, the U.N. General Assembly approved a new Convention on the Rights of the Child. Weaving together the scattered threads of earlier international statements of the rights of children, the convention's articles cover civil, political, economic, social, and cultural rights. The convention addresses not only basic survival requirements, such as food, clean water, and health care, but also rights of protection against abuse, neglect, and exploitation, and the right to education and to participation in social, religious, political, and economic activities. It is a comprehensive legal instrument, binding on all nations that sign and ratify it.

To implement the convention, Article 43 calls for the creation of the Committee on the Rights of the Child, consisting of ten elected experts whose main functions are to receive and transmit reports on the status of children's rights. Article 44 requires signatory nations to submit "reports on the measures they have adopted which give effect to the rights recognized herein and on the progress made on the enjoyment of those rights." Article 46 entitles UNICEF and other agencies to work with the committee within the scope of their mandates.

The Convention on the Rights of the Child is an important advance, and should be vigorously supported by all governments and all advocates of children's interests. But its implementation mechanisms are much too weak. The same problem arises with respect to the implementation of earlier human rights agreements. The United Nations has a number of committees in place to implement human rights law, such as the Committee on the Elimination of Racial Discrimination, the Human Rights Committee, the Committee on Economic, Social, and Cultural Rights, the Committee on the Elimination of Discrimination Against Women, and the Committee Against Torture. They do useful work, to be sure, but their resources and their mandates are not nearly adequate to the needs in these areas. The Committee on the Rights of the Child is not likely to be any more effective.

We can look to other agencies. The preeminent organization attending to children worldwide is the United Nations Children's Fund, UNICEF. It does magnificent work. But it is no criticism of the organization to point out that it, too, falls short of the need.

UNICEF is conservative. It does well in promoting technical interventions such as immunization programs, but it avoids politically sensitive activity. In 1984 UNICEF's Executive Board commissioned a study on children in especially difficult circumstances, "a euphemism for the range of sensitive subjects which include victims of labour exploitation, abandonment, sexual abuse, and conflict."[8] There was some follow-up action which held the promise that UNICEF would come to grips with these enormously important and widespread problems. However, by the end of the 1980s these issues were hardly visible on UNICEF's agenda. UNICEF instead continued to focus on politically safe, technical approaches to reducing children's mortality.

On questions of child labor, UNICEF defers to the International Labor Organization (ILO). The ILO has done a great deal of useful work in promoting the adoption of minimum ages for employment in various industries, and it has sponsored many good studies and conferences on child labor. Like UNICEF, the ILO has made a great contribution to the advancement of children's welfare. But the problems persist, on a very large scale.

Nongovernmental organizations (NGOs) had originally proposed that UNICEF might serve as the principal agency to monitor compliance with the Convention on the Rights of the Child, but UNICEF rejected the idea. The NGOs came to agree:

the NGO Group, fully aware of the mandate of UNICEF, has taken full account of the fact that any UNICEF role in this connection must be limited strictly to responding, directly or otherwise, to requests for technical assistance from States Parties, and would in particular not involve any monitoring function under the terms of the Convention.[9]

A number of member states sensibly "expressed concern that a perception of UNICEF as a 'watchdog' could complicate its Third World assistance programmes which rely on cooperative relationships with host governments."[10]

UNICEF does less than advocates of children's interests might wish, but "the extent to which UNICEF is bound and gagged has always been well understood by its own officials."[11] Roger Sawyer explains:

The representatives of United Nations agencies and funds, all of whom are nominees of governments of member states, are expressly forbidden to engage in any activity without the knowledge and approval of the government of the host country; they therefore enjoy negligible independence. Moreover, many of the states in which UNICEF works are subject to one-party systems of government under the dictatorial rule of a "President for Life" or a military despot. Like other organizations, they are welcome only in so far as they do not seem to de-stabilize the régime by so much as a word of criticism; provided they do not step out of line, they can do invaluable work combating hunger, disease and ecological disasters of various kinds.... [UNI-CEF's] lips are effectively sealed on human rights violations.[12]

UNICEF's conservatism is demonstrated by its national *situation analyses*. These documents compile a great deal of useful information on the situation of children and women in particular countries. But they are rarely critical of the national governments' policies toward children. If governments are mentioned, it is to praise them for "working on" the problems. Governments are given credit for improvements in bad conditions, but they are not associated with the existence of those bad conditions. Little is said about what governments fail to do.

This is very understandable. The UNICEF office operating in a nation's capital cannot be very critical of its host country, or it will not be allowed to work in that nation. There are always limits on the extent to which one can speak truth to power and still remain effective.

These constraints are fully recognized at headquarters. As an international governmental organization whose immediate constituency is its Executive Board, representing its member nations, UNICEF could not be expected to be anything but conservative and constrained. Similarly, we may bemoan the fact that the ILO does not give more attention to child labor, and that the Food and Agriculture Organization of the United Nations does so little to alleviate world hunger, but we have to recognize these realities and understand that their pinched behavior is inescapable, given the ways in which these organizations are structured. When they are blessed with directors of vision, the envelope of possibility is enlarged, but the most effective directors also understand their constraints very well.

Within the U.N. system, in addition to UNICEF and ILO, the Working Group of Experts on Slavery also is concerned with the exploitation of children. Human rights in general is the responsibility of the Economic and Social Council of the United Nations; it has a subsidiary Commission of Human Rights, which in turn has a Sub-Commission on Prevention of Discrimination and Protection of Minorities. The latter Sub-Commission receives reports from a number of working groups, one of which is the Working Group of Experts on Slavery. Since 1975 it has held sessions each summer at U.N. headquarters in Geneva.

The 1986 meeting of the Working Group of Experts on Slavery was canceled because of the U.N. system's economic crisis, precipitated by the U.S. and the Soviet failure to keep up with their payments. Cancellation of the slavery meetings suggests that human rights issues are of low priority even within the U.N. system. Indeed, even in normal years "only 0.7 per cent of the United Nations budget is allotted specifically for the promotion and protection of human rights."[13]

NGOs are not so constrained in what they can do for the advancement of children's rights. Indeed, the Ad Hoc Group of NGOs that was formed in

1983 to participate in the drafting of the Convention on the Rights of the Child played a leading role in the negotiations.[14] The problem with NGOs is that while they have considerable freedom of action in some ways, their lack of official mandates limits them in other ways, and they always suffer from inadequate funding.

DESIGN FOR THE FUTURE

Roger Sawyer observes that "international conventions exist to protect children and their parents from all manner of abuses, but there is no international inspectorate to monitor, let alone compel, their implementation."[15] The Convention on the Rights of the Child will not remedy that problem. It falls short of what is needed to effectively address the massive problems of children throughout the world. A legalistic approach to the advancement of human rights in general and of children's rights in particular alone is not adequate; it tends to ignore the political bases of human rights problems. Claims to rights and resources must rest on power. The problems of children are fundamentally political problems.

Effective international human rights law must be tied to appropriate international institutions to implement its rules. Not only the rules but also the charter of the organization that is to implement those rules need to be drafted. If the nations of the world agree, say, that children under ten years of age should not be employed outside the home, they ought also to propose institutional arrangements to assure that the rule is honored. Historically, international human rights agreements have included some provisions regarding implementation, but those arrangements have been extremely weak. They have been so weak that in many cases the agreed rules have not been taken seriously.

Children's advocacy is splintered among many governmental and nongovernmental agencies, both within countries and internationally, with each of them carving out narrow areas of specialization. The unfortunate fact is that children's advocacy organizations have not found the motivation and the means to pull their resources together. Important gains could be achieved if strong relationships were established between governmental and nongovernmental organizations. Their capacities complement one another. Governmental organizations have resources but a limited scope of action, while NGOs have the opposite. Some governmental organizations, such as the U.S. Agency for International Development, have discovered the many advantages of working with and through NGOs. Alliances should be built systematically, within nations, across nations, within particular regions, and globally.

Chapter 8 showed that there are several international organizations dealing with the problems of children in situations of armed conflict. They are doing excellent work, but collectively their coverage of the problems is spotty and incomplete. I have suggested the creation of a Liaison Group on Children in

Armed Conflict to deal with this fragmentation. When I tried to float the idea at an international conference on children, it sank like a rock. None of the established organizations showed any interest in arranging even a small meeting on the issue.

Apparently an established organization will not take on new work unless it benefits the organization directly, in terms of its own current agenda. In a world of thin and fragile funding, in which all organizations of this sort are already overstretched, they cannot volunteer for new tasks of any kind. The conclusion is simple and unsurprising: *new action requires new resources.* There is nothing that attracts attention and generates energetic activity so much as a new infusion of money.

New assignments are resisted, and the proposal for collaboration is viewed with particular suspicion. The idea that children's advocacy organizations have substantial common interests is naive because each of them carves out its own distinctive niche. The smaller ones fear proposals for collaboration because they may be swallowed up. The larger ones don't see that they have anything to gain. The same pattern applies in other areas. For example, the many different organizations concerned with the hunger issue do not work together very much.

One could try to find a funding agency that would see value in, and agree to sponsor, occasional low-key liaison meetings of agencies concerned with children's welfare. But, given the magnitude and diversity of the problems of children around the world, something more ambitious is needed.

Sometimes when really good ideas are put together, so good that the benefits are obvious, they will attract the support they require. Perhaps, if a highly effective new global children's agency could be designed to complement the work of UNICEF, WHO, ILO, and the NGOs, and that design was then circulated, either governments or private agencies would agree to fund it. Fundability would be a major test of the merits of the design.

The immediate objective here is not to propose a particular design, but to propose that the design effort should be undertaken. Ideas should be pooled from many different sources, in a collaborative effort involving all the established global agencies concerned with the welfare of children.

The quality of our future depends on the quality of life of our children and their children. If we do not begin to do much more to look after their interests, the prospects are bleak. We should create more effective institutional arrangements for improving the lives of children, and thus brighten our collective future.

If we could somehow transcend the traditional parochialism of the various agencies working on the issue and find ways in which they could join forces, it might be possible to break through to much higher levels of effectiveness in child survival work. If concerned individuals and agencies act in unison toward the common objective, undertaking coordinated action, they will have tapped the very roots of social power. Joint action requires sustained dialogue on the issues, both horizontal and vertical. The dialogue on child survival should be extended in every direction to help every individual, every agency, and every government see more clearly how it could help. This greatly enlarged development dialogue could result in a fundamental transformation of the social structure, saving our children in ways we had hardly dared to imagine.

NOTES

1. I made a similar point, even in the title, in *The Political Economy of Hunger: The Silent Holocaust* (New York: Praeger, 1984).

2. Christopher D. Stone, *Should Trees Have Standing: Toward Legal Rights for Natural Objects* (Los Altos, Ca.: William Kaufmann, 1974), pp. 3–4. The quantity of law protecting the interests of children is probably smaller than the quantity of law protecting inanimate entities such as ships or corporations.

3. See Maria Enrica Agostinelli, *On Wings of Love: The United Nations Declaration of the Rights of the Child* (New York: Collins, 1979), for an interpretation and illustration of the principles designed for children.

4. Rebecca J. Cook, "Human Rights and Infant Survival: A Case for Priorities," *Columbia Human Rights Law Review,* 18, no. 1 (Fall/Winter 1986/87), 1–41.

5. The application of the Geneva Conventions and the protocols to children is analyzed in Denise Plattner, "Protection of Children in International Humanitarian Law," *International Review of the Red Cross,* May–June 1984, pp. 140–52; and Sandra Singer, "The Protection of Children During Armed Conflict Situations," *International Review of the Red Cross,* May–June 1986, pp. 133–68.

6. Resolution 3318 (XXIX) of 14 December 1974.

7. For details see Everett M. Ressler, Neil Boothby, and Daniel J. Steinbock, *Unaccompanied Children: Care and Protection in Wars, Natural Disasters, and Refugee Movements* (New York: Oxford University Press, 1988), pp. 246–61.

8. Maggie Black, *The Children and the Nations: The Story of Unicef* (New York: UNICEF, 1986), p. 376.

9. *Statement Submitted to the 1987 UNICEF Executive Board by Defence for Children International,* E/ICEF/1987/NGO/2, (New York: United Nations Economic and Social Council, 17 April 1987), p. 2.

10. Ian Steel, "A New UN Convention: 'Every Child Has the Right to...,'" *Development Forum,* 17, no. 2 (March–April 1989), 1, 6.

11. Roger Sawyer, *Children Enslaved,* (London: Routledge, 1988), p. 178.

12. Ibid., p. 179.

13. Ibid., p. 177. See pp. 189–90 for an account of the limited scope of the Working Group's activity.

14. Nigel Cantwell, *The Future UN Convention on the Rights of the Child: Implications for Amnesty International* (Geneva: Defence for Children International, 1989).

15. Sawyer, *Children Enslaved,* p. 183.

SELECTED REFERENCES

Acker, Alison. *Children of the Volcano*. Westport, Conn.: Lawrence Hill, 1986.

Agostinelli, Maria Enrica. *On Wings of Love: The United Nations Declaration of the Rights of the Child*. New York: Collins, 1979.

Ahluwalia, Montek S., Carter, Nicholas G., and Chenery, Hollis B. *Growth and Poverty in Developing Countries*. Washington, D.C.: World Bank, 1979.

Alderson, Michael R. *International Mortality Statistics*. New York: Facts on File, 1981.

Antonovsky, A., and Bornsten, J. "Social Class and Infant Mortality," *Social Science & Medicine,* 11 (1977), 454–70.

Aries, Philippe. *Centuries of Childhood: A Social History of Family Life*. New York: Alfred A. Knopf, 1962.

Austin, James E. *Confronting Urban Malnutrition: The Design of Nutrition Programs*. Baltimore: Johns Hopkins University Press/World Bank, 1980.

Barnum, H., Barlow, R., Fajardo, L., and Pradilla, A. *A Resource Allocation Model for Child Survival*. Cambridge, Mass.: Oelgeschlager, Gunn & Hain, 1980.

Bell, David E., and Reich, Michael R., eds. *Health, Nutrition, and Economic Crises: Approaches to Policy in the Third World*. Dover, Mass.: Auburn House, 1988.

Black, Maggie. *The Children and the Nations: The Story of Unicef*. New York: UNICEF, 1986.

Boothby, Neil. "Children and War," *Cultural Survival Quarterly,* 10, no. 4 (1986), 28–30.

Boulding, Elise. *Children's Rights and the Wheel of Life*. New Brunswick, N.J.: Transaction Books, 1979.

Bryce, Jennifer W. *Cries of Children in Lebanon: As Voiced by Their Mothers*. Amman, Jordan: UNICEF Regional Office for the Middle East and North Africa, 1986.

Caldwell, John C. "Routes to Low Mortality in Poor Countries," *Population and Development Review,* 12, no. 2 (June 1986), 171–220.

———. *Children of Calamity*. New York: John Day, 1957.

Cantwell, Nigel. "The Draft Convention on the Rights of the Child: And Now for the Good News . . . ," *International Children's Rights Monitor,* 4, no. 1 (1987), 4–7.

Cash, Richard, Keusch, Gerald T., and Lamstein, Joel, eds. *Child Health and Survival: The UNICEF GOBI-FFF Program.* London: Croom Helm, 1987.

Child Study Association of America. *Children and the Threat of Nuclear War.* New York: Duell, Sloan & Pearce, 1964.

Children in Situations of Armed Conflict. E/ICEF/1986/CRP.2. New York: UNICEF, 1986.

Children on the Front Line: The Impact of Apartheid, Destabilization and Warfare on Children in Southern and South Africa. New York: UNICEF, 1987.

"Children under Attack by Governments," *Amnesty Action,* January/February 1988, p. 2.

Children's Defense Fund. *A Children's Defense Budget, FY 1988: An Analysis of Our Nation's Investment in Children.* Washington, D.C.: CDF, 1987.

———. *American Children in Poverty.* Washington, D.C.: CDF, 1984.

Cobb, Alice. *War's Unconquered Children Speak.* Boston: Beacon Press, 1953.

Cook, Rebecca J. "Human Rights and Infant Survival: A Case for Priorities," *Columbia Human Rights Law Review,* 18, no. 1 (Fall/Winter 1986/87), 1–41.

Cornia, Giovanni Andrea. "A Survey of Cross-Sectional and Time-Series Literature on Factors Affecting Child Welfare," *World Development,* 12, no. 3 (March 1984), 187–202.

Cornia, Giovanni Andrea, Jolly, Richard, and Stewart, Frances, eds. *Adjustment with a Human Face: Protecting the Vulnerable and Promoting Growth.* Oxford: Oxford University Press, 1987.

Dodge, Cole P. "Child Soldiers of Uganda: What Does the Future Hold," *Cultural Survival Quarterly,* 10, no. 4 (1986), 31–33.

Dodge, Cole P., and Raundalen, Magne, eds. *War, Violence and Children in Uganda.* Oslo: Norwegian University Press, 1987.

Dodge, Cole P., and Wiebe, Paul D., eds. *Crisis in Uganda: The Breakdown of Health Services.* New York: Pergamon Press, 1985.

Edelman, Marian Wright. *Families in Peril: An Agenda for Social Change.* Cambridge, Mass.: Harvard University Press, 1987.

———. "How the Military Budget Hurts America's Children," *Food Monitor,* no. 41 (Summer 1987), 3–5, 23.

Eliot, Gil. *Twentieth Century Book of the Dead.* London: Penguin Press, 1972.

Ford Foundation. *Child Survival/Fair Start: A Working Paper.* New York: Ford Foundation, 1983.

Freud, Anna, and Burlingham, Dorothy T. *War and Children.* New York: Medical War Books, 1943.

Galway, Katrina, Wolff, Brent, and Sturgis, Richard. *Child Survival: Risks and the Road to Health.* Columbia, Md.: Institute for Resource Development/Westinghouse/USAID, 1987.

Gardner, R. W. "Ethnic Differentials in Mortality in Hawaii, 1920–1970," *Hawaii Medical Journal,* 39 (1980), 221–38.

George, Susan. *A Fate Worse Than Debt: The World Financial Crisis and the Poor.* New York: Grove Press, 1988.

Gran, Guy. *Development by People: Citizen Construction of a Just World.* New York: Praeger, 1983.

Grant, James P. *The State of the World's Children.* New York: Oxford University Press/UNICEF, annual.

Gwatkin, Davidson R. *Signs of Change in Developing Country Mortality Trends: The End of an Era?* Washington, D.C.: Overseas Development Council, 1981.

——. "How Many Die? A Set of Demographic Estimates of the Annual Number of Infant and Child Deaths in the World," *American Journal of Public Health,* 70, no. 12 (December 1980).

Gwatkin, Davidson R., and Brandel, Sarah. *Reducing Infant and Child Mortality in the Developing World.* Washington, D.C.: Overseas Development Council, 1981.

Gwatkin, Davidson R., and Grant, James P. "Using Targets to Help Improve Child Health." Paper prepared for Fifth International Health Conference of the National Council for International Health, May 1978.

Gwatkin, Davidson R., Wilcox, Janet R., and Wray, Joe D. *Can Health and Nutrition Interventions Make a Difference?* Washington, D.C.: Overseas Development Council, 1980 pp. 1286–89.

Harbison, Jeremy, and Harbison, Joan. *A Society Under Stress: Children and Young People in Northern Ireland.* Somerset, England: Open Books, 1980.

Hobcraft, J. N., McDonald, J. W., and Rutstein, S. O. "Socio-Economic Factors in Infant and Child Mortality: A Cross-national Comparison," *Population Studies,* 36 (1984), 193–223.

Hughes, Dana, Johnson, Kay, Rosenbaum, Sara, Simons, Janet, and Butler, Elizabeth. *The Health of America's Children: Maternal and Child Health Data Book.* Washington, D.C.: Children's Defense Fund, 1987.

International Children's Rights Monitor. Geneva: Defense for Children International, quarterly.

Jacobs, Dan. *The Brutality of Nations.* New York: Alfred A. Knopf, 1987.

Jolly, Richard, and Cornia, Giovanni Andrea, eds. *The Impact of World Recession on Children.* Oxford: Pergamon Press, 1984.

Jupp, Michael. *Children Under Apartheid.* New York: Defense for Children International-USA, 1987.

——. "The Human Rights of Children," *International Health News,* 8, no. 1 (January 1987), 1.

——. "Apartheid: Violence Against Children," *Cultural Survival Quarterly,* 10, no. 4 (1986), 34–37.

——. et al. *The Children's Clarion: Database on the Rights of the Child.* New York: Defense for Children International-USA, 1987.

Kent, George. *War and Children's Survival.* Honolulu: University of Hawaii Institute for Peace, 1990.

——. "Security and Hunger," *WHY: Challenging Hunger and Poverty,* no. 1 (Spring 1989), 18–19.

——. "Answer Is Power Not Just Bread," *UNICEF Intercom,* no. 47 (January 1988), 2–3.

——. "Children as Human Capital?" *Food and Nutrition Bulletin,* 10, no. 4 (December 1988), 54–58.

——. "Nutrition Education as an Instrument of Empowerment," *Journal of Nutrition Education,* 20, no. 4 (July/August 1988), 193–95.

——. "Who Would Not Save Their Own Children? The Impact of Powerlessness on Child Survival," *Development Forum,* 16, no. 6 (November–December 1988), 11.

————. *The Political Economy of Hunger: The Silent Holocaust.* New York: Praeger, 1984.

Kielmann, Arnfried A., and McCord, Colin. "Weight-for-Age as an Index of Risk of Death in Children," *Lancet* (1978), 1, 1247–50.

Kohler, Lennart, and Jakobsson, Gunborg. *Children's Health and Well-being in the Nordic Countries.* London: Mac Keith Press, 1987.

La Farge, Phyllis. *The Strangelove Legacy: Children, Parents, and Teachers in the Nuclear Age.* New York: Harper & Row, 1987.

Lappé, Frances Moore, and Schurman, Rachel. *The Missing Piece in the Population Puzzle.* Food First Development Report no. 4. San Francisco: Institute for Food and Development Policy, 1988.

Leowski, Jerzy. "Mortality from Acute Respiratory Infections in Children Under 5 Years of Age: Global Estimates," *World Health Statistics,* 39, no. 2 (1986), 138–44.

MacCormack, Carol P. "Health and the Social Power of Women," *Social Science & Medicine,* 26, no. 7 (1988), 677–83.

Mandl, Pierre E., ed. *Going to Scale for Child Survival and Development.* Special issue of UNICEF's *Assignment Children,* 65/68 (1984).

McDevitt, Thomas M. *Child Survival, Fertility, and Population Policy: Implications of an Analysis of Provincial-Level 1971 Census Data.* Boroko, Papua New Guinea: Institute of Applied Social and Economic Research, 1981.

McKeown, Thomas. *The Modern Rise of Population.* New York: Academic Press, 1976.

————. *Medicine in Modern Society: Medical Planning Based on Evaluation of Medical Achievement.* New York: Hafner, 1966.

McLaren, D. S. "The Great Protein Fiasco," *Lancet* (1974), 2, 93–96.

Miller, C. Arden. "Infant Mortality in the U.S.," *Scientific American,* 253, no. 1 (July 1985), 31–37.

Morley, David, Rohde, John E, and Wiliams, Glen, eds. *Practicing Health for All.* New York: Oxford University Press, 1983.

Mosley, W. Henry, and Chen, Lincoln C., eds. *Child Survival: Strategies for Research.* Cambridge: Cambridge University Press, 1984.

Murdoch, William W. *The Poverty of Nations: The Political Economy of Hunger and Population.* Baltimore: Johns Hopkins University Press, 1980.

Murray, Christopher J. L. "A Critical Review of International Mortality Data," *Social Science & Medicine,* 25, no. 7 (1987), 773–81.

Nabarro, David, and Chinnock, Paul. "Growth Monitoring—Inappropriate Promotion of an Appropriate Technology," *Social Science & Medicine,* 26, no. 9 (1988), 941–48.

National Commission to Prevent Infant Mortality. *Death Before Life: The Tragedy of Infant Mortality.* Washington, D.C.: NCPIM, 1988.

Newland, Kathleen. *Infant Mortality and the Health of Societies.* Washington, D.C.: Worldwatch Institute, 1981.

Organski, A. F. K. *Births, Deaths, and Taxes: The Demographic and Political Transitions.* Chicago: University of Chicago Press, 1984.

Osada, Arata. *Children of the A-Bomb: The Testament of the Boys and Girls of Hiroshima.* Tokyo: Uchida Rokakuho, 1959.

Overview: Children in Especially Difficult Circumstances. E/ICEF/1986/L.6. New York: UNICEF, 1986.

Plattner, Denise. "Protection of Children in International Humanitarian Law," *International Review of the Red Cross,* May–June 1984, pp. 140–52.

Preston, Samuel H. *Mortality Patterns in National Populations.* New York: Academic Press, 1976.

Prosterman, Roy L. *The Decline in Hunger-Related Deaths.* Hunger Project Paper no. 1. San Francisco: The Hunger Project 1984.

Puffer, R. R., and Serrano, C. V. *Patterns of Mortality in Childhood.* Scientific Publication no. 262. Washington, D.C.: Pan American Health Organization, 1973.

Ressler, Everett M., Boothby, Neil, and Steinbock, Daniel J. *Unaccompanied Children: Care and Protection in Wars, Natural Disasters and Refugee Movements.* New York: Oxford University Press, 1988.

Rohde, Jon E. "Why the Other Half Dies: The Science and Politics of Child Mortality in the Third World," *Assignment Children,* 61/62, no. 1 (1983), 35–67.

Rohde, Jon E., and Hendrata, L. "Development from Below: Transformation of Village-Based Nutrition Projects to a National Family Nutrition Programme in Indonesia," in Nevin S. Scrimshaw and Mitchel B. Wallerstein, eds., *Nutrition Policy Implementation: Issues and Experience.* New York: Plenum, 1982.

Rosenblatt, Roger. *Children of War.* Garden City, N.Y.: Doubleday, 1983.

Sagan, Leonard. *The Health of Nations: True Causes of Sickness and Well-Being.* New York: Basic Books, 1987.

Sanders, David, and Carver, Richard. *The Struggle for Health: Medicine and the Politics of Underdevelopment.* London: Macmillan, 1985.

Shade, John A. *America's Forgotten Children: The Amerasians.* Perkasie, Pa.: Pearl S. Buck Foundation, 1981.

Singer, Sandra. "The Protection of Children During a Armed Conflict Situations," *International Review of the Red Cross,* May–June 1986, pp. 133–68.

Sivard, Ruth Leger. *World Military and Social Expenditures 1987–88.* Washington, D.C.: World Priorities, 1987.

Tolley, Howard, Jr. *Children and War: Political Socialization to International Conflict.* New York: Teachers College Press, 1973.

Underwood, Barbara, ed. *Nutrition Intervention Strategies in National Development.* New York: Academic Press, 1983.

UNESCO. *UNESCO-UNICEF Co-operation in Asia and the Pacific,* Bangkok: UNESCO Regional Office for Education in Asia and the Pacific, 1986.

United Nations, Department of International Economic and Social Affairs. *Demographic Yearbook.* New York: United Nations, annual.

———. *Socio-Economic Differentials in Child Mortality in Developing Countries.* ST/ESA/Ser. A/97. New York: United Nations, 1985.

———. *World Population Trends, Population and Development Interrelations and Population Policies: 1983 Monitoring Report,* vol. 2. New York: United Nations, 1985.

United Nations, Secretariat. "Infant Mortality: World Estimates and Projections, 1950–2025," *Population Bulletin of the United Nations,* no. 14 (1982), 31–53.

United States Agency for International Development. *Child Survival: A Second Report to Congress on the AID Program.* Washington, D.C.: USAID, 1988.

Vornberger, William, ed. *Fire from the Sky: Salvadoran Children's Drawings*. New
     York: Writers and Readers Publishing Cooperative, 1986.
Wilson, Francis, and Ramphele, Mamphela. "Children in South Africa," in *Children
     on the Front Line: The Impact of Apartheid, Destabilization and Warfare on
     Children in Southern and South Africa*. New York: UNICEF, 1987.
Woodbury, Marda. *Childhood Information Resources*. Arlington, Va.: Information
     Resources Press, 1985.
Woodbury, R. M. *Infant Mortality and Its Causes*. Baltimore: Williams & Wilkins, 1926.
World Health Organization. *World Health Statistics Annual*. Geneva: WHO, annual.
Zeitlin, Marian, Ghassemi, Hossein, and Mansour, Mohammed. *Positive Deviance in
     Child Nutrition: With Emphasis on Psychosocial and Behavioural Aspects and
     Implications for Development*. Tokyo: United Nations University, 1989.

INDEX

ences among leaders of, 151; economic growth and, 84, 138; gender
discrimination by, 115; poverty and,
86; spending priorities by, 86, 111,
116–18; UNICEF and, 151, 184–85
Grant, James, 42, 44, 141, 154, 155
green revolution, 67, 69, 70, 72, 81
growth monitoring, 42–43, 47–48
Guyana, 10

Hardin, Garret, 127
Harvard University, 87
Haryana, India, 81, 83
Hawaii, 126
health: care for: See health care; caregivers and, 66; economy and, 125,
141–46; factors of good, 55; government priorities and, 118–19; growth
faltering and, 66; income level and,
118; nutrition and, 63; poverty and,
85; powerlessness and, 161; productivity and, 143–44, 145–46
health care: AIDS and, 20; child mortality and, 34–35; comprehensive, 55–
56; death rates and, 124–25; developing countries and, 36; education
and, 27, 35; gender discrimination
and, 32; in Ghana, 35; GOBI program and, 50; government spending
for, 86, 118; international conference
on, 39; modern, 53–54; national ideology and, 134; research emphasis in
51; selective primary, 50–52; in Thailand, 120; war and, 97
HEALTH-GOM (Communication for
Child Survival), 41
Hesperian Foundation, 162
Hiroshima, 10–11, 94, 98
Honduras, 43
Hong Kong, 136
hospitals, 54
human rights, 183, 185, 186

Iceland, 136
ICRC (International Committee of the
Red Cross), 102–4
immunization: ARI and, 51; breast-feeding and, 43; child survival and, 44–

45; criticism of programs for, 49–50;
diseases focused on for, 44; effectiveness of, 49–50, 51, 52; El Salvador
and, 44; Grant and 44; neonatal tetanus and, 21–22; Nicaragua and, 44;
UNICEF and, 44, 51–52; USAID
and, 41, 51–52; warfare and, 44;
WHO and, 40, 44
India: child mortality in, 7; food supply
in, 67–68; gender discrimination in,
114–15; green revolution and, 81,
83; Haryana, 81, 83; health priority
in, 118; immunization and, 50; Kerala, 62, 89, 118, 151; malnutrition in,
62, 67–68; overpopulation and, 130;
Punjab, 62, 81, 83, 114–15; religion
and infant deaths in, 30; social services and, 134; wealth distribution in,
127
Indonesia, 7, 42, 64
industrialization, 158
industrial revolution, 39, 123–24
infancy period, defind, 15
infanticide, 182
infant mortality rate(s): breast-feeding
and, 61; child mortality rate compared with, 8; countries leading
United States in, 9; decline of, 5; defined, 4; education and, 89; errors in
calculation of, 4–5; government
spending and, 98–99, 120; health
progress indicated by, 39; in Karala,
62, 89; malnutrition assessment and,
67; maternal education and, 89; in
Middle East, 161; national ideology
and, 135; neonatal death and, 16;
neonatal period and, 8; neonatal tetanus and, 21; in 1980, 5; official violence and, 112; political power and,
113; poverty and 77; prenatal care
and, 35; racial differences and, 9–10,
113–14; revolution and, 150; smoking mothers and, 17; in Soviet Union,
8, 134; in Sri Lanka, 62; in Tanzania,
1985, 4; in Thailand, 119; in United
States, 8–10, 11, 17, 34, 120; water
supply and, 33. See also child mortality rate

ABOUT THE AUTHOR

GEORGE KENT is professor of political science at the University of Hawaii. His interest in child survival evolves from his continuing concern with structural violence in the world system. His previous books include *The Politics of Pacific Islands Fisheries, The Political Economy of Hunger: The Silent Holocaust,* and *Fish, Food, and Hunger: The Potential of Fisheries for Alleviating Malnutrition*; he was coeditor of *Marine Policy in Southeast Asia*. He has worked with the Food and Agriculture Organization of the United Nations and other governmental and nongovernmental organizations. He is currently preparing a study on child prostitution in Asia.